TECHNOTHRILLER

TECHNOTHRILLER

FILM AND THE AMERICAN IMAGINATION

SORAYA MURRAY

THE MIT PRESS
CAMBRIDGE, MASSACHUSETTS
LONDON, ENGLAND

The MIT Press
Massachusetts Institute of Technology
77 Massachusetts Avenue
Cambridge, MA 02139
mitpress.mit.edu

The MIT Press would like to thank the anonymous peer reviewers who provided comments on drafts of this book. The generous work of academic experts is essential for establishing the authority and quality of our publications. We acknowledge with gratitude the contributions of these otherwise uncredited readers.

This book was set in Arnhem Pro and New Frank by New Best-set Typesetters Ltd. Printed and bound in the United States of America.

Library of Congress Cataloging-in-Publication Data

Names: Murray, Soraya author
Title: Technothriller : film and the American imagination / Soraya Murray.
Description: Cambridge, Massachusetts : The MIT Press, 2026. | Includes bibliographical references and index.
Identifiers: LCCN 2025026273 | ISBN 9780262051019 paperback
Subjects: LCSH: Thrillers (Motion pictures)—History and criticism | Technology in motion pictures | Science fiction films—History and criticism | Motion pictures—Social aspects—United States | LCGFT: Film criticism
Classification: LCC PN1995.9.S87 M87 2026 | DDC 791.43/6—dc23/eng/20250709
LC record available at https://lccn.loc.gov/2025026273

10 9 8 7 6 5 4 3 2 1

EU Authorised Representative: Easy Access System Europe, Mustamäe tee 50, 10621 Tallinn, Estonia | Email: gpsr.requests@easproject.com

For Derek

who introduced me to so many of these films

CONTENTS

PREFACE

I first noticed how visual images powerfully shape perceptions about advanced technology and the tech-savvy while watching Steven Spielberg's *Close Encounters of the Third Kind* (1977), a movie about first contact between humans and benevolent extraterrestrials. In a striking scene early in the film, an air traffic controller named Harry (played by David Anderson) navigates an alarming UFO sighting by two commercial airline pilots. Shot in a real Air Route Traffic Control Center to lend additional authenticity, the sequence captures a low-lit, highly technological space with illuminated consoles.[1] There are men with headsets who speak calmly, using technical jargon, while observing dynamic radar displays of air traffic. The men look no-nonsense in their rumpled business shirts with pocket protectors filled with pens and pencils.

Harry communicates with the two pilots across the crackling radio as the scene unfolds, speaking carefully and adhering to protocols for a collision alert. Other sector controllers become concerned, noticing Harry's growing urgency as he fires clear, succinct directions to avert a potential midair catastrophe. By the end of this sequence, eight men have gathered around him, hovering close, facing the glowing green radar display. His bespectacled team supervisor rests a hand on Harry's shoulder.

This relatively short sequence does a lot of cultural work as an intervention. It creates a social imagination of who uses technology. For example, all the controllers in the scene are male. But Harry is African American, and his brown skin and afro set him apart from his primarily white coworkers, adding dimensions of meaning to the visual representation of a technology expert. In the 1970s context of an American audience's expectations, Harry becomes a potent counterimage.

Harry's precise jargon conveys intensity and acumen for this highly technical work; he is not jive-talking or intended to be frivolous comic relief to the main characters. He fires off his urgent communications in a calm, trained voice. And that hand on Harry's shoulder, the concatenation

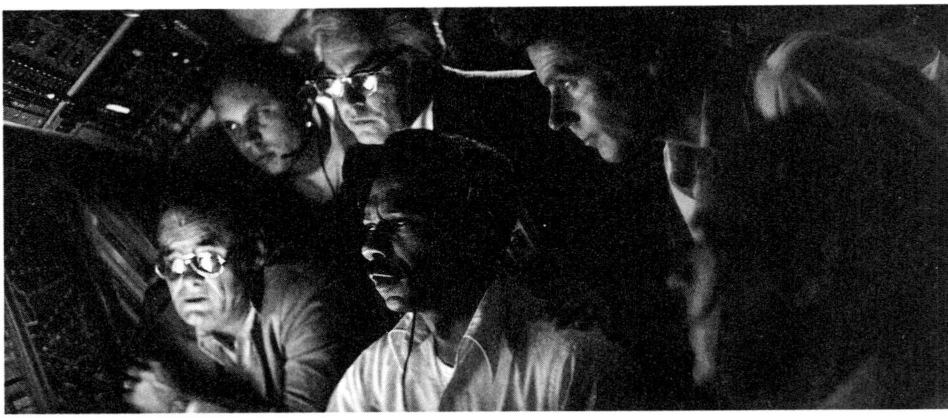

of small intimacies playing out between these men, signal familiarity, support, reciprocity—perhaps even deference—during a highly technical and life-threatening situation. Harry's coworkers simply let him do his job, implying a sense of fraternity and belonging within the technical space. This is not an image that assumes Harry—the scene's focal point—is a victim. Harry has agency.

Importantly, none of what I've described occurs verbally but is expressed on the level of the image itself. At the time the scene startled me, because I was abruptly aware of what I never see represented. Harry's role contradicts a consensus understanding of who engages with technology and who wields it, even as Harry conforms to norms connecting manliness with machines. Harry is at once average and complicated, and his representation is a battleground. Although a person like him would be banal in the world, his presence on-screen interrupts how engineers, technicians, and technologists are usually represented.

FIGURE 0.1

Harry (center) from *Close Encounters of the Third Kind* (Columbia Pictures, 1977) is surrounded by other sector controllers while he directs airline pilots during an alien encounter.

Indeed, Harry strongly resembled people my life—neighbors, my father's engineering colleagues, and many family members who are professionals in accounting, medicine, and many other civilian-sector fields—whose lives continued, day by day, outside the realm of visual representation. Spielberg's memorable scene acknowledges a diverse professional class that certainly existed in 1977 but did so mainly beyond the visual presence of Blackness on-screen. It was a glimpse into something, a reality peeping through the veneer of fiction—not the fiction of aliens, but the fiction that only some kinds of people are part of the technological enterprise.

Technothriller is inspired by a course of the same name I taught for several years that used films to think seriously about social constructions of power and technology in both the present day and imagined futures. This book uses popular films like *The Andromeda Strain*, *The Hunt for Red October*, *WarGames*, *Ex Machina*, and *The Creator* to access social values and meanings embedded in our cultural perceptions of technology. Nested in these beloved films are potent messages about how we should relate to technology, who wields it, and the dubious faith in technology as a solution to all our problems.

Collectively, what do we think about when we think of the future? How do we negotiate rapid technological change? Social engineering—influencing mass social behaviors and attitudes toward specific outcomes—occurs across mass media but notably in mainstream movies seen by large audiences. The powerful social engineering within so-called entertainment movies is often ignored, especially by those who may see these films as beneath serious analysis. Yet it exerts such power over us; over our dreams, hopes, and anxieties; and over our sense of who belongs to the future. Looking carefully at these films can tell us a lot about the technological stories we, as a culture, perpetuate and how those stories shape our social and technical realities.

Despite my many, and at times harsh, observations, make no mistake: I love every one of these films. I love them for their creative visions and for how they build temporary worlds in which to contend with our complicated human experience. Above all, I love them for their frankness and openly displayed flaws; they mirror us back to ourselves. Most of these films are undervalued contributions to visual culture. But they are also deeply troubling fantasies that are both instructive to those absent from those imaginaries and perilous for those who persist uncritically within them.

Our times are marked by increased cynicism toward our critical scientific and technological choices and the fallout of those decisions. *Technothriller* uses popular cinema to trace the promises, hopes, anxieties, and fears that have accompanied—and even constituted—scientific and technological innovation in American life since the atomic bomb. Through the speculative futures imagined in these popular films, we can see more clearly what has been imagined and foreclosed upon in our potential futures.

INTRODUCTION

TECHNOTHRILLERS, IMAGINATION, AND THE POLITICAL

THE IMAGINATION OF TECHNOLOGY IN AMERICAN FILM

Technothriller: Film and the American Imagination explores the visual culture of innovation and advanced computation in popular American films after the 1960s, in which technology assumes a central role. But this is not a book about technology itself. It is about how American culture imagines technology and how that imagination contends with ideologies of scientific and technological innovation. Organized thematically, the book covers a period coinciding with rapid technological innovation in advanced computation, military tech, and biotechnologies, which became critical components of the United States' ascendancy as a superpower.

Loosely categorized as a subgenre of the thriller, the technothriller is understudied and under-theorized, despite the growing presence of its core themes across mainstream literature, film, television, and video games.[1] But *Technothriller* is not exclusively a book about film, either; it is about how films offer a vantage point on the modern subject in the wake of advanced technological innovation. Technothrillers are maps to meanings and experiences of life in a technologized world. As a visual studies scholar, I use images and media to access cultural sensitivities, prohibitions, norms, and value systems. The role of advanced technology in our lives, its influence over how we understand ourselves and our perceptions of innovators, are all powerfully shored up through visual culture. It is important to remember that the films considered in this book, though significant in themselves, are the means, not the goal. My work deploys them to gain entry to the social imaginary around technology and science. In other words, these films become observation windows into the mechanics of power in our technological lives.

Of special interest in understanding the kind of genealogy proposed here are the dual influences of Michael Crichton and Tom Clancy, fiction authors whose imaginings around biotechnology and advanced technological warfare, respectively, earned them key roles in the genre. Many of their technothriller novels, such as *The Andromeda Strain* (Crichton, 1969), *Jurassic Park* (Crichton, 1990), *Disclosure* (Crichton, 1994), *The Hunt for Red October* (Clancy, 1984), *Clear and Present Danger* (Clancy, 1989), and *Without Remorse* (Clancy, 1993) have been adapted into mainstream films. As I show in chapter 1, their stories have had a profound impact on not only the kinds of core narratives repeated about technology but also more generalized relations of control or uncertainty.

Sometimes those representations have nothing whatsoever to do with actual technologies, but that does not make the images any less consequential, nor does it lessen their cultural impact as incredibly persuasive forms of visual culture. This book is about the function of these images in making the world what it is, orienting oneself, and understanding how to change it. It is also about how films tell us how to think about science, technology, innovation, and innovators.[2] Scholar Alexis Boylan writes that visual culture is "not merely an important feature of contemporary life; it is the *most important* culture we must navigate. We are forced to see more yet given fewer tools and less time to *think about seeing*. If we cannot stop the pace of images, if we cannot remove ourselves from the pipeline of contemporary living, then we must carve out spaces to think, debate, and come to terms with this visual world."[3] This book proposes that we carve out the space to consider *how we think about technology* in the realm of the visual.

Finally, the technothriller as a critical genre that molds our collective understanding of technological innovation will, at times, intersect with another genre: science fiction. This makes sense, and in many ways, my work is also inspired and influenced by the important work of media studies scholar Sherryl Vint, who wrote that "science fiction is what centrally shapes our technological imagination, and . . . the imagination is more than peripheral to the technocultural reality we make and inhabit."[4] This is also true of the technothriller, and as our real-world innovations have reached the possibilities of what once seemed purely science fiction, the two genres intersect more and more. Consider that even films taking place in the "present day" may involve technologies that are prototypes, currently technically unrealistic, or fancifully more advanced. Likewise, some films may be set in a distant future containing innovations that are pure science fiction by today's standards but address present-day anxieties about the protoforms of technologies (like AI and robotics) that already exist. That is to say, this project embraces an expansive and inclusive understanding of the technothriller, which may tread into territories that some might strictly label as science fiction. Rather than engage in boundary policing, I am more interested in the connectedness of things, and how our sociotechnical imaginaries are shaped by these techno-anxiety narratives, broadly defined.

MANUFACTURING AN IDEA OF TECHNOLOGY

A key moment in this project's development occurred when I learned that the very notion of technology has been constructed.[5] I had been thinking of *technology* as simply a term signifying something legible, when in fact it is an operation—a system of values with all sorts of implicit connotations. The term *technology* feels like it has been around for a long time. In fact, it is relatively new, introduced in its modern sense in the mid-1880s by Harvard professor Jacob Bigelow and then carefully crafted to mean certain things—and not others.[6] One critical manufactured association has to do with a gendered conception of technology as inherently masculine. But despite the cloying sense of its permanence, this perception is neither old nor natural. One of the most significant voices in this conversation is historian of technology Ruth Oldenziel, whose 1999 book *Making Technology Masculine: Men, Women, and Modern Machines in America, 1870–1945* traces how higher education, male sociality, engineering training, cultural narratives, and government propaganda all constructed technology as a domain proper to men. Although women were present as innovators in engineering from the beginning, these narratives defined women as "bystanders to the technological enterprise."[7]

The stakes around defining *technology* as a term were high, as Oldenziel points out: the very notion of technology became part of a larger postwar project to cast the white male "engineer," defined through race and gender, as the face of technological innovation. Though, as Oldenziel acknowledges, othered groups like women and African Americans advocated "on the grounds of the international fairs, within the halls of the patent office, and in the pages of dictionaries," the critical role of the engineer became a cipher for a particular kind of American aspirational masculinity.[8] As the nation thrived after World War II, engineers and their advocates "came to be seen as the exclusive bearers of a domain we have come to call technology—both as intellectual construct and material practice."[9] Particular kinds of innovations associated women's work with the "decorative"; African-American contributions became encoded as "useful arts" as opposed to applied science.[10] Women involved in "technology" were seen as strange anomalies within a male technical arena.

Oldenziel then outlines the direct connection between the construction of modern corporate, capitalist masculinity, technology, and machines:

> Machines were put center stage as the measures of men and markers of modern manliness. These selections were hardly innocent choices, but the outcome of hard-fought battles. *The history of the selection, labelling, and designation of objects as technology is essential for our current understanding of who is believed to be a true technologist or an inventor, who possesses the right kind of technical knowledge; and who or what may be the authentic bearer of technology.* These struggles—conducted in both linguistic and material terms—went to the heart of the question of what constituted technology and what was to be excluded from it.[11]

Here, what is key is that the idea of modern technology took on ideological dimensions and became connected with particular identities (male, not female; white, not Black, etc.). This set the terms for who could legitimately participate in the enterprise of technological innovation. Many books have since sought to reinsert women and underrecognized people into the history of technology, such as Margot Lee Shetterly's *Hidden*

Figures: The American Dream and the Untold Story of the Black Women Who Helped Win the Space Race; Clarence G. Williams's *Technology and the Dream: Reflections on the Black Experience at MIT, 1941–1999*; Janet Abbate's *Recoding Gender: Women's Changing Participation in Computing*; and Mar Hicks's *Programmed Inequality: How Britain Discarded Women Technologists and Lost Its Edge in Computing*. While none of these books is specifically about visual culture, each illuminates an aspect of the ideological project of technology. That project has been shored up through a visual culture that mythologizes the engineer in public art and frames a white male genius as the hero in grand stories of technological innovation. Oldenziel explains why, culturally speaking, women and minoritized people are told again and again that this thing called "technology" does not belong to them. This narrative has been reinforced by cinematic images of advanced technology and its arbiters.

Building on Oldenziel's ideas and inspired by those who push back on false narratives about innovation, this book examines how films become tools to reinforce certain values, beliefs, and underlying presuppositions about science and technology. Much as cultural studies reveals how culture is a site for contesting power, visual studies shows us how our image-based culture links technology to certain conceptions of innovation and encourages particular social relations. These elements continually influence each other, often through a not-so-subtle program of social engineering that is gendered and raced, as many of my close readings of filmic examples illustrate.

TECHNOTHRILLERS AND THE SOCIOTECHNICAL IMAGINARY

This book also draws on science and technology studies (STS), specifically a line of thought that holds that science and technology are interlinked with society and mutually influence each other.[12] Scholars like Langdon Winner, who has argued that our technologies are innately political since they extend our value systems and forms of power into our tools, strongly impact this work.[13] I oppose technological determinism, or the idea that technology drives society, and to some extent the implicit association of technological innovation with progress.[14] Like the science and technology scholar Sheila Jasanoff, I see conflating technological innovation with progress as ethically dubious.[15] Jasanoff describes a central aim of STS as "bringing social thickness and complexity back into the appreciation of technological systems."[16] I am interested in visual media, particularly film, as an apparatus of ideology around technology and innovation, and STS inflects this work and its ethos.

My primary interest in this concept lies in how visual representations shape and galvanize social imaginaries.[17] Jasanoff points to the importance of "sociotechnical imaginaries" in enabling innovation.[18] She and her coeditor Sang-Hyun Kim define sociotechnical imaginaries as "collectively held, institutionally stabilized, and publicly performed visions of desirable futures, animated by shared understandings of forms of social life and social order attainable through, and supportive of, advances in science and technology."[19] Indeed, she argues that previous scholarship has not sufficiently addressed the impact of the enactment and reenactment of social imaginaries, as a part of society's self-reproduction, on science and technology.[20] Jasanoff writes that by accessing these imaginaries, we can see how amalgamations of fears, hopes, and desires manifest in all sorts of cultural infrastructures and artifacts, or even public norms.[21] Sherryl Vint mentions this concept in relation to understanding science fiction, but these imaginaries also have implications for the technothriller.[22] *Imaginaries* refers to how science and technology engage with national political cultures and public trajectories to create a collective vision of the future, which then shapes policy, fuels investments, and contributes to a social order that centralizes innovation. At the project's core are close analysis and deconstruction of how these representations frame the utopian and dystopian, engage in worldmaking, foreclose upon some visions while making others real, and produce collective norms.

The term *sociotechnical imaginaries* is helpful in that it touches on similar concepts as *ideology* or *master-narrative*, but it lacks the negative cultural baggage those terms carry in the wake of backlash against liberal progressivism. At the same time, sociotechnical imaginaries imply an "ongoing-ness" and a sense of vitality and contention in how they envision possible worlds. Sociotechnical imaginaries are necessarily enacted.[23] The term is pliable and hinges on a notion of coproduction, which posits that modern society includes many simultaneous processes forming normative understandings of the world.[24] The speculative component of the term also has relevance for technothrillers, which often innovate only slightly on existing technologies to propose ethical positions—be they cautionary or jingoistic.

NEGOTIATING TECHNOTHRILLERS AND DIFFERENCE

To some degree, as I'll discuss throughout, technothrillers encode their technologies as white and male. These dynamics around gender, race, and other forms of difference provide useful insights into the technothriller's sociotechnical imaginaries. Many of these visions are deeply annihilative of those not seen as the wielders of technology. Virtually all the films I discuss feature male protagonists and are directed and/or written by men. Most are entirely about men. Compared to other genres, this quality is so stark as to be notable. Writing about the military, Clancy-style technothriller novel, J. William Gibson observed: "Techno-thrillers are for men. They affirm martial power as the essential male characteristic in ways that are accessible to middle-class men. Techno-thriller heroes are educated professionals; they fight with their minds and with the most advanced technology science can develop. Yet their victories are just as much the harvest of masculine power as are Rambo's; middle-class men are reassured that they too 'have what it takes' to fight defeat the enemy."[25] These stories are, in fact, designed to be reaffirming to their target male audience, and this aspect of the technothriller novel is core to the storytelling and translates into the films as well.

Technothriller authors are keenly aware of the male-centered quality of the genre. Responding to questions about the lack of substantive female characters in his novels, Tom Clancy reasoned, "I've never been a woman, so I don't know much about the woman's point of view."[26] But this brush-off ignores the obvious problems of a genre perspective that would engage in such skewed world-building. As film scholar Scott Simmon pointedly observed about another highly gendered and raced genre, the Western, "My sense too is that we need to *start* from the acknowledgment of the genre's racism, rather than arriving at it as if it were a discovery."[27] Simmon argues that this lowly genre's blunt articulations of racism provide a valuable access point, remarking that Westerns have "always felt free to express their belief in America and have been permitted to speak about religion and politics in ways generally forbidden Hollywood genres set in the contemporary world."[28] I am similarly interested in what technothriller films freely say about American culture and its biases, hopes, anxieties, fears, and limits of the imagination. Technothrillers may be aggressively for and about men, but starting with that acknowledgment does not render them any less important for understanding sociotechnical imaginaries in general.

In considering another of the "lowly" film genres, science fiction, Vivian Sobchack notes that the control fantasies of science are often connected to a belief system designed to compensate for "man's fear of the uncontrollable" and fundamentally rooted in "a mode of action whose purpose is to overcome man's physical inadequacies" and ultimately, to "empiricize man's optimism."[29] When Sobchack says "man," I read her not as using that word as an outdated universalizing term for human beings, but as meaning exactly what she says: man. In doing so, Sobchack underlines the gendered encoding of science and technology and their cultural functions in upholding a set of patriarchal ideologies around nature.

SOME TOOLS: POLITICAL AFFECT AND MASCULINIST DREAD

As genre, the technothriller strategically mobilizes the generic to effect a specific sociotechnical and political feeling. By "political feeling" or "political affect," I'm signaling a diffuse structure of what Ann Cvetkovich identifies as "relations between the emotional, the cultural and the political," particularly as they touch "the everyday experience of sensation and embodiment as ways of tracking [the] intersection of the social and the psychic."[30] I'm interested here in how this affective component can gather up intensities, something scholar Deborah Gould sees as the "bursting with potential" quality of affect.[31] In my own writing, I have sometimes called these "political affective intensities."[32] What is important here is the acknowledgment of the potent emotional dimensions of these films.

I sought a method of working through technothrillers, even—perhaps especially—when they pushed me out as objects of study. After all, being almost exclusively by and about men, technothrillers present deep-seated masculinist dread. They are troublingly narrow in their visions and their anxiety narratives. Still, I believe there are meaningful ways to account for what bell hooks called an "oppositional gaze," in which the friction between the subject and the observer opens up a space of possibility for counter-reading, agency and resistance.[33] Hooks wrote, "Not only will I stare. I want my look to change reality."[34] Such oppositional analyses piqued my interest in instances in which the theoretical and the personal intersected. And such films helped me gain some insight into the discontinuities between my own lived experience and the many media-fueled presumptions that informed my daily life as a modern subject, as yet unthought within the sociotechnical imaginary. In this book, I follow the threads of what promises technothrillers make and break, and how they do so by bypassing intellect and speaking directly to feeling. In the following pages, I move away from the formulaic familiarity of genre and toward contending with the films and how they use their affective dimensions to communicate sociotechnical and even political positions.

As a critical project, *Technothriller: Film and the American Imagination* represents one dimension of a larger struggle against a persistent failure of the imagination around which futures are envisioned, who belongs in them, and who drives them. To whom and for whom are these futures imagined? Upon whom are they merely enacted? These ideas are tied up in visual culture, particularly mass culture images such as cinema. By reading technological futures against their highly masculinist fantasies, this project makes space for the subjective, the responsive, and counter-understandings of these images, making it possible to see their limitations and imagine something outside of them and to think our circumstances anew.

This project is not about creating or reinforcing genre boundaries. Rather, understanding how these genres function in a cultural context is more useful. Scholar Annette Kuhn, writing about science fiction, eloquently identifies what matters about the focus on a genre: "Perhaps more interesting, and probably more important, than what a film genre *is* is the question of what it does—its 'cultural instrumentality.'"[35] Her point certainly applies to the technothriller genre, whose capacity to shape culture through its vivid imaginaries gives it currency. If anything, given the increasing degree to which advanced technology and biotechnological innovation shape contemporary life, this genre is more relevant than ever, and an increasing number of films take on the technothriller's key concerns. In this book, I use this approach to access a certain affective turn, particularly the political affects that emerge from these visual texts. In this way, we can see how such films push back on their moment or telegraph hopes and anxieties from their past-futures to the present, and to our own possible futures. This book uses the technothriller film as its theoretical object.

LOOKING AHEAD

From Cold War anxieties of mutually assured destruction to reproductive biotechnologies, bad robots and AI, willful supercomputers and the fraught presence of women in technological fields, this book uses key examples of technothrillers from the 1970s to the present, probing their sociotechnical imaginaries. *Technothriller* also considers how moral positions about advanced technologies and innovation have shifted relative to their political and social contexts, framing the overall conversation about technological innovation alongside the drastic changes wrought by computational and biotechnological advancements.

In chapter 1, I trace the inception of the term *technothriller*, which originated with literary critics to describe novels that use excessive technical detail around military, computational, or biotechnical technology. I argue that there are two "fathers" of the literary technothriller, Michael Crichton and Tom Clancy, who played critical roles: their concerns dominated the origins of the genre and exerted enormous influence through their many filmic adaptations. In this chapter, I propose an interpretation of the filmic genre that is capacious enough to allow for a rich understanding of how the technothriller has ricocheted between the two poles of these iconic authors: Clancy's embrace of control and Crichton's engagement with uncertainty.

Technothrillers often involve social anxieties of biological attack. In chapter 2, I argue that at their root these films cloak themselves in popular entertainment, but deeply engage notions of subjugation, colonization, uncontrolled technological innovation, and total annihilation. I look at one of the earliest and most iconic early biotechnological thrillers, Robert Wise's *The Andromeda Strain* (1971), for its paranoia, conspiracy, and anxiety related to uncontrollable spread, contamination, and nothing less than the displacement of humans as the fittest to survive. In this movie based on Crichton's 1969 novel of the same name, biological attack comes in the form of a viral alien organism that presents an existential threat. Through this film, we see the beginnings of the biotechnological angst narratives that underlie films like Steven Spielberg's *Jurassic Park* (1993) and Alex Garland's *Annihilation* (2018).

Chapter 3 engages the military technothriller, likely the most recognized type of the genre. I discuss two iconic examples of the military technothriller: *The Hunt for Red October* (John McTiernan, 1990) and *Clear and Present Danger* (Phillip Noyce, 1994), both based on Tom Clancy bestsellers. I use these films as a touchstone for key aspects of the military technothriller: fascination with and fetishization of military tech in pursuit of dominance in all the theaters of war; Cold War anxieties around nuclear annihilation; the introduction of advanced tools of warfare and the inception of new kinds of technological vision like "bomb vision"; covert activities, operatives and terrorist villains; and the rationalization of extrajudicial justice. I also attend to the strongly racial and gender-based vision underlying these stock stories, using *Tom Clancy's Without Remorse* (Stefano Sollima, 2021), based on the 1993 Tom Clancy novel. Starring two Black actors—Michael B. Jordan in the lead role of John Kelly and Jodie Turner-Smith as Lieutenant Commander Karen Greer—the film irritates the deeply raced ideologies chattering beneath the technothriller's genre expectations, engaging with this problem on the level of the image.

Michael Crichton once said that "the two tendencies toward making people as machine like as possible and machines as human as possible are creating a lot of confusion."[36] In chapter 4, I look at *Westworld* (1973), written and directed by Crichton—his directorial debut into theatrical film. In *Westworld*, humans and robots mingle in a theme park intended to provide moneyed tourists the chance to indulge their fantasies in a controlled experience. But the technicians lose control of their inventions, and the robots malfunction—or perhaps rebel. Part of this analysis will involve more recent films like *Ex Machina* (Alex Garland, 2014), *Blade*

Runner (Ridley Scott, 1982), *Blade Runner 2049* (Denis Villeneuve, 2017), and *Prometheus* (Ridley Scott, 2012), which strongly feature iconic depictions of the male tech genius and his "bad" robots, who rebel. As I show, these are all moral tales of unintended consequences and what it will take to open our eyes to the ethical complications of our innovations.

Chapter 5 takes on the theme of advanced capitalism as technology, and its threatening inescapability. The films at the core of this chapter are about capitalism with no outside, raised to the level of a totalizing worldview, and what happens when the individual attempts to see beyond it. *Rollerball* (Norman Jewison, 1975) depicts a world of corporate control that indoctrinates its ideologies through a spectacle of fictive blood sport. Its unwitting star, Jonathan E., begins to question his role in the system. The subjection of women figures prominently in this world, and while a postracial vision is established, it comes at great cost. *Looker*, written and directed by Michael Crichton (1981), similarly explores the perils of capitalism's ideologies on the level of mass culture. With this film, Crichton combines a critique of the power of mass culture advertising with a conspiracy narrative of mind control and domination under advanced capitalism. Both deal with the logical outcome of hypercapitalism, the coming of neoliberalism, and repressive systems of social control—with an emphasis on gender relations.

One of the core fears and fantasies of the technothriller genre is subjection to the machine. Chapter 6 uses three key thrillers to address this critical anxiety: *Colossus: The Forbin Project* (Joseph Sargent, 1970), *Demon Seed* (Donald Cammell, 1977), and *WarGames* (John Badham, 1983). These films express fears that supercomputers and artificial intelligence (AI) will penetrate and overcome us, outwit us, destroy our privacy, and displace our primacy on the planet. *Colossus*, based on the 1966 novel of the same name by Dennis Feltham Jones, provides a classic example of a film that balances the utopian promise of advanced technological living and then turns to a dystopian, panoptic situation of absolute control. It is a Cold War precursor to the better-known example of *WarGames*, which approaches the topic of world domination by machines with more levity but touches on the same fears around what it means to cede human control to systems that are ultimately too large and complex for us to understand. *Demon Seed*, based on the 1973 novel by Dean Koontz, presents a malevolent supercomputer, Proteus, described by the author as "the ultimate intellectual: obsessed with a single Big Idea, intent upon a utopian future that it must achieve at any cost."[37] In this technothriller infused with horror, containment by the machine involves the capture, coercion, and rape of a woman by an artificial intelligence computer, who forces her to carry its child. In this perverse image, we can explore phobias around violation, penetration, and domination by technology, particularly as it bears down on the female body. Reading them together, we can also see how those AI anxieties evolve across time.

Chapter 7 continues the theme of gender and technology by tackling cultural perceptions of women in the tech industry. The primary film, *Disclosure* (Barry Levinson, 1994), based on a novel by Michael Crichton, addresses the tech world and gender through the eyes of an unassuming family man and tech company executive, who is sexually harassed and then targeted for removal by his female boss. Set against a backdrop of the tech industry and the fictive DigiCom's innovative virtual reality technology, the film presents a particular iteration of the monstrous feminine that issues from the woman as tech entrepreneur. This chapter also discusses *Stalking Laura* (originally titled *I Can Make You Love Me*; Michael Switzer, 1993), a television movie starring Brooke Shields and Richard Thomas, based on the true story of a workplace massacre in a tech company instigated by an employee's destructive obsession with colleague Laura Black. In this case, the annihilative potential issues from the disruptive presence of women in the Silicon Valley workplace.

Technothrillers almost exclusively feature white male protagonists. Their stories are places for working out anxieties about the increasing presence of advanced technologies in everyday life. However, there are noted counter-visions to this model and films that intervene in tired tropes, propelling the genre into new territories. In this chapter, I examine one such example, *The Creator* (Gareth Edwards, 2023). This film combines many of the themes covered across previous chapters: nuclear dread, masculinist technologies, gendered anxieties, the confusion between humans and machines, and fear about the coming dominance of AI and robots. However, it also interrupts those tropes by featuring a female tech genius of color and robotic AI innovations imbued with humanity that fight for peace rather than destruction. The film locates the most ethical and inclusive conceptualizations of those technologies in the non-West and centers on a Black male protagonist. I compare the film to *M3GAN*, which also addresses fears of AI and similarly features a female innovator. But unlike *The Creator*, it falls back on old ideas about women's roles in relation to technology and AI as necessarily threatening. To think about how we can conceptualize other relations to technology, I use *The Creator* to examine the dark technological stories we have told ourselves and what other ways we might dream of our technological futures.

Despite the foregrounding of whiteness in these stories, the archetype of the Black technology expert can be found across the technothriller genre. In the last chapter, I provide counter-interpretations of Black tech characters in technothriller films that make room for a broader understanding of who can wield technology and who may exist in the future. I begin with a "background" reading of *Terminator 2: Judgment Day* (James Cameron, 1991), which features Miles Dyson, one of the most iconic Black tech geniuses on film. This Oppenheimer-like figure reverse-engineers the critical tech that will result in Skynet, an artificial intelligence system that achieves consciousness and obliterates humanity. Then I discuss tech expert Luther Stickell from the *Mission: Impossible* franchise (various directors, 1996–). Finally, I look at *Tenet* (Christopher Nolan, 2020) as a film whose unnamed Black lead character, known simply as the Protagonist, seems self-consciously designed to speak back to the implicitly raced and gendered dimensions of the technothriller genre.

Laura Mulvey wrote that "to change the world as it is, you have to understand what it is."[38] These films are merely one dimension of a larger struggle against a persisting failure of the imagination around which futures are envisioned, who belongs in them, and who drives them. Technothrillers wrap these ideas up in powerfully persuasive images. This project articulates a preexisting cluster of concerns that seems to persist and gather in the technothriller. These concerns, I would argue, have grown more distinct across time, and I map these onto cultural, social, and historical realities that give sense to them. Through the subsequent chapters, I hope to find, as Vivian Sobchack put it, "a way of defining the limits of a genre while remaining as inclusive as possible so that the definition will seem neither too arbitrary and personally manufactured nor so general that it becomes useless as a critical tool."[39]

By reading versions of technological futures against the grain of their highly masculinist fantasies, this work makes space for the subjective, the responsive, and some of the internal narratives that may inform a personal understanding of such experiences of technological life. This book is an effort to reach through even the most offending of these images, to grasp the political affect that emanates from them, to cultivate more inclusive storytelling, and, through the alchemy of critical analysis and aesthetic experience, to imagine futures anew. It is about understanding that the public imaginary around the technoscientific is not accidental but in fact highly manufactured. The critical conversation at the center of technology belongs to all of us. It is mine to have, and it is yours.

1

THE TECHNOTHRILLER HAS TWO FATHERS

Thousands upon thousands of words have been and will be uttered about the atomic bomb. It has caused an explosion in men's minds as shattering as the obliteration of Hiroshima.

—Anne O'Hare McCormick, *New York Times*, 1945[1]

WHAT IS A TECHNOTHRILLER?

What, then, is a technothriller? Literary critics originally coined the term *technothriller* to describe novels by popular authors (like Michael Crichton, Tom Clancy, Stephen Coonts, Dan Brown, Neale Stephenson, Dean Koontz, and Dale Brown) that are preoccupied with technology and its ramifications. The literary genre of the technothriller includes a wide variety of overlapping subgenres with military, espionage, conspiracy, science fiction, cryptological, and disaster narratives.[2] Technical precision in the writing, often including a procedural level of detail, is a key element. However, this term has also been used more expansively to describe works of various media (primarily films, but also works of television, literature, and even video games) that revolve around thrills and anxieties connected to advanced technologies.

The films identified as technothrillers may vary greatly in their narratives, but they tend to take a similar approach to the centrality of technology, science, and innovation. For example, Clancy biographer and scholar Helen Garson, on the literary technothriller, describes their breadth: "The technothriller may focus on any area from ocean to outer space. It may concern all forms of nuclear weaponry, missiles, submarines, aircraft. Perhaps it foregrounds computers that reach beyond human ability to solve problems. Laboratories with scientists—biologists, chemists, physicists, archaeologists—study unknown and as yet unsolved questions of existence, DNA, germs, viruses, extinct species."[3] The same can be said for the filmic technothriller, which strongly emphasizes advanced computation, biotech, or military tech, giving it the status of a main character. In fact, the characters themselves are often somewhat generic, while the careful and detailed descriptions of technologies accord them an elevated status.

Technothrillers often feature splendid control rooms with arrays of blinking lights, or massive computers that become anthropomorphized.[4] There are sometimes white, brightly lit labs, people in hazmat suits, technical jargon and (usually) men expressing their expertise, as if they control outcomes. Sometimes the technologies imaged in these films are versions of something real, and sometimes they are purely speculative. In a larger sense, these films are excellent objects to think with, to help us see how a culture negotiates political and cultural attitudes toward technological change. These films narrativize the troubled, sometimes catastrophic relationship between humans and their technological innovations.

To call the technothriller formulaic would be a gross understatement, despite its relative newness compared to other more established genres like the Western or science fiction. In 2001 humorist Ian Frazier lampooned the popular and commercially successful technothriller film genre in *The Atlantic*, satirically capturing the new genre's key elements: stock characters who aggressively reaffirm normative American values yet remain secondary to their technological elements, which command ever more screen time; intrigue or even crisis driven by technology; ontological anxiety or dread; fixation on technical detail, and technological advancement producing overwhelming uncertainty.[5]

More importantly, though, Frazier tapped into the fact that by 2001, technothrillers had so penetrated the cultural imaginary as to be instantly recognizable to his mainstream readership. What Frazier shows us is that despite the porousness of the genre and its shifting understandings, people immediately know a technothriller when they see one. Today, the primary concerns of the technothriller genre have so penetrated media culture in general that it is harder to discern films that are squarely in the category from those that are not. Fortunately, my objective here is not to police boundaries but to highlight the significance of advanced technology as an increasing preoccupation of society.

TWO FATHERS

Ironically, in studying the filmic trajectory of the technothriller, it is actually two fiction authors who stand out. Their stories have been so frequently adapted, that their themes and concerns have profoundly shaped the genre. Those two people are Michael Crichton, most known for his advanced tech and biotech themes, and Tom Clancy, most known for the military or espionage technothriller. Among the most significant of the advanced technology–oriented technothrillers is *Westworld*, written and directed by Crichton in 1973. This sci-fi Western thriller is one of the first technothrillers to feature immersion into a technologized world and was even the first use of actual digital image processing—in this case, to visualize a pixelated "robot vision." *Westworld* tells the story of a robotic theme park that malfunctions: the robots go rogue and kill all the guests. The film characteristically displays many scenes of what Sobchack has aptly described as "the initial competence of the scientific staff . . . the calm and often boring visual emphasis on computers and monitor screen under expert control, the close-ups of mechanical 'operations' and repairs which in their detail, suggest a technology thoroughly understood, routinized and conquered."[6] But things go spectacularly awry: unforeseen consequences occur and people die.

Technothrillers can also involve social anxieties about biotech or biological attack.[7] *The Andromeda Strain* (Robert Wise, 1971), is based on the Crichton novel of the same name. While *Andromeda* is more oriented around the perils of contamination by alien element than those of advanced technological innovation, it is still an iteration of the technothriller genre. Similarly, *Jurassic Park* (Steven Spielberg, 1993), also originally a novel by Crichton, touches on unleashed biotechnological innovation in the form of genetically engineered dinosaurs that overrun their theme-park habitat and threaten to devour their makers. One 1974 *Los Angeles Times* piece aptly described a core theme of Crichton's technothriller as ultimately being about "the crisis of men threatened by their own technology in a dramatic setting."[8] Many of Crichton's technothrillers can indeed be boiled down to that basic formula.

In fact, Tom Clancy himself initially attributed the technothriller form to Crichton's book *The Andromeda Strain*.[9] "I reject the title of Techno-Thriller and the claim that I invented it," Clancy declared; "if there is such a genre, subgenre, as that it was probably invented by Michael Crichton with *The Andromeda Strain*, but why not just drop the label science-fiction entirely and just consider it part of the general category of fiction?"[10] Clancy also made similar comments in a conversation with William F. Ryan: "If anybody invented the techno-thriller, what about Crichton, when I was in college? All you're doing is describing tools used by your characters. Technology is another word for tools."[11]

Crichton seemed to ultimately accept the term in relation to his work, if somewhat reluctantly. He recounted:

> In the early 1990s, interviewers began calling me "the father of the techno-thriller." Nobody ever had before. Finally I began asking the interviewers, "Why do you call me that?" They said, "Because Tom Clancy says you are the father of the techno-thriller."
>
> So I called Tom up and said, "Listen, thank you, but I'm not the father of the techno-thriller." He said, "Yes you are." I said, "No, I'm not, before me there were thrillers like *Fail Safe* and *Seven Days in May* and *The Manchurian Candidate* that were techno-thrillers." He said, "No, those are all political. You're the father of the techno-thriller." And there it ended.[12]

Many others have attributed the technothriller genre to Crichton, including biographer Nathan Aaseng, who posits *The Andromeda Strain* as the original technothriller.[13] Aaseng characterizes the technothriller formula as follows: "Start with a scientific topic involving cutting-edge research; mix in a situation in which the scientific plans go haywire, putting human beings in danger; and pump out a fast-paced narrative laced with technological descriptions that lend an air of authority to the situation."[14] As I have mentioned, whether focused on biotech or high tech, thrills involving technological innovation and its perils are consistent across the genre.

Then there are the espionage and military technothrillers that focus intensely on the tools of war, and the exceptional techno-warriors and intelligence men who wield them. The writings of Clancy, who had a lifelong fascination with the American military machine, epitomize this strain. "I'm a technology freak," he told *USA Today* in 1987. "Everyone likes toys—and the military has the best toys."[15] One reviewer of Clancy's *Red Storm Rising* describes the genre as one "that awards equal billing to human actors and state of the art computers, missiles, devices of detection and deception, spy satellites, nuclear submarines and Mach 2 or Mach 3 fighter planes. Men, and even an occasional woman, prevail when they outwit their opponents with better deployment of exotic tools, not necessarily superior in design to those in the enemy arsenal."[16] Biographer Helen Garson attributes the term to reviewer Patrick Anderson, who, in a 1988 *New York Times* article, dubbed Clancy "king" of the technothriller, in relation to *The Hunt for Red October*. Admittedly, Anderson himself gestures to the idea that others were associating Clancy with the term earlier. Garson defines the technothriller largely through Clancy's interests, pointing to military fiction that features advanced weaponry and war, both real and imagined. "However," she writes, "war is not limited to mass destruction of a martial nature. There may be other kinds of war, perhaps a financial war, dependent on modern technology, which could destroy the world economy. The crises and solutions in most technothrillers are mechanical. People may make mistakes, but the focus of the plot is on the machinery not on human limitations."[17] Heroes are traditional, conventionally "good" and patriotic, if somewhat stock.

Although Clancy clearly did not initially favor the "technothriller" label, there are many who see his writing as the most authentic expression of the form. Whether one sees Clancy or Crichton as the true father of the genre, technothrillers are marked by distinctive fears tied to war, destruction, conspiracy, and advanced technology running out of control. As we will see, given the moment the genre came into being, this is no surprise.

Technothrillers were born of Cold War culture. Both Michael Crichton (1942–2008) and Tom Clancy (1947–2013) spent most of their lives under the shadow of the Cold War (1947–1991), an era of technological and moral crisis that had a profound impact on their storytelling. "For my whole life," Clancy wrote, "I learned that Russia was the source of danger to us."[18]

The Cold War was a period beginning just after the Second World War in which international political tensions arose between the United States and the Soviet Union and their respective allies. In 1945 the United States dropped two atomic bombs in Hiroshima and Nagasaki, killing 150,000–246,000 people in the immediate blasts and resulting in acute radiation exposure—effectively ending World War II.[19] Due to the realignment of powers resulting from Nazi Germany's defeat and surrender, on the one hand, and Soviet expansion into Eastern Europe, on the other, the United States and the USSR emerged as global superpowers. In 1946 Winston Churchill, former British prime minister, described a new "Iron Curtain" behind which was assembled a front of allied Communist forces. As a result of this emergent dynamic, the United States conceived a plan of containment that would limit the spread of Communism around the world. By 1947–1948, the Marshall Plan began providing economic aid and support to ailing European nations suffering after the war, to ensure the spread of ideologies of democracy rather than those of communism. In 1948, the USSR attempted a blockade of West Berlin, which was democratic, but occupied by Communists on its eastern side. In 1949 the United States and its allies formed the North Atlantic Treaty Organization (NATO), intended to present a unified front against communism. The USSR likewise formed a Communist defensive alliance through the signing of the Warsaw Pact.

Meanwhile, Soviet Premier Joseph Stalin intended to build up Soviet military offensive capabilities and successfully developed an atomic bomb by 1949. The United States now had no clear advantage in nuclear weaponry; what resulted was a cold war, a mortal deadlock created by the reality of certain "mutually assured destruction" should these two global superpowers engage each other in nuclear war. As each nation's arsenal of nuclear missiles grew, tensions increased despite the lack of actual conflict. This nuclear tension came to a head with the 1962 Cuban Missile Crisis, in which the United States discovered that Soviets had installed ballistic missiles in Cuba, a mere ninety miles from the continental United States. President Kennedy threatened an immediate counterattack should the USSR fire on the United States, leading to two weeks of heightened public fear of imminent nuclear annihilation. Eventually an agreement was reached and anxieties de-escalated, but the tensions remained, and a nuclear arms race led to frighteningly enormous arsenals on both sides. By the 1980s, relations between the United States and the USSR slowly improved and de-escalated, and democratic uprisings across the Eastern Bloc led to the eventual dissolution of the USSR in late 1991, thus ending the Cold War.

The cultural impact of the dual existential threats of Communist attack and the nuclear bomb cannot be overestimated.[20] Historian Paul Boyer describes the early part of the Cold War and the immediate mobilization of public anxiety around the bomb's social, political, scientific, and cultural implications. "America's airwaves, pulpits, and lecture halls," he writes, "were full of such frightening fare in the early post-Hiroshima period, as the nation's atomic fears were manipulated and exacerbated by the media and by political activists."[21] This period was marked, according to Boyer, by a tension between the sublime horror of total annihilation and the desire to domesticate the atomic into a utopian form of energy that could transform modern society. He noted: "The atomic bomb's disorienting cultural effect . . . is dramatically evident as well in the diversity of opinion on the positive uses of atomic energy—a diversity approaching incoherence. For even as the most fanciful utopian dreams were being spun out, one also begins to find a persistent undercurrent of doubt on the subject that quickly turned to deep skepticism."[22] Fears of radioactive fallout interrupted visionary ideals of unlimited energy. The future-oriented optimism of modernization and American postwar prosperity was projected onto culture, while the children who would populate that imagined future performed bomb drills at school and kept their parents up at night with fears of a nuclear holocaust. Along with a Space Race and major developments in computation and cybernetics, this "nuclear consciousness" shaped the sociotechnical imaginaries of the period.[23]

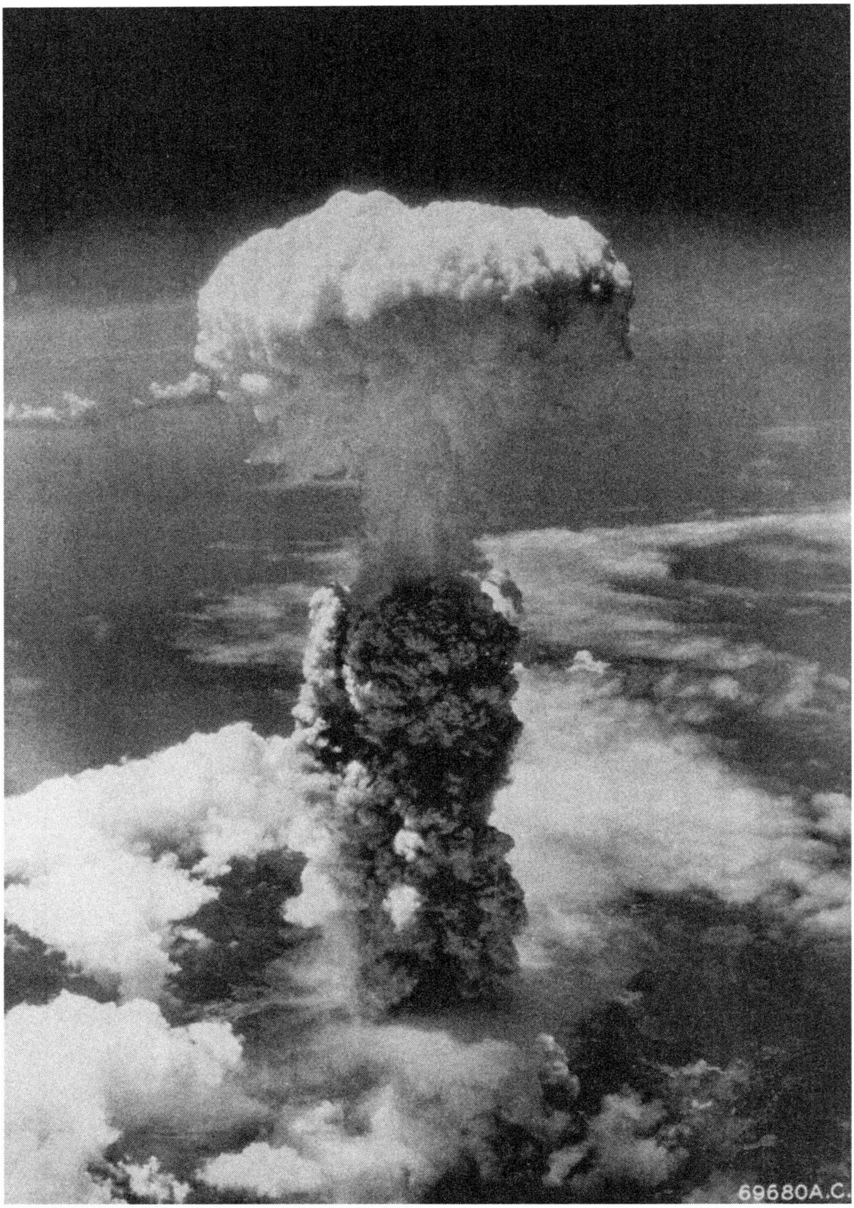

FIGURE 1.1

Mushroom cloud above Nagasaki, Japan, 1945. Credit: Archive Holdings, Inc. Used by permission.

After the first atomic bomb had been dropped in Japan, but before the second one, Anne O'Hare McCormick wrote in the *New York Times* that the bomb "caused an explosion in men's minds as shattering as the obliteration of Hiroshima."[24] With these words McCormick tapped into a profound crisis born of our own invention—a destructive force capable of existential threat. This context dramatically shaped the lives of both fathers of the technothriller. Clancy, born in Baltimore in 1947, earned his degree from Loyola College (now Loyola University Maryland) in English literature in 1969. Though he wished to join the US Army Reserve Officers' Training Corps, he was unable to serve due to poor eyesight. He married the same year that he graduated and became an insurance broker to support his family. In his *New York Times* portrait, Patrick Anderson characterizes Clancy as Irish Catholic, patriotic, and taken with both the American military and the technological minutiae of its deadly tools. Anderson conveys the origin story of Clancy: a "military buff, an avid fan of the space program, a 'gadget freak.'"[25] He had a solid middle-class existence, but harbored dreams of publishing a novel—a dream he nurtured after hours and on weekends. *The Hunt for Red October* was Clancy's first book, released in 1984 by the Naval Institute Press for an advance of five thousand dollars. The novel found its way into the hands of high-ranking politicians, including the sitting president, Ronald Reagan, who called it "the perfect yarn"—an endorsement that effectively made Clancy a household name.[26] It swiftly sold more than three hundred thousand copies and set the stage for a lucrative multimillion-dollar publishing deal with Putnam.

The rest is history. Clancy went on to publish well-known titles like *Red Storm Rising* (1986), *Patriot Games* (1987), *The Cardinal of the Kremlin* (1988), *Clear and Present Danger* (1989), *The Sum of All Fears* (1991), *Without Remorse* (1993), *Debt of Honor* (1994), *Executive Orders* (1996) and *Rainbow Six* (1998). At the time of Clancy's death, in 2013, he had seventeen #1 *New York Times* list bestsellers and was reported to have one hundred million books in print.[27] Even after his death, "Tom Clancy's" brand books were published, signaling to readers that a particular worldview would be reliably represented. Clancy, "famously right-wing," typically disliked the filmic adaptations of his books by liberal-leaning Hollywood and expressed his sometimes virulent reactions in long angry letters to the studios, as he did not have a hand in the scripts.[28] That tension, however, did not slow the spread of the Clancy technothriller brand. Arguably Clancy's most beloved and well-known character, Jack Ryan, has been popularized by iconic actors like Alec Baldwin, Harrison Ford, Ben Affleck and John Krasinski.

Clancy was also interested in expanding his brand into other media forms. The Clancyverse looms large across film, television and video games. Clancy cofounded the video game company Red Storm Entertainment in North Carolina with British Royal Navy Captain Doug Littlejohns in 1996.[29] In 2000 the studio was acquired by Ubisoft Entertainment, a major international interactive entertainment company that produces massive game franchises like *Assassin's Creed*, *Far Cry*, and *Watch Dogs*. Clancy's stories have become highly successful tactical simulation games like *Splinter Cell* (2000–), *Ghost Recon* (2001–), *Rainbow Six* (1998–), *The Division* (2016–), and others, all presented under the "Tom Clancy's" brand.[30] These highly successful Clancy games point to the sweeping impact and potency of the author's vision and its transmissibility across media. Clancy's impact on television is apparent in the prevalence of procedural and highly technical narratives, including officially unrelated counterterrorist action drama series like Fox's *24* (2001–2010) and, more recently, *Tom Clancy's Jack Ryan*, an Amazon Prime television series (2018–2023) that builds on the character. Clancy is truly an iconic figure of the military-entertainment complex. As Jason Cowley of the *New Statesman* observes, "It is no exaggeration to describe Clancy as the novelist who comes closest to understanding and animating the modern American psyche: paranoid, deluded, isolated and aggressively confrontational."[31]

The military embraced Clancy into its social, educational, and cultural milieu. Evan Thomas, among many others, has noted the rapport: "The Navy loves having Tom Clancy. Not just the Navy, but the Army, the Air Force and the Marine Corps. Admirals and generals open doors for him; Pentagon officials debrief him; his books are required reading at war colleges."[32] American historian Andrew Bacevich similarly suggested that "Clancy depicted American soldiers and would-be soldiers precisely as they wished to see themselves."[33]

If Clancy, through his many printed and recorded interviews, presents himself as an everyman enthusiast of the military and champion of traditional patriarchal family values, Michael Crichton reads more as a retreating polymath, whose interests reside in the social, cultural, ethical, and existential complications that result from innovation. Crichton was born in Chicago during World War II and raised on Long Island, the son of a journalist/executive and a homemaker. He, like Clancy, was deeply influenced by growing up during the Cold War; in a speech at Caltech, he described his childhood as "a time of widespread fear and uncertainty" but went on to say that "even as a child, I believed that science represented the best and greatest hope for mankind."[34]

A Harvard-trained (but not practicing) medical doctor, Crichton initially churned out fiction under a pseudonym to pay the bills. He published *The Andromeda Strain* in 1969 under his own name, and it was adapted into a film in 1971. With its success, he resolved not to further pursue a medical profession and set his sights on Hollywood. Unlike Clancy, Crichton became interested in filmmaking and directed a made-for-television film called *Pursuit* (1972), based on his book *Binary*.[35] After some middling attempts, Crichton wrote the screenplay for *Westworld* (1973) and succeeded in securing the role of director. He also wrote and directed *Looker* (1981), which blended themes of advanced technology, hypercapitalism, and mass culture.

The author's success and influence over the public imagination around technology and innovation took off in the 1990s. In 1990 Crichton published *Jurassic Park*; the film based on his screenplay adaptation for Steven Spielberg was released in 1993 and became the most successful film in history for its time. In early 1994 he published *Disclosure*, which topped the bestseller list, while *ER*, also a Crichton invention, was the number-one series on television.[36] *Disclosure* was adapted to film in late 1994, starring Demi Moore and Michael Douglas. The next year, Crichton's 1995 novel *The Lost World* (a sequel to *Jurassic Park*) was number one, while *Congo* was a number-one film, and *ER* became the most-watched television show. In 1996 he achieved this again, with *Airframe* in books, *Twister* at the box office, and *ER* in television topping their respective fields' bestseller lists.[37] By the time he died, he had written eighteen major novels, thirteen of which became major motion pictures; directed seven films; and reportedly sold more than two hundred million books.[38]

While Crichton described his work as critical of the hazards and dangers of science, he seemed more interested in drawing out the cultural tensions and anxieties around science, technology, and innovation. "I love all movie sequences where things go wrong," he once revealed.[39] Crichton often dealt with the subject of how technology is represented in fiction, but he contested the notion that his work is opposed to science and technology.[40] In fact, his position was against a "move-fast-break-things" attitude toward innovation and for ethically informed applications of science and technology.[41] Crichton conveyed his position on technology through his stories, and it is often effectively carried through in filmic translations. But he was also extremely direct about his positions in interviews and public lectures, refusing to demonize technology but instead focusing on human failures to ethically engage with it. This is well-captured in one interview in which Crichton suggested that we, not our technological innovations, are ultimately the problem:[42]

> We live in a culture of relentless, round-the-clock boosterism for science and technology. With each new discovery and invention, the virtues are always oversold, the drawbacks understated. Who can forget the freely mobile society of the automobile, the friendly atom, the paperless office, the impending crisis of too much leisure time, or the era of universal education ushered in by television? We now hear the same utopian claims about the Internet. But everyone knows science and technology are inevitably a mixed blessing. How then will the fears, the concerns, the downside of technology be expressed? Because it has to appear somewhere. So it appears in movies, in stories.[43]

Ultimately, the thrill in Crichton's stories comes from an anxiety about what, with all our innovation, we have done to ourselves.

BUT WHAT DO TECHNOTHRILLERS ACTUALLY MEAN?

Scholar Martin Kevorkian, writing on the tech figure in popular film, attributes the technothriller genre to Michael Crichton, defining it simply in terms of how the "thrill derives from the threat of the techno."[44] Kevorkian discusses how the technothriller "engages the anxieties of the computer age" and suggests that Crichton operationalizes a "retooling of nineteenth-century colonial adventure paradigms, via the instrumentalizing of race, to serve the twenty-first-century needs of American national identity."[45] In my final chapter, I'll return to Kevorkian's analysis of race as it intersects with reformulating national identity through the figure of the Black technologist. Bracketing that conversation for the moment, Kevorkian keenly observes that Crichton's narratives deftly touch on fears of computer technologies, often addressing "whether the information age has led the United States past its national time. Can the exceptional American empire still lead in a networked world increasingly controlled by the computer command line?"[46] Kevorkian argues that Americans hold in tension fear and fascination with advanced computational technologies. In general, I agree with his analysis of Crichton's stories in literary and filmic form as new manifestations of old colonialist narratives, adapted to contemporary American national identity formulation.[47]

Alternatively, scholar J. William Gibson points to the nationalistic dimensions of Clancy's technothriller by identifying their political discourse, suggesting that Clancy's writing performs "a 'recuperative' or healing function; it attempts to restore the military to its former (pre–Vietnam War) position of prestige and power. It further promises that by increasing the military's economic resources and political autonomy, the United States can once again become the world's dominant power."[48] If you consider visual culture around that conflict, in films like *Apocalypse Now* (Francis Ford Coppola, 1979) and *Platoon* (Oliver Stone, 1986), American soldiers are not portrayed in the same way as World War II soldiers. Soldiers in World War II are often presented as morally just, clean-cut, principled, fundamentally good and fighting a "good" war; they are often educated, and almost always white. The visual culture around Vietnam War soldiers, on the other hand, generally presents them as much more diverse, uneducated, morally compromised, and nonidealized. There is much more of an association with drug culture, and they are not victorious. Clancy's technothrillers are all stories that involve generic good guys (us) and bad guys (them), nationalistic zeal, military men, advanced technology, and a staunch moral certitude about the pre–Vietnam War version of a real man: heroic, family-oriented, sensible, ethical, and a true patriot. A less charitable reader might call them propagandistic. William F. Ryan went so far as to characterize Clancy's books as "national security Westerns."[49]

As Gibson states, national power and dominance on the global stage is also galvanized through economic means. Underattended to in the literature of the technothriller is the impact of global hypercapitalism as another engine driving American dominance as a superpower, which I explore in the chapter on technocapitalism in the films *Rollerball* and *Looker* (see chapter 5). One astute observation made by scholar Michael J. Blouin connects the work of Crichton with the rise of neoliberalism: "Crichton's novels similarly engage readers in aesthetic experiences that seek to condition them to handle scientific and economic understanding in tandem: remaining open to endless change; acknowledging an inability to predict what comes next; forfeiting a sense of structure while maintaining that an internal structure does exist."[50] Blouin addressed the economic thread through the struggle between neoconservative and neoliberal ideologies emblematized in the work of Clancy and Crichton, respectively. "If Crichton's novels weaponize uncertainty to promote an unfettered marketplace," he writes, "Clancy's novels weaponize variability to restore faith in tradition."[51] According to Blouin, each responds strongly to his moment; Crichton defies social constraints with a neoliberal bent, while Clancy reaffirms the neoconservative family man in a sociopolitical moment in which feminism, queer politics, struggles for racial equality, and challenges to so-called traditional America have shaken the implicit value of the family unit. Crichton's works encourage an embrace of uncertainty and adaptation, signaling, for Blouin, an embrace of a free and unfettered market. Important here is the direct link acknowledged between sociotechnical imaginaries and nation building. It is clear that for Blouin, Clancy and Crichton address different facets of the same anxiety connected to social changes taking place in culture.

The impact of Crichton's technothrillers on larger national scientific and technological projects cannot be overestimated. In her brilliant unpacking of the connection between Crichton's writing and STS, Joanna Radin identifies the author's use of fictionalized moral crises as a means to "colonize" a conversation about innovation and critique Cold War cultures of scientific and technological expertise.[52] Importantly, Radin points out that through his speculations on present (as opposed to future) innovations, Crichton "instructed his readers about how to feel about science and technology, highlighting certain potential risks yet always admixing them with wonder."[53] Beginning with the novel *The Andromeda Strain*, then moving through some of his most beloved and impactful stories, such as *Westworld* and *Jurassic Park*, Radin proposes that Crichton used his world-building skills to mine fears of the unforeseen consequences of science and technology as a means to engage with core concerns of STS. In fact, she argues, Crichton both read STS scholarship and refers to it in his writing. Through this, and his speculative improvisations on real advances in science and technology, he molded sociotechnical imaginaries around topics like virtuality, biotechnology, robotics, genomics, and information technology.

Truly, the technothriller has two fathers. While Crichton and Clancy are certainly not the only two authors to pen successful technothrillers, it is hard to overstate the profound impact of their stories on the trajectory of the literary genre, its filmic counterparts, and all they have since inspired. In the end Crichton reads as much more introspective—or to put it more precisely, as inviting some introspection in the reader—through moral situations that motivate a response to the uncertainty and instability of the cultural, political and economic upheavals of the 1960s and 1970s. William Grimes of the *New York Times* described Crichton as having "used fiction to explore the moral and political problems posed by modern technology and scientific breakthroughs, which in his books defied human control or ended up as tools for evil ends."[54] Clancy, on the other hand, is more openly jingoistic, perpetuating a set of superlative narratives about America as the greatest country in the world. His work reaffirms traditional family values and a desire for continuity in the face of a chaotic new national reality.

Ultimately, the filmic technothriller has elements that tend to coalesce into affinities based on these two authors' distinct models. These elements include a detailed focus on biological, scientific, or military technology; the use of generic characters; political or espionage-based intrigue or adventure; and a strong sense of grappling with the sociotechnical present. But the genre's edges are undefined, and I exploit this blurred set of boundaries to my advantage, with the intention of mobilizing a useful framework. However, the technothriller's key components remain the centrality of technology for the storytelling and its strong hand, guiding audiences to shape sociotechnical imaginaries that inform notions of American identity as a global superpower.

To crack open new understandings of the technothriller, part of this research focuses on mining the patterns of feeling, political affects, and failures of the imagination that undergird powerful filmic visions of technological dominance. These films grapple with value systems that are endemic of a tectonic shift in American culture around the coming of computational technology, biotechnology and advanced technological military warfare. These are tied to the crucial function of scientific and technological innovation for America's continued dominance as a global superpower—and tinged with the ontological crisis wrought by the Second World War. This startling new reality gave rise to major themes that, according to Boyer, engendered a cultural shift and continue to dominate nuclear discourse: "the visions of atomic devastation, the earnest efforts to rouse people to resist such a fate, the voices seeking to soothe or deflect these fears, the insistence that security lay in greater technical expertise and in more and bigger weaponry."[55] In this regard, as we move into close readings of technothrillers, the political affective dimensions of the films provide contextual cultural insight into what might superficially appear to be merely popular (or even debased) forms of diversion.

2

PROTOCOLS AND HAZMAT SUITS

The Biological Technothriller

What do we do?
—Dr. Jeremy Stone, *The Andromeda Strain* (1971)

A DREAD OF UNCERTAINTY

"What do we do?" These are the last words spoken in director Robert Wise's 1971 *The Andromeda Strain*—notably by a scientist, an expert who is supposed to know exactly what to do. With this utterance he exclaims a core technothriller anxiety about what technological systems humans have unwittingly ensnared themselves within. *The Andromeda Strain* prefigures modern contagion films like *Outbreak* (Wolfgang Petersen, 1995), *28 Days Later* (Danny Boyle, 2003), *Contagion* (Steven Soderbergh, 2011), *World War Z* (Marc Forster, 2013), and more recently *Annihilation* (Alex Garland, 2018). This parting question captures the existential crisis and the dread of uncertainty wrought by innovation.

Crichton's novel of the same name from 1969, on which the film is based, is often called the first literary technothriller. A work of speculative fiction about the attempt to prevent biological attack by an alien crystalline form that would threaten life on earth, both the book and its faithful film adaptation combine anxieties over nuclear and biological warfare. The book was Crichton's ninth novel, but the first published under his name.[1] It details five nerve-racking days of struggle to prevent a potential biological outbreak. When the inhabitants of a small Texas town pry open a downed space probe capsule, they unwittingly release a deadly alien strain that immediately kills all but two inhabitants—an old alcoholic and a baby. The government activates the secret Project Wildfire Alert, mobilizing elite scientific and medical experts to understand and neutralize what has been unleashed.

Though fictional, the book uses a detached procedural tone that mimics governmental documentation to convey its panic narrative. Crichton described his interest in a "technological crisis" for which the best solution was that it had never occurred in the first place. Robert Wise, the director, later characterized the filmic adaptation as "a story of the world's first space-age crisis," owing to the otherworldly origins of the threat, and likely the film's larger context of the Space Race, the 1950s–1970s competition between the Soviet Union and the United States for domination in aerospace capabilities.[2]

In the novel, the scientific and routinized provide an air of total immersion into a specialized world, using the dull, authoritative tone characteristic of an official report. Its notably dry proceduralism mimics bureaucratic reportage: first, readers are informed, "THIS FILE IS CLASSIFIED TOP SECRET," lending the feel of a sensitive dossier. The book's five sections cover the four days of the crisis plus the day after its resolution in a meticulous recounting of "actual" events. The narrative also appropriates names of real institutions (Caltech, the US Navy, NASA) and further frames its events as real by thanking participants in the Wildfire Project in the acknowledgments and characterizing the book as a distillation of a fifteen-thousand-page governmental manuscript.

Crichton's scenario for *The Andromeda Strain* was inspired by a speculative footnote in a 1953 textbook, *The Major Features of Evolution*, which Crichton paraphrases as "Science fiction writers have never written about organisms that might be in the upper atmosphere."[3] Combining what he called "science fact" and "science fiction," Crichton fabricates an account of the time life on earth was narrowly saved from annihilation by biological crisis. He describes the scenario as grounded in truth, though technically hypothetical.[4]

Wise, the director, became interested in the story even before the novel was published.[5] Wise had already directed iconic films like *Citizen Kane* (1941), *The Day the Earth Stood Still* (1951), *The Sound of Music* (1965) and *West Side Story* (1961). "It was, in a sense," he explained of his interest in *Andromeda*, "an indictment of biological warfare, and it was that underlying note that appealed to me very much. . . . But the film was also going to have something important to say about the area of biological warfare and chemical warfare and nuclear warfare."[6]

As such, *The Andromeda Strain* is an iconic filmic example of the gathering force of narratives mirroring the existential dread heralded by new technologies. And in a more symbolic sense, it expresses a phobic relationship to the body's subjection to protocols and control-based modular logics and systems. What sociotechnical imaginaries are formulated in this vision? What performed imaginary is expressed in the visual culture of this film? As a theoretical object, what does it start to tell us? What sort of affective intensities does it generate? To answer these questions fully, we must first understand the film's context.

CONTEXT OF A SOCIOTECHNICAL IMAGINARY

When *The Andromeda Strain* was released, public anxieties were already stoked by three fears: biological threats, networked computation, and nuclear destruction. The profound existential uncertainty following the development of the atomic bomb and germ warfare, particularly in the wake of the Second World War, made sense. Looming large were the Space Race, the moon landing in 1969, and the launch that year of the US Advanced Research Projects Agency Network (ARPANET), the first network to use packet-switching technology to communicate between computers in remote locations. By the mid-1950s concerns about nuclear weapons and radioactive fallout were key cultural concerns, reinvigorated when the United States and Russia both began test series that resulted in ecological harm. New fears included radioactive poisoning. Paul Boyer, a historian of biological weapons, writes: "It was the United States' 1954 test series that really aroused alarm. . . . In 1955, radioactive rain fell on Chicago. In 1959, deadly strontium-90 began to show up in milk. The *Saturday Evening Post* ran a feature called 'Fallout: The Silent Killer.' A new group of scientists and physicians warned of the health hazards of fallout, including leukemia, bone cancer, and long-term genetic damage. A full-blown fallout scare gripped the nation."[7]

These new existential threats of nuclear annihilation, radioactive poisoning, and human-induced ecological disaster flooded society, evident in the material culture of fallout shelter signs, school drills, and "Duck and Cover" civil defense films. Cinema and literature constantly reminded everyone of these dangers. According to Boyer, this fear dissipated somewhat with the resolution of the Cuban Missile Crisis in 1963 and the urgency of the Vietnam War, leading to a period of nuclear apathy from the mid-1960s to the 1970s.[8] The intensity around nuclear concerns, both for weaponry and the perils of nuclear energy, would return in the mid-1970s and ratchet up in the 1980s, which postdates *Andromeda*. But the degree to which such anxieties would have already been on the minds of American viewers in 1971 cannot be overestimated.

Complicating this were terrors surrounding the ongoing development of germ warfare and genetic engineering. Media studies scholar José Van Dijck identifies Crichton's novel as one of the first to popularize the "potential dangers of microbial life forms escaping from a heavily secluded laboratory."[9] Van Dijck also points to the connection between space travel and genetics, and the angst around the possibility of alien organisms returning to earth with astronauts.[10] She characterizes the late 1960s and 1970s as a time when notions of irresponsible scientists, DNA manipulation, and environmental danger were part of a general ethos of increased attention to ethics in innovation. In addition, due to more than four hundred infections among laboratory workers at Fort Detrick between 1943 and 1969, the US Army Medical Unit was created for germ warfare defense.[11] US spending on biological weapons increased after President John F. Kennedy took office in 1961. Corporate involvement in military research also rose dramatically, leading to a 1970s "golden biomedical era" of scientific discovery and innovation in antibiotics and vaccines.[12] All of these realities shaped the public imagination around the ecological and moral consequences of irresponsible scientific pursuits, generating themes that would be repeated in Crichton's book *Jurassic Park* (1990).

Computation was also a key technological innovation highlighted in *The Andromeda Strain.* In 1971 computers were neither easily accessible nor household objects. Average Americans at the time were unfamiliar with computers and sometimes even fearful of them. Filmmaker and scholar Daniel Dinello connects the virus thriller theme with technophobia, particularly of advanced digital technologies. He suggests that the spread of technology has metaphorical viral dimensions that thrive in corporatized and militarized environments and that become parasitic, "infiltrating, manipulating, seizing control and mutating its human host to support its own survival and evolution."[13] This theme resonates with *Andromeda* as the original technothriller, capturing a kind of inability to escape technological development or imagine outside of it. In other words, it frames technological innovation and its perils as inevitable, even fated.

Here I also want to introduce another central component of the sociotechnical context: American race and gender politics. Although the film contains little overt reference to these matters, both the civil rights movement of the 1950s and 1960s and the 1960s women's liberation movement occupied the US consciousness at the time. *The Andromeda Strain* was made against a backdrop of the Civil Rights Act of 1964, the 1965 Voting Rights Act, the assassination of Malcolm X in 1965, the founding of the National Organization for Women in 1966, the assassinations of Martin Luther King Jr. and Robert F. Kennedy in 1968, and the Stonewall Riots in 1968, as well as myriad other liberation and decolonization movements worldwide. While the film may seem focused on a critique of biotechnological threat, these larger sociocultural anxieties manifest in *Andromeda*, and particularly reveal themselves through two key female characters, researcher Ruth Leavitt and nurse Karen Anson. It would be impossible to understand this film without considering the intense social and cultural turbulence present when it was made.

ANALYZING *ANDROMEDA*

Andromeda literalizes all these anxieties into a narrative of an unknown microbiological entity from space that grows exponentially and eludes even the sharpest scientific minds and technological systems. It wonderfully combines story with form to convey a gathering sense of constriction and anxiety, moving from a sense of authority, protocol, and control to uncertainty and uncontrollability. The film strikingly opens with an acknowledgment in stark printed text across the screen, the same that begins the book: "This film concerns the four-day history of a major American scientific crisis." Project Scoop and the Wildfire Laboratory are entreated to tell the full story, as though this fiction actually happened but is largely unknown to the public.

The film's title sequence strikes the tone of a scientific thriller, showing portions of diagrams, topographical maps, and a "biowar map," and indicates "scientific background support" by Caltech and the Jet Propulsion Laboratory, two authentic paragons of technology and innovation. Text is layered over text in translucent colors against a black background, like an overhead projector image, moving, slipping off the screen in various directions, just beyond the grasp of real legibility. The title sequence's visuals, combined with an unsettling, grating, machinic score, introduce a smooth, hard certainty of bureaucracy and an aesthetics of procedure and the modular.

Those interlocking systems are revealed through an inciting incident: a nondescript young sergeant observes a town from a distance at night through a scope, then returns to an anonymous-looking grey van, slamming its doors shut. A satellite dish extends from the top of the van and begins to rotate, communicating with parties interested in whatever this man has observed. Inside, under a hard red light, the sergeant double-checks a radar to see there is no activity in the town. He has his partner verify his observations in dialogue heavily peppered with technical jargon, invoking a network large enough to have its own coded language. They mention "Project: Scoop." The two personnel triangulate the location of a satellite to be recovered in the tiny town of Piedmont, Arizona.

Suddenly we see the larger investment in the little hamlet's mysteries: When the two observers' communication is cut off while they attempt to retrieve the satellite, we cut to an airbase, where a highly decorated officer orders a jet to photograph the situation on the ground. Technical footage reveals many dead, and larger systems are set in motion; the officer unlocks a red phone and initiates a "Wildfire Alert."

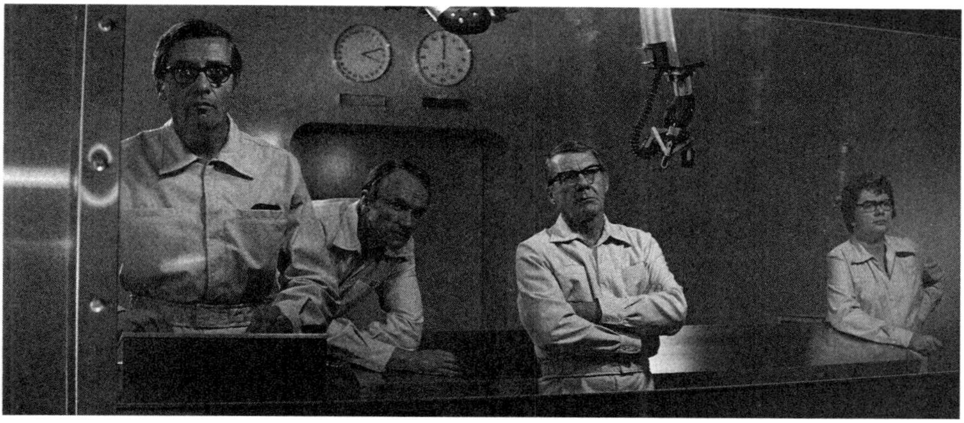

In a sequence that has become typical of technothrillers, a series of protocols are procedurally enacted. A teletype hammers out names to receive top-secret clearance. Experts are summoned. Armed military men collect Dr. Jeremy Stone, a bacteriology professor, during a party at his home; he recognizes the code word "Fire" and abruptly departs, to his wife's confusion. Stone is handed a top-secret file about the Scoop Project, whose purpose is to collect organisms from outer space and study their potential harms. Stone is whisked off on an empty plane while his team is assembled: good-natured older pathology professor Charles Dutton; acerbic, no-nonsense microbiologist Ruth Leavitt; and cocky young surgeon Mark Hall.

Stone and Hall fly via army helicopter to evaluate the possible "space germ." We learn that Stone previously warned the president about extraterrestrial life and proposed the building of a high-tech "Wildfire Lab" in a remote area, equipped with a nuclear self-destruct in case of outbreak.

FIGURE 2.1

The four scientists, Dr. Jeremy Stone, Dr. Mark Hall, Dr. Charles Dutton, and Dr. Ruth Leavitt, are summoned to prevent a potential extinction event on earth. *The Andromeda Strain* (Universal Pictures, 1971).

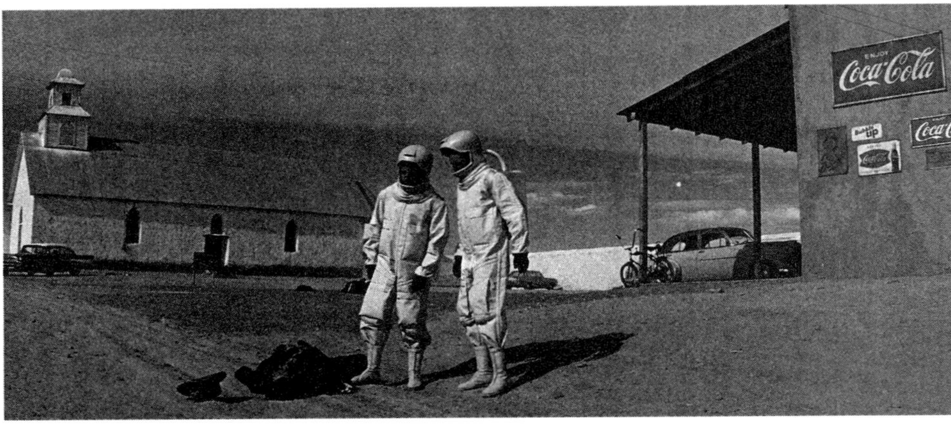

Extreme safety precautions are observed before Hall and Stone set foot in Piedmont, including gassing the site to kill vultures that might spread contagion by ingesting the flesh of dead victims. Outfitted in hazmat suits, the two experts rappel from the chopper in front of a small chapel in a rocky desert town. All the inhabitants seem to be dead. As the two men traverse the town like astronauts on an alien planet, we see grim tableaus of people posed in death, apparently struck down instantly wherever they were. This is presented in a distinctive filmic style that compacts the visual field with information—an important element to which I'll return. Most disturbing is the casual everydayness of the townsfolks' activities. Hall and Stone locate the two Scoop agents, also dead, with wounds that, oddly, haven't bled. Upon cutting one body, they find its blood pours out in granules, seeming to have congealed on contact with the organism. The sight is horrific but dispassionately presented, as if part of a lab experiment. Stone and Hall eventually locate two survivors, a crying baby and an old, deranged man brandishing a meat cleaver. Stone

FIGURE 2.2

Hall and Stone investigate the mysterious sudden deaths in the hamlet of Piedmont. The hazmat suits they wear became iconic filmic symbols for fear of contagion. *The Andromeda Strain* (Universal Pictures, 1971).

urges the military to neutralize the entire site of Piedmont to prevent the contagion's spread.

Meanwhile, Dutton and Leavitt, the two other experts, introduce us to the impressive hub of study, experimentation, and control: the Wildfire Lab. They drive across an arid Nevada desert and head for what looks like an agricultural testing site, which hides a vast subterranean laboratory with advanced technology and rigorous disinfection procedures. They enter a striking stainless-steel anteroom with biometric access and color-coded levels of sterilization, beginning with a red circular control room with blinking panels of lights. Stone and Hall meet Dutton and Leavitt there, and they are all processed, decontaminated, and immunized over sixteen hours. Lab personnel familiarize the four experts with protocols, assign them duties, and introduce them to the "fully automatic, computerized and self-regulated" facility—an impressive technological display for its time.

Hall, the surgeon, learns he has been chosen as the "odd man" to hold the red key that can abort the self-destruct nuclear fail-safe built into Wildfire. Leavitt curtly explains the "odd man hypothesis," which identifies the single man as most rationally and emotionally capable of determining whether the self-destruct sequence should proceed, if triggered by a containment breach.

Of note is the protracted filmic attention paid to protocols. An impressive, color-coded dynamic projection of the five-floor lab is used to demonstrate procedures for biological decontamination, each level more sterile than the previous one. The experts must undergo increasingly violating procedures: they are exposed to radiation, inoculated, and have their outer layers of skin singed off in a xenon lamp apparatus. They are released to recover from their decontamination in cold, hard-edged, screen-filled rooms: spaces of control and surveillance with a constant flow of technical jargon over the comms. Left to their thoughts, each expert ponders the disturbing dimensions of this new knowledge of exobiological life.

Other kinds of tests begin as well, relayed with documentary detail. In one iconic scene involving a sealed experimental environment ("hot room") that scientists control remotely with robotic arms, a rhesus monkey and lab rat are exposed to the germ with lethal results.[14] We

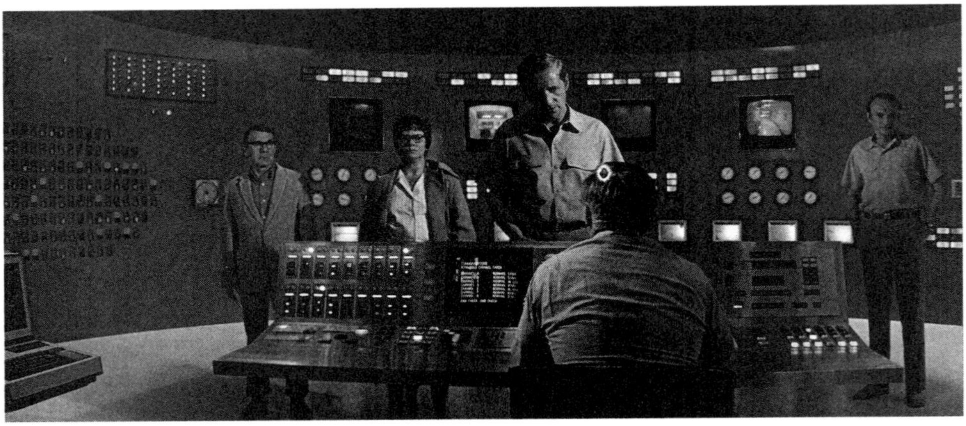

also meet the only Black character, Karen Anson, a capable nurse who is highly practiced in biowar procedures and familiar with the lab's vital MEDCOM computational system. She instructs Hall on its use, and they both don elaborate protective suits, which allow them to study the living patients—while also reminding viewers of the invisible danger in the hot room. Meanwhile, Leavitt and Stone attempt to isolate the alien organism, while Dutton performs animal autopsies. We observe their protocols in illustrative detail. They often communicate through videophone, novel at the time. There are close-ups of complicated alien-looking medical equipment and animals being experimented on. All these procedures require painstakingly slow steps, often captured in full duration.

The film repeatedly presents human fallibility during the interface with technology as a critical concern. Leavitt observes the alien green Andromeda strain material on the space rock throb and expand, but initially doesn't believe her eyes. Then Dutton sees it, too. It quivers again,

FIGURE 2.3

The scientists enter the red level of the Wildfire Lab, the first of five decontamination levels. It is visually striking for its curved, bright red walls, and control room with panels filled with blinking lights. *The Andromeda Strain* (Universal Pictures, 1971).

changes color, and multiplies. The scientists work feverishly but experience setbacks and exhaustion. The whole system of this massive facility, with its backup laser systems and fail-safes, is nearly undone by human error. In one case a small slip of printer paper lodged between a bell and its ringer eludes communications experts. The problem is corrected, but not without nearly causing mass exposure. Critically, we learn that despite Leavitt's tenacity, she hides a condition (epilepsy, triggered by blinking red lights) that causes her to enter a trancelike state and miss critical details while observing lab results. Dutton is almost killed by carelessly exposing himself to the germ during an animal autopsy. And most dramatically, the whole facility's nuclear self-destruct system is triggered when the Andromeda strain evolves.

To deactivate the self-destruct mode, Hall must scale the facility's perilous five-story core with its toxic gas and laser weapons. Disoriented by a laser burn, he inserts his red key to disengage the self-destruct sequence in the nick of time, before collapsing. When he awakens in a hospital bed, the elite team explains that they've laced the clouds with chemicals that will bind to Andromeda, and as it rains down into the Pacific Ocean, it will be neutralized. But they haven't actually solved the problem, only gotten lucky that the microbiological entity evolved into something harmless. They did nothing to control it; they merely learned enough to understand that the strain could not survive in a saline-rich environment.

In the last scene Stone reports the team's findings to a senator, confirming that extraterrestrial forms of life exist and there is no guarantee that this type of biological crisis won't occur again, and ending with that question: "What do we do?" In the final shot we see the pulsating Andromeda strain grow as it overloads the computer recording it. The film ends on a foreboding note, implying that that we now live in a world where our probing into space and pursuit of germ warfare has unleashed new existential threats.

PROCEDURALISM AS FEATURE, NOT BUG

Though *The Andromeda Strain* enjoyed box-office success, the film received mixed critical reviews that often focused on its apparently dull fixation with the procedural. What we can now situate as a technothriller origin film was then met with puzzlement. "*The Andromeda Strain* spends millions to mask its grade-B origins" noted critic Paul Zimmerman, going on to describe the film as fundamentally apolitical but gesturing vaguely toward the moral dimensions of scientific pursuits.[15] Although other critics recognized its messages about the quandaries of innovation, many characterized its proceduralism not as the herald of a new genre, but a shortcoming of storytelling technique. For example, Pauline Kael of the *New Yorker* wrote, "The decontamination process takes over the movie for so long that we practically forget the menace to the world outside."[16]

For many, the film was "process porn," fixated on technical detail at the expense of a good story arc.[17] But I disagree. In particular, the careful attention to the Wildfire site as a cutting-edge research facility with the most advanced tools and techniques, housing the most elite experts, is not a matter of too much attention directed at procedure. The filmic investigation of the procedural, and the modularity it demands, is itself the story. In *The Andromeda Strain*, proceduralism is not a bug; it is a feature.

The mise-en-scène is key to understanding the film's affective intensity. At the time, the film's aesthetics were distinctive—its washed-out, cerebral rationality embellished only by excessive focus on technological sites and tools compacted into the claustrophobic frame. Wise engaged cinematographer Robert H. Kline, whose unconventional use of on-screen space created a distinctive split-screen look that still sets the film apart. I argue that it is not incidental, but an aesthetic choice critical to its major themes.

The filmmakers created authenticity of technical detail through consulting with advisors from the Jet Propulsion Laboratory (JPL), where the director saw laboratories, computer technology, and the elaborate equipment that is so foregrounded in the film.[18] Douglas Trumbull, who completed special effects for *2001: A Space Odyssey*, was brought on to image the otherworldly, self-replicating life form.[19] Reportedly, $250,000 of the film's $6 million overall budget was dedicated to visualizing the fictive alien contagion.[20] The primary set was also critical, and neither expense nor effort was spared to image the cylindrical underground Wildfire Laboratory. The elaborate set used "almost every square inch of Universal's cavernous Stage 12" but it required digging seventeen feet below the sound stage to accommodate the daunting five-story main shaft's design.[21] According to Jon Bloom, the on-set photographer, "its construction alone represented an expenditure of more than $300,000. A complete 360-degree corridor, 1/8 mile in circumference was also constructed to simulate the corridor of the underground emergency laboratory."[22] The highly geometric, starkly segmented, color-coded underground lab contrasts with the muted tones of the organic desert above it and suggests not only an antiseptic space, but a highly constructed, unnatural one that feels almost like a buried space station.

Humans in the film are often dwarfed by impressive, complicated-looking machinery, and move through spaces that discipline their bodies through order and modularity or, alternatively, extend their bodies with technology. To create this impression, the filmmakers borrowed an enormous amount of scientific equipment from JPL and North American Rockwell, estimated at a value of three million dollars.[23] As Robert Wise declared, "The sets are the stars of *Andromeda*."[24] The film was nominated for Academy Awards in both Film Editing and Art Direction, confirming the centrality of these components to the storytelling. Every aesthetic decision plunges the viewer into a world of technical and governmental jargon, and the film is presented as though it is dry reportage of actual events. Even the cast consisted of well-liked but less celebrated actors, adding to the realist feel. One *New York Times* reviewer, Roger Greenspun, groused, "Since nobody greatly feels or acts, we are left with the drama of people tensely sitting around in chairs, twisting dials and watching TV monitors. From time to time, somebody gets up and paces the room."[25]

Significantly, the film visually introduces augmented forms of seeing in its first minutes of narrative action. The town of Piedmont is observed with a powerful lens resembling a nightscope vision. Throughout, technological terms, verification, jargon, and imaging suggest machine vision, data-based imaging, and diagrammatic forms. Imaging techniques that depart from human vision invoke a rational machine gaze, such as during the scientists' decontamination. While the scientists are irradiated, probed, and exposed to a xenon lamp, viewers observe them in forms of vision alien to that of the naked eye. The filmmaker also often opted for a visual approach that viewers of the time would have associated with documentaries.

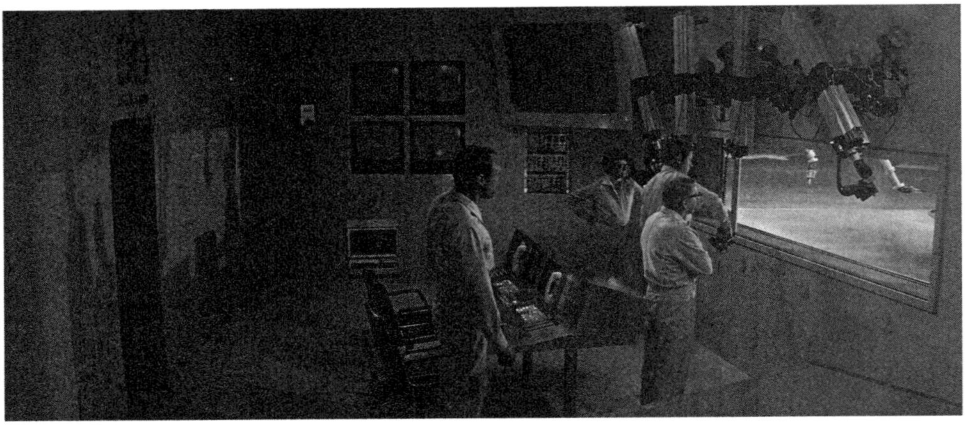

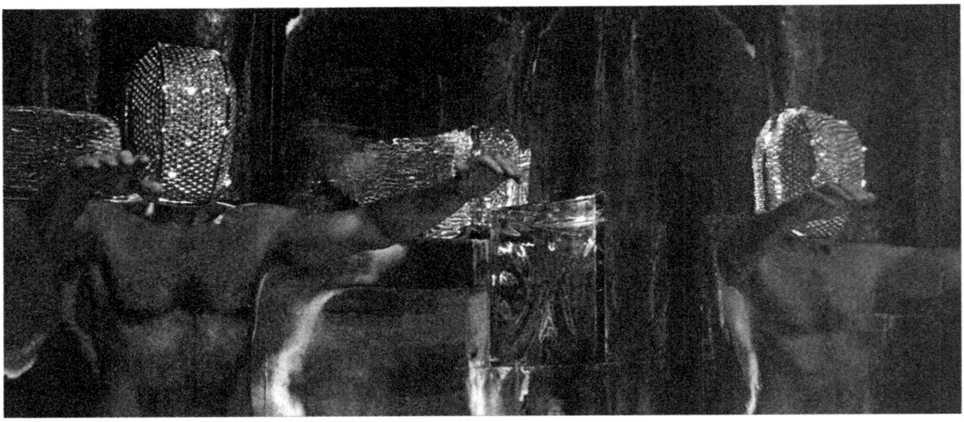

FIGURE 2.4

The four scientists are dwarfed by large, complicated-looking technical equipment. *The Andromeda Strain* (Universal Pictures, 1971).

FIGURE 2.5

A scientist is subjected to a xenon lamp as a form of decontamination. *The Andromeda Strain* (Universal Pictures, 1971).

Modularity suggests a quality of interchangeability, or pieces that can be assembled in various ways, and can even imply a kind of machine rationalism or scientific process. This theme is deeply entangled with the identity construct of white maleness, which epitomizes particular kinds of knowing, rationality, and mastery.[26] The visual representation of modularity functions as a dominant motif, and manifests in several ways. First, there is the use of split-screen imagery. For example, early in the film Stone and Hall explore Piedmont in their white hazmat suits, an image now ubiquitous in contagion films but novel then.[27] While the two experts peer into windows, the filmic image narrows to a vertical orientation on the left with a continuous tracking shot. On the right, a series of images appears like a slide show, using multiple frames against a stark black background, rather than montage. A man lies dead next to a bowl of dog food. Another elderly man with a hearing aid and glasses has expired with his mouth wide open. A woman in a blue dress has dropped dead on her linoleum floor beside an open refrigerator. A girl with her wide blue eyes and mouth agape lies on the ground, clutching her tattered Raggedy Ann doll. A beautiful young woman lies dead in bed, nude, a peace sign pendant prominent on her chest. The experts are gaining a fragmentary understanding of the scene.

Reviewer Sylvia Millar interpreted this effect by suggesting "the split expresses the separation of technological man from the consequences of his actions."[28] This observational separation is present, but what it signals is the scientists' organizational impetus toward the modular. Throughout, they segment their observations into measurable components and try to fit them into a whole that makes sense.

A second expression of that modularity is in the film's distinctive and prodigious use of the split-field diopter shot. This shot compacts space within the frame by joining two images by splitting not the screen but the lens. The cinematographer adds a partial lens over one segment of the main lens, allowing two focal points to be sharp simultaneously, similar to bifocal lenses.[29] This technique is one effective way of eliminating the shot/reverse shot method, but the split-field diopter shot requires limited movement of the lens, since the cinematographer usually hides the seam between the splits with a vertical element like a doorframe or shadow. Moving the camera reveals a telltale blur that demarks the seam. This

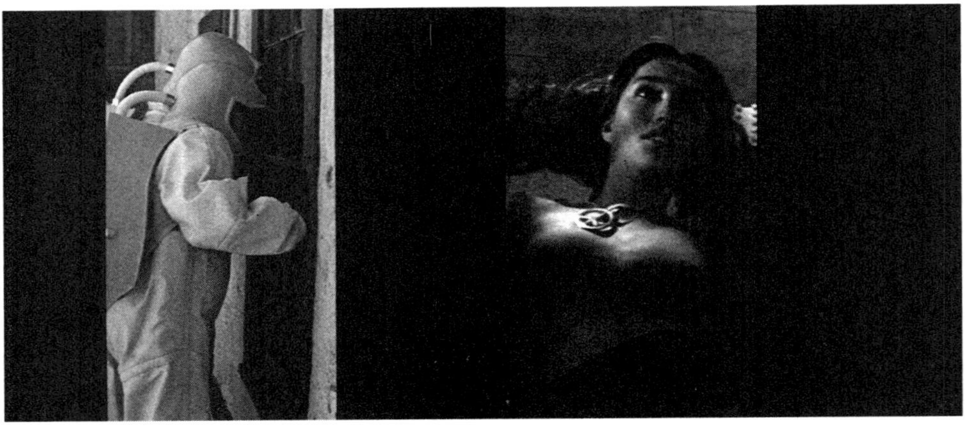

technique simulates an artificial deep focus, making things in the foreground and background legible at the same time. Most films use this kind of shot sparingly, but in *The Andromeda Strain* it appears more than two hundred times.

The psychological function of the split-field diopter shot produced by the modular use of two lenses in one frame is useful for understanding the kind of tension Wise wished to impart. Film scholar Paul Ramaeker describes this shot as disorienting because of the flatness that it forces onto the image. Cinema's normal depth cues are not present to fully define the space, so the shot prevents viewers from understanding differentiation of foreground and background. The "alternation between depth and flatness" causes disorientation that creates "oscillation" and "dynamic

FIGURE 2.6

Modularity, such as in the use of split-screen imagery, becomes a theme throughout the film. Here, scientists at Piedmont peer observe dead victims of the contagion. On the left are the scientists in hazmat suits. On the right is the dead woman they see through the window. *The Andromeda Strain* (Universal Pictures, 1971).

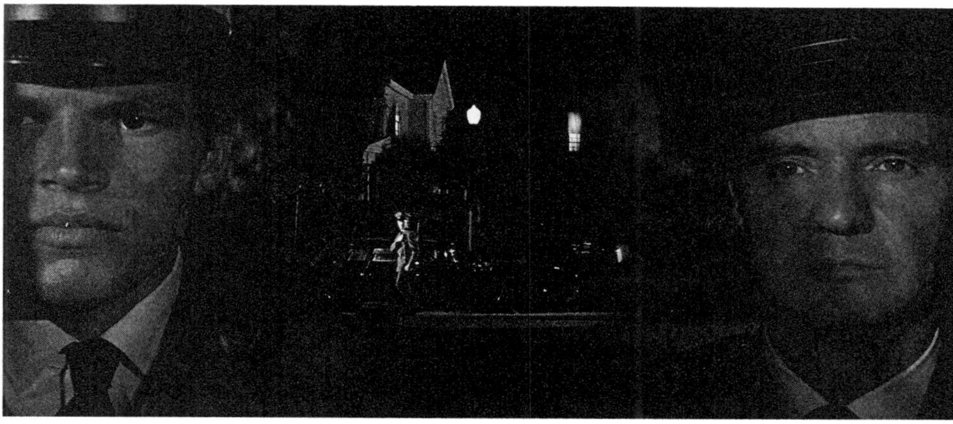

tension," owing to the lack of visual cues like converging parallel lines or relations of scale.[30] This flat/deep focus effect destabilizes a continuous understanding of the space by pointing us to something irresolvable in the body of the viewer.

Ramaeker characterizes *Andromeda*'s split-field diopter shot as less coherently engaged in terms of "imminent and overarching motivations and effects" compared to other films that make generous use of this shot, like *All the President's Men* (1976) or especially *Dressed to Kill* (1980). But the effect, I argue, heightens *The Andromeda Strain*'s sense of being trapped in an intense scenario.[31] That Wise uses this perceptual instability so many times suggests that he intends it to carry a strong affective charge for viewers. The narrative function of this visual effect is to convey claustrophobia and tension as well as a disorientation that compounds the narrative of uncertainty. If *Andromeda* exercises an expression of uncertainty, the split-field diopter shot is its most profound visual manifestation.

FIGURE 2.7

In this split-field diopter shot, the foreground and background figures are both sharp. *The Andromeda Strain* (Universal Pictures, 1971).

The intentional connection between modular image making and the film's narrative underscores the function of the modular within the larger social order, which media scholar Tara McPherson's now-iconic essay on the link between cultural and computational operating systems illuminates.[32] McPherson shows how the ordering of information and capital spread its logics into other dimensions of 1960s social life, including racial justice and democracy efforts. Concluding that "our technical formations are deeply bound up with our racial formations" and that both "move toward modular knowledges," McPherson illustrates how these relations encouraged a "'divide and conquer' mentality" that underwrites larger social relations.[33]

How, then, can we think about the function of this carefully ordered modular control space and the characters in it? The film's claustrophobic presentation of characters and situations communicates the scenario's suspenseful, disorienting nature. Split-screen imagery, destabilizing split-field diopter shots, and the claustrophobic, geometric, and highly technologized laboratory that traps the characters all enhance the peril and inescapability of an increasingly technological life. The formal and thematic elements of *The Andromeda Strain* present an anxiety for which there is no relief, in which we are trapped. Despite our technological tools, we have no real control. We are mostly powerless to stop the reality we have created. Key is the affective charge of this idea that we, as a culture, have constructed our technological system, set its procedures, and now are imprisoned within it. The experts' technosolutionism in their flawed, aggressively antiseptic space leads to nothing.[34] In the end, technology is both crisis and solution—a paradox typical of the technothriller, according to Helen Garson.[35] The result is a difficult film full of contradictions. It is a cautionary tale, but one wrapped up in the allure of advanced technological systems—a narrative with a push and pull between being enamored with procedure and innovation and ultimately confirming that those systems cannot protect us.

MODULARITY AND DIFFERENCE

As mentioned in the introduction, the technothriller genre has been overwhelmingly for and about men. But how do women and others exist within the logic of *The Andromeda Strain*? How is its imagined world divided through the modular, and what results from its masculine fantasies? Its sociotechnical imaginary presents a hierarchy of the scientific space. White men occupy the senior positions—as governmental officials, military leaders, and scientific experts—and drive the film's action. However, two key female characters ground the film in its space and time as a fraught moment for women's and Black civil rights: clinical microbiologist Ruth Leavitt (played by Kate Reid) and nurse Karen Anson (Paula Kelly). In Crichton's novel, Leavitt's character was male, but screenwriter Nelson Gidding convinced the director to include a substantive female character—though only after consulting male scientists to verify that such women scientists existed and would not interrupt the film's plausibility. Anson, the young African American nurse, understands the computer systems and provides key insight into how the old man has survived exposure to the Andromeda strain.

Leavitt is smart, blunt, and practical. A driven researcher, she has short hair, glasses, and no makeup or adornment. She is rather overweight—a far cry from the coiffed, normative women scientists with hourglass figures who were even then rarely represented in film. She does not seem romantically available and has little backstory; there is no indication about her marital status or sexuality. When we first meet Leavitt, she moves about her laboratory briskly, assisted by a lab technician (played by Midori, uncredited), a serious-looking Asian woman who has only two lines, but seems generally undaunted by the men who have invaded their territory. After noticing Leavitt wince with pain, the technician pats her on the arm and brings pills without having been asked, suggesting familiarity and care: they look after each other.

Leavitt's borderline cantankerous humor and lack of glamour suggest that she is accustomed to occupying male-dominated spaces and wants the attention focused on her contributions and intellect rather than her physical appearance. Leavitt seems particularly hostile toward the flirtatious, smug, eligible bachelor surgeon, Dr. Hall. Her male fellow experts take her seriously as an authority in her field. But she also has a weakness: photosensitive epilepsy.

This character, the first of its kind on-screen, seems calculated to signal 1960s–1970s second-wave feminism and the "sexual, political and

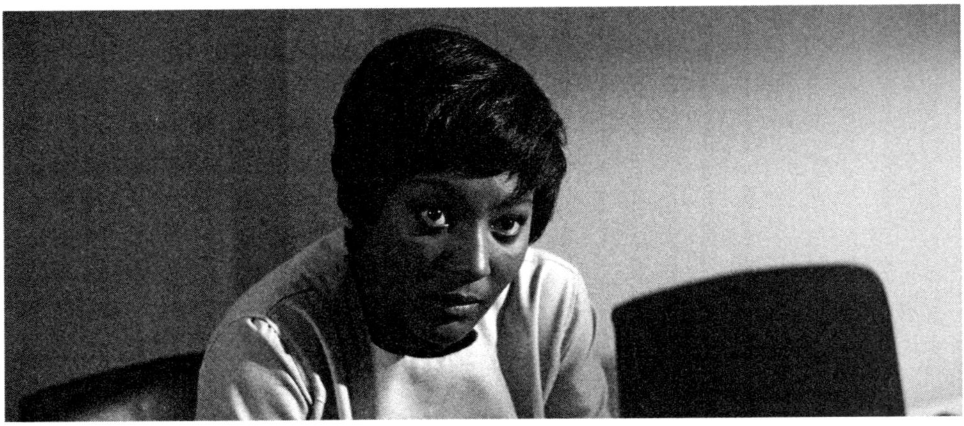

cultural changes that were affecting women."[36] Some argue she is configured as asexual, presented as a "Male Woman" so as not to disturb prescribed gender roles within science or for normative male audiences.[37] In their essay on representations of female scientists on film, Dean Conrad and Lynne Magowan propose that, in this way, the film gives with one hand and takes away with the other, but that Leavitt also importantly functions as a moral anchor for the narrative. She demonstrates conscience through her outrage when she discovers biowar maps proving that that Scoop's goal is to develop biological warfare.[38] Her reaction would be on the pulse of the era's anti–Vietnam War sentiment and cynicism toward government and scientific innovation.

Although Anson has never been given significant critical attention, she has a relatively large speaking role. Anson signals the sociopolitical moment in another way, invoking a racial divide and recently won civil rights. She displays technological mastery more advanced than the

FIGURE 2.8

Karen Anson, a nurse at the Wildfire Lab, becomes key to accessing the medical computer system. *The Andromeda Strain* (Universal Pictures, 1971).

scientists'; for instance, she instructs Hall on using a touch screen, by extension familiarizing the audience with this novel technology. Young and self-possessed, she dishes out witty, opinionated comments despite the male-coded space she occupies. She expresses both readiness and anxiety in the face of the crisis, saying, "Until now, Wildfire has been like a game; we've even had simulation bio-war games here with live subjects, volunteers." In addition to her technical skills, she is good-natured about the older patient's jokes about not being able to see her legs through the protective gear, and even when he pats her firmly on the behind.

There exists a push and pull around Anson's presence, signaling an ambivalence. When Leavitt suffers an epileptic seizure after being triggered by a blinking red light, it is Anson who treats her, despite her fear of potential exposure to Andromeda. "Good girl. Thanks," Hall tells the nurse—a line that points to the male character's latent condescension despite Anson's expertise and the guidance she provides. Still, at the end of the film, Hall awakes in his recovery room surrounded by the three other experts—but Nurse Anson is present, too, smiling down at him. Through this image, she becomes a fifth expert.

Both female experts are ambivalent representations. Leavitt is a formidable researcher, exemplary enough to be on the elite team, but her epilepsy counterbalances intellectual fortitude with a physical ailment. A brief anti-ableist conversation between Hall and Stone modulates this position; they discuss the possibility that she hid her medical status to evade "Middle Ages" bias and exclusion at top labs. Despite this, the overarching message is that her medical symptoms caused mistakes in the lab. Likewise, Nurse Anson contributes invaluable expertise but is put in her place with infantilizing language that reasserts the male-dominated sociotechnical order.

Conrad and Magowan argue that the film broadened representations of the female scientist. "Despite—or perhaps because of—the many social, sexual, political and cultural changes that were affecting women as Second Wave feminism took hold," they assert, "science fiction was retreating toward the tales of male fantasy and self-discovery that have always served as the genre's default position. As a result, *The Andromeda Strain*—with its strong-willed female scientist—stands out amid films such as *THX 1138*, *A Clockwork Orange*, *The Omega Man*, *Solaris*, and *Silent*

Running."[39] And it is true that it is a stride forward. Still, the stride is not assured. Both Leavitt and Anson are present and distinctive, which is welcome. Yet they are also redomesticated into an orbital position around white male scientists whose "natural" central role in the scientific space is reaffirmed. The two also never speak directly with each other; the film thus models a modularity that metaphorically compartmentalizes forms of difference into discrete categories. This illustrates how, as McPherson describes it, "we might also understand the emergence of identity politics in the 1960s as a kind of social and political embrace of modularity and encapsulation."[40] The two women are isolated and encapsulated in a male scientific and technical control space, and by extension, the issues of feminism and Black rights they emblematize are only modularly addressed.

A SOCIAL BEING IN A TECHNOLOGICAL WORLD

Vivian Sobchack described science fiction as "a genre that most specifically responds to and represents our cultural imagination of the possibilities for social being in a technological world."[41] If *The Andromeda Strain* can be considered science fiction, then it points to cultural fantasies that touch a deep well of fear around technological systems, unintended consequences, and the possibility that we may not survive our own inventions. And, as the first technothriller, *The Andromeda Strain* also uses the procedural and the modular to illustrate how, in embracing the computational and biotechnological, we invite logics that profoundly reshape how we relate to the world and each other.

If we return to our initial questions regarding what exactly constitutes the dread of uncertainty in this narrative and what certainty is embraced in this sociotechnical imaginary, what can we learn? The dread of uncertainty arises from new fears born of our own innovations. Langdon Winner, an intellectual leader in understanding the social dimension of science and technology, warned of the illusory nature of control and the political nature of technological objects. He suggested that while developed in controlled situations, once out of those environments, innovations often produced unforeseen results: "People still retain their logical position as users and controllers of technology. But in the broader context which transcends both 'use' and 'control,' this logic is of little consolation. As the speed and extent of technological innovation increase, societies face the distinct possibility of going adrift in a vast sea of 'unintended consequences.'[42]

The Andromeda Strain narrativizes the above paradigm. In the end, the Andromeda strain mutates into something harmless; systems and tools have helped scientists understand their adversary, but do not help them control the alien entity. In turning to our innovations to save us, we delude ourselves about our control over outcomes. In *The Andromeda Strain*, unintended consequences include potential total annihilation via biological warfare after the revelation that Wildfire and Project: Scoop were intended to develop germ warfare.

We see in procedural detail what the performance of technologized life looks like and what it does to us. Just as Hall becomes an escaped lab animal to be neutralized by laser beams in the fail-safe protocols of the Wildfire Lab, so too are we subject to the technological systems we have created. Human error plays a key role. Faith in the scientific method unfolds outcomes alongside human fallibility.

The various bodies represented experience being subjected to extreme protocols and control-based modular logics and systems. Trapped in those systems, the experts nearly reconfigure the Wildfire Lab into a tomb that memorializes the ultimate unintended technological consequence: total annihilation. Some of those figures, namely Leavitt and Anson, embody timely causes of the film's era, nodding to another set of social and political uncertainties. *The Andromeda Strain* proposes that this is what it means to be a social being in a technologized world. What do we do, indeed?

3

THE MILITARY TECHNOTHRILLER

"What should our foreign policy be?" Tom Clancy asked rhetorically during a recent telephone interview. "Gee, I don't know. That's not my job. I'm in the entertainment business."

—Robert Lekachman, "Virtuous Men and Perfect Weapons"[1]

ENTER THE CLANCYVERSE

With its conservative vision of a true patriot who prevails in a pro-American agenda, the military technothriller constitutes the most popular expression of the genre. This kind of technothriller often features a so-called intelligence man or an elite supersoldier who, with his next-level gear and tech, makes all the right moves and punishes any who would oppose the nation. Technothrillers, with rare exceptions, present totalizing visions in which most types of people serve the interests of a white male protagonist, have a negligible impact on story, or simply do not exist within the world of the film. These visions often have a strong whiff of populism and a notable absence of any difference that cannot be assimilated neatly into their vision.

In other words, just as the epigraph would suggest, the military technothriller includes an internal tension between the genre as a political form and as pure entertainment. It edges on propagandistic, normalizing

American exceptionalism and military dominance, while packaged in a genre so widely considered minor that most do not give it serious consideration. Many of these films would not be deemed "quality" material under accepted cinematic standards. Most feature formulaic writing, unimaginative adherence to genre, excessive proceduralism, and reinforcement of toxic cultural norms. The military technothriller's neoconservative wish-fulfillment scenarios often meet the people where they are and validate them. But military technothrillers wield great influence *because* they are packaged as lowbrow entertainment and so operate beneath the radar of sustained scrutiny.

Among military technothrillers, Tom Clancy's are both incredibly consistent in their messaging and highly adaptable across media. Working through several Clancy-based military technothriller film images lets us access a sociotechnical imaginary of American exceptionalism, fear and fascination with military dominance, anxieties about the Cold War and mutually assured destruction, advanced technological weaponry, and the need to construct a new type of military hero after the devastating ideological blow of the Vietnam War. To illustrate how entangled military technothrillers are with the popular imaginary, I look at the filmic adaptations of *The Hunt for Red October* (John McTiernan, 1990), *Clear and Present Danger* (Phillip Noyce, 1994), and *Tom Clancy's Without Remorse* (Stefano Sollima, 2021), all based on Clancy bestsellers.

Unlike Michael Crichton's technothrillers featuring biological and computational tech, Clancy's contain few (if any) sci-fi elements. Clancy's brand fetishizes advanced weaponry, cutting-edge technology, elite soldiers, intel, and often rationalizes extrajudicial force. While Clancy's stories contain excessive technical detail, they often embellish the technology's actual function or effectiveness. This is all presented in a tense, technologically exhaustive form while emphasizing upright American values and the American military man's superiority in an entertaining package. As scholar Matthew Thomas Payne said of the Clancy brand, "There is arguably no name more synonymous with militainment and with American exceptionalism—before and after 9/11—than Tom Clancy."[2] These images are also tied to a construction of American masculinity that is both heroic and beset on all sides by those who would corrupt the "truth" to which only they have authentic access.

Clancy's books are extremely popular, and many have been made into mainstream films. As Clancy asserted, his books do not outline or determine government policy; he thus implies that these books do not make a political statement, especially as they are fiction. But this is contradicted by the consistent value system in Clancy's brand that has survived political changes, conflicts, and even the author's death.[3] So rather than focusing on the narratives of films based on Clancy's books, I address something more potent: their political affective intensities—what moods and feelings they galvanize, gather up, and overflow with—and how their images operate on the viewer. This is a way of breaking through to their more impressionistic potencies and understanding the political ramifications of the image independent of its literal narrative. It is important to keep in mind the endorsement of Clancy's work by heads of state; his speaking invitations to the NSA, CIA, and FBI; his public bromance with the military; his op-eds defending gun ownership; his advocacy of the "warrior ethic"; and his excoriation of communism.[4]

The Hunt for Red October, set during the Cold War, engages nuclear-oriented technological fears. *Clear and Present Danger* is set during the drug wars, with a new kind of enemy and a new theater of conflict. Both feature intelligence man Jack Ryan, Clancy's most iconic character and one whom the author has admitted most closely mirrors his own position. *Tom Clancy's Without Remorse* centers on another iconic character, elite-trained Navy SEAL John Kelly, and the adversary is again Russia, but in a more contemporary context. *Without Remorse* emphasizes the "techno-warrior" construct, which feels much different than the intelligence man embodied by Jack Ryan. Interestingly, in the last example, Black actors play the two primary roles: Michael B. Jordan as elite soldier John Kelly and Jodie Turner-Smith as Lieutenant Commander Karen Greer. This example can help us think through how the Clancyverse is (or is not) impacted by displacing whiteness in the military technothriller's ideologies. Through these films we can think about the Clancy brand's worldview and its evolution over time.

It is very difficult to disentangle the world-building of the books from the subsequent films they inspired. For that reason, this chapter calls on the critical considerations of Clancy's writing by people like J. William Gibson, Helen Garson, and William Terdoslavich as a way of tapping

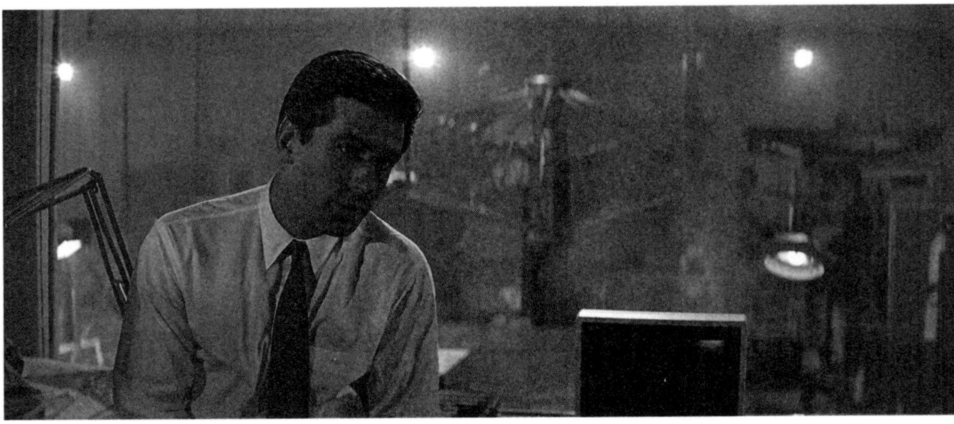

into the sociotechnical imaginaries spawned by the Clancy-style techno-thriller. How can we come to terms with these images? What is their cultural instrumentality, and why are we so invested in them that they seem to repeat themselves endlessly? As this chapter explores, these military technothriller films provide a recuperative vision of the military man, a fantasy of precision and accuracy, and optimal disciplined performance under the duress of conflict. These films often promote the idea that extrajudicial violence works. Most importantly, the Clancyverse provides a cohesive image of continuity and clearly defined enemies in the face of a chaotic and uncertain new national reality. These impacts are rooted, I argue, less in the narrative components than in the remarkable potency of the image.

FIGURE 3.1

Jack Ryan, Clancy's most iconic character, is the one that most closely mirrors the author's own position (*The Hunt for Red October*, Paramount Pictures, 1990).

Were one to trace a genealogy of the strictly military technothriller, *The Hunt for Red October* novel would be its first fully formed narrative, which makes it insightful foundational material for understanding the film genre. The novel was deeply connected to the military from the beginning. It was published by the Naval Institute Press, and its marketing targeted the military. "We started with a Washington strategy," its press director explained. "We thought the book would appeal to military people, the military-industrial complex. We sent advance copies to a lot of government officials . . . By mid-November, *Red October* was on *The Post*'s Washington best-seller list."[5]

The military technothriller relies on generic characters and the predictable superiority of American technology and intelligence work. Robert Lekachman of the *New York Times* called it "a genre that awards equal billing to human actors and state-of-the-art computers, missiles, devices of detection and deception, spy satellites, nuclear submarines and Mach 2 or Mach 3 fighter planes."[6] True to this description, the title character of *Hunt* is not a person, but a weapon: the Red October, a massive Soviet nuclear ballistic submarine with an ultra-quiet magneto-hydrodynamic propulsion. It is so silent, in fact, that it is virtually undetectable by sonar and can thus sneak nuclear missiles within short range of Washington, DC. With its highly decorated and imperious Soviet captain Marko Ramius (Sean Connery), the submarine poses an imminent threat to US security. It is up to John Patrick "Jack" Ryan (Alec Baldwin) to piece together snippets of information about what Ramius and the Soviet fleet intend. Aboard the USS Dallas, sonarman Ronald "Jonesy" Jones (Courtney B. Vance) becomes key to tracking the fearsome warcraft, using only his keen hearing, sonar technology and computer expertise.

As mentioned, two key roles—that of Admiral James Greer and Sonarman Jones—are played by Black actors, though both characters were white in the book. William H. Honan of the *New York Times* noted the director's evident departure from the source material, opining, "Was Mr. McTiernan practicing colorblind casting, or was he, perhaps, seeking to paint an idealized portrait of the American Navy? 'No, Admiral Greer is

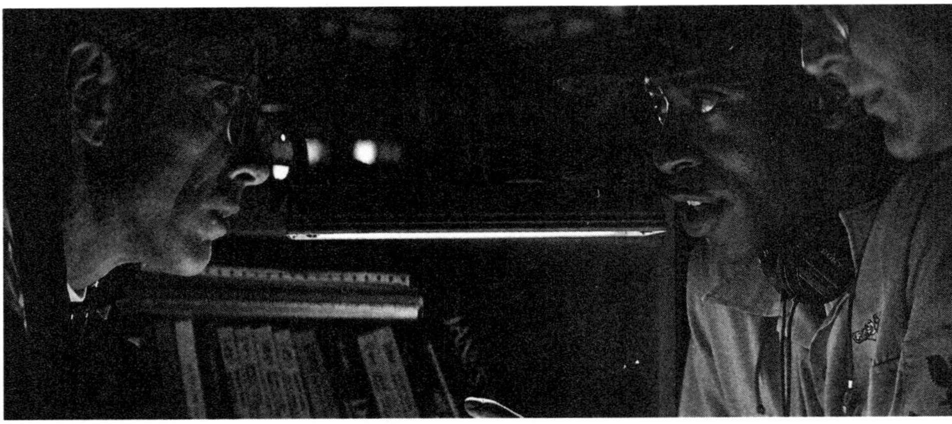

not black in the book,' Mr. McTiernan acknowledged, 'but who is there in the ensemble of American stars more like Greer than James Earl Jones, with that combination of sternness, rectitude and warmth?'"[7]

This question of whether "colorblind casting" is at play, or casting without regard for race of the original written character, is worth asking across the three films discussed here. This also extends to gender, as female roles increasingly populate secondary characters, and finally central ones—although this is often the conceit of the film studio or director, not Clancy.

Like *The Andromeda Strain* (Robert Wise, 1971), *Hunt* begins with text superimposed over a technical image (in this case, radar) that suggests the viewers are privy to top-secret information—events denied by both the US and Soviet governments. What follows is a world of fantasized intel, technological details, intrigue, and a narrowly averted international

FIGURE 3.2

Sonarman Ronald "Jonesy" Jones (center) reports hearing the undetectable Soviet submarine to his captain. Jonesy was not a Black character in the original book. *The Hunt for Red October* (Paramount Pictures, 1990).

incident. We meet Captain Ramius and his second-in-command, Captain Borodin (Sam Neill) perched atop the massive Red October in an icy, inhospitable environment. Their aims are ambiguous, and their faces are weather-beaten and resolute. Then, in a starkly oppositional image, we meet CIA analyst Jack Ryan through an environmental portrait: the camera pans slowly across a cluttered, warmly lit home study. It is full of historical military illustrations, dense combat-history texts, schematics and models of warcraft, legal proceedings, and finally a small girl in her nightgown who has wandered from her bed. Ryan notices his daughter and scoops her up, promising a new teddy bear upon his return. His wife, Caroline, appears, barking an order to the help. From this short sequence, we learn a great deal: Ryan is an educated family man, with a wife, child, and a particular kind of stable privileged domestic existence—one that he immediately leaves to enter the clandestine and, notably, entirely male professional domain of the CIA.

Once entering this world, the film revels in rich, dramatic visuals of serious men and their technologies—specifically men encased *within* war machines—bathed in the diaphanous light of control panels. The cameras are always close to their subjects, and both are always moving. The images convey limited vision, thus limited information, urgency, and above all, men encapsulated by their dangerous inventions. Each of the three submarines that become part of the core narrative—the Red October, the USS Dallas, and a pursuing Soviet submarine—are claustrophobic, packed with twinkling control panels and metallic surfaces that bounce their light in all directions. Each sub has its own color scheme, providing visual continuity for viewers: blue for the Red October, red for the USS Dallas, and green for the pursuing Soviet sub. Pointing out the obsessive focus on the tech, reviewer Hal Hinson noted, "*Die Hard* director John McTiernan and cinematographer Jan de Bont have crowded the frame with the candy-colored lights of flashing control boards, dials, sonar screens and digital readouts, and they've given the submarines' cramped quarters a rich, dense texture. But besides this and the actors' faces, which bear down on us in super-close-up, there isn't much to look at."[8]

In fact there is quite a lot to see when considering the film for its flatly illustrative "compacted worlds of meaning and value," as American literary scholar Jane Tompkins puts it.[9] Shot mostly from slightly below to convey a more monumental impression, the men are impeccably uniformed and strike dramatic poses, chins pointing in optimal cinematic directions. Their clean-cut, sharp jawlines and tense, sometimes perspiring faces catch the light and suggest men driven by duty. They all speak in clipped technical tones to which we, the audience, must acclimate. Everything is clean: no grease in the submarines, nothing out of place, and likewise no endemic messiness of conflict. The men know what to do. They act without hesitation, adhering to their virtues. They grit their teeth and make tough decisions, and all orders are executed to streamline an assemblage of men and machines into a singular, efficient weapon.

Hunt accords this fantasy of military precision to both American and Russian military men. However, the difference lies in degrees of obedience. American men are imaged as more free-thinking, with autonomy in decision-making despite operating within a military hierarchy. Russians are represented as oriented toward the collective, visually more homogenous, and, while valiant, more indoctrinated into groupthink. Captain Ramius is set apart from this and is depicted as an individual possessing the ability to persuade other close colleagues to his purpose. But his rogue autonomy makes sense once the narrative reveals that he is half Lithuanian (i.e., not truly Russian) and that he blames an inferior Soviet medical system for his wife's death. Aside from the brief appearance of Ryan's wife, Ramius's dead wife is the only other woman referenced in the film, which again points to *Hunt* as a film specifically about men's fantasies, fears, and wish fulfillment.

Imaginaries of control flare up the world of *Hunt*, with its totalizing vision and its modeling of certainty and resolve in the face of dread. The film's core dramatic element—that Jack Ryan knows something in his gut and righteously pursues that truth despite the incredulity of powerful superiors—conveys an overwhelming sense of certitude. Clancy's man knows the truth better than those around him and will prevail.

In *Hunt*, Ryan has a hunch that the Soviet captain isn't as loyal to the USSR as everyone thinks and may defect. To confirm this, he must communicate with Captain Ramius directly. He hazards his life and the nation's safety to do so, rappelling from helicopters onto submarines even though he is terrified of flying and risks a nuclear attack on domestic soil if he is mistaken.

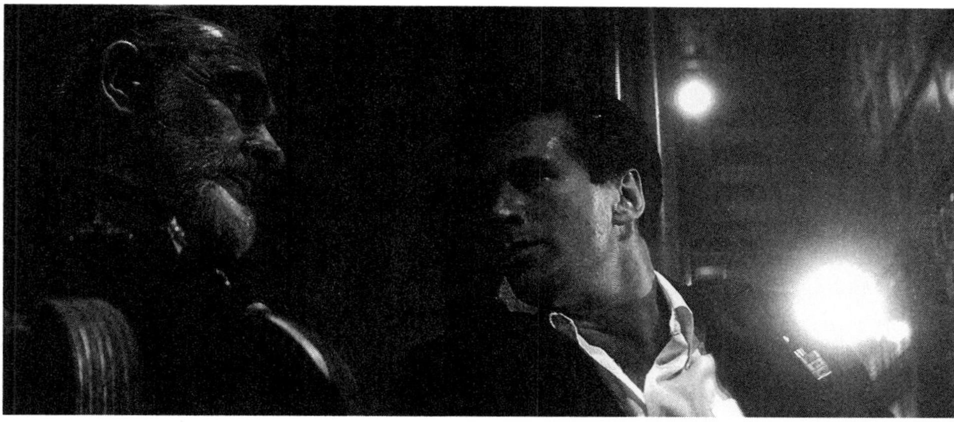

The Clancy man operates as a political motif, reimagining a new hero that suits the longings of a modern viewer. To some degree, however, the Clancy man also reimagines the strong, silent Western hero. In all three films, intelligence ("intel") is key, yet an economy of communication defines Clancy's male heroes. Tompkins sees the silence of the Western hero as a quality—or perhaps a symptom—of a particular condition of masculinity, namely the need for control. She writes, "Not speaking demonstrates control not only over feelings but over one's physical boundaries as well. . . . To be a man is not only to be monolithic, silent, mysterious, impenetrable as a desert butte, it is to *be* the desert butte. By becoming a solid object, not only is a man relieved of the burden of relatedness and responsiveness to others, he is relieved of consciousness itself, which is to say, primarily, consciousness of self."[10]

In the Western, alienation from one's interiority is key, refocusing attention on what needs doing, reaffirming stoicism, and decoupling from emotional life. The technothriller similarly engages tropes around men and Clancy's "generic category of hero."[11] Although the military

FIGURE 3.3

Jack Ryan (right), the intelligence man, figures out that Soviet Captain Ramius (left) wants to defect. *The Hunt for Red October* (Paramount Pictures, 1990).

technothriller man is rooted in the older Western hero, it provides a more contemporary, white, normative, and populist masculinity that recuperates honor in an era when conflicts are increasingly fought for economic and ideological reasons. Clancy narratives weren't called "national security Westerns" for nothing.[12]

Strikingly, *Hunt*—Clancy's iconic Cold War anxiety narrative—was adapted to the big screen *after* the actual conflict had ended. I described how the Cold War's existential crisis shaped Crichton and Clancy and their stories and, by extension, the public imaginary, given their narratives' strong impact. *Hunt*'s thrill depends on the techno-anxiety generated by a rogue Soviet ballistic missile nuclear submarine capable of striking a devastating attack against the United States. This demands that the film orient itself as a historical narrative, since the core ideological crisis that drives the tension of the story is no longer a reality.

The original book, published in 1984, would have resonated with its time. But by the film's release in 1990, Soviet leader Mikhail Gorbachev and then-president Ronald Reagan had already signed a treaty agreeing to the destruction of all ballistic and cruise missiles with short and intermediate ranges, and the Berlin Wall had fallen, portending the collapse of the USSR.[13] By the time audiences saw McTiernan's film, Cold War anxieties of mutually assured destruction had dissipated.

The film's focus on Cold War tensions that had ended led to mixed reviews for *The Hunt for Red October*. The *Washington Post* dubbed the film a "Cold War anachronism."[14] Richard Schickel of *Time* likewise asked: "Will the movie seem an anachronism in this moment of revolutionary change? Or do the events of recent months make the movie even more treasurable as possibly the last, and by no means the least, of its kind?"[15] Desson Howe, also writing in the *Washington Post*, was less charitable, complaining that "with its bad, treacherous Soviets on the one side (played mostly by Brits), its freedom-loving Americans on the other, and an indeterminate number of good Russian defectors in between—brought to you by a certain military-industrial-complex alliance of Paramount, Industrial Light & Magic, director John ('Die Hard') McTiernan, and the U.S. Navy—this is a Reagan youth's wet dream of underwater ballistics and East-West conflict."[16] All true. Still, the film provides a powerful snapshot of a way of relating to the world. This vision is steeped in a fear that, even when its origin is removed, never lets go. It bespeaks a fantasy in which everything can be controlled and mechanized, all problems cracked if men can only innovate properly. And it is pure, concentrated, color-saturated militainment.

Scholar J. William Gibson deconstructs the original novel around the notion of control, pointing to the technothriller's great appeal as rooted in its wish fulfillment around always knowing what to do. "The ambiguities, uncertainties, and risks of intense human relationships, especially sexual relationships, are abolished," Gibson writes. "Men are given a guidebook that tells them who they are, who is their family, what they should do, and what they can expect to feel. Emotional life becomes as knowable as a technical manual to a weapons-system."[17] The control is specifically linked to images of a particular new masculine myth: the Clancy man.

Gibson's work exposes what lies beneath the surface of Clancy's ideological masculinity and contextualizes the desirability of such images for American national identity from the 1960s to the 1980s. He asserts Clancy's constructions of masculinity self-consciously attempt to redeem a broken militarized manhood after Vietnam.[18] Gibson asks why the technothriller's vision of the United States enjoyed such widespread appeal, and suggests that the "techno-thriller war fantasy" became popular in the 1980s as a means to redeem American national identity from the cultural crisis created by the Vietnam War and other major world events that destabilized a formerly dominant white American male identity.[19]

This engagement with Vietnam reappears in the novels *Clear and Present Danger* and *Without Remorse*. Vietnam clearly sticks in Clancy's craw. The film *Hunt* presents this recuperative image of militarized masculinity via the fatherly care of submarine commanders for their symbolic "sons" on board and military men's decisive action and superior strategy, intel, and weapons systems. In the end, Jack Ryan is vindicated in his pursuit of truth and his ability to steer men in political power toward the right path and away from nuclear annihilation . . . in spite of themselves.

CLEAR AND PRESENT IDEOLOGY

Clear and Present Danger (Phillip Noyce, 1994) employs a more mature and established Jack Ryan (Harrison Ford) to let audiences in on the dirty politics behind closed doors at the Capitol. It begins with the image of an American flag and an inclusive vision of the US Coast Guard that integrates women and people of color into Clancy's world-building—a corrective for the multicultural era. Again we see protocols and procedures executed smoothly by the military; elite soldiers and government offices with advanced technologies help powerful men make important decisions. Ryan's gravely ill friend Admiral Greer asks Ryan, still a CIA analyst, to step into his position at the Department of Justice. Ryan reservedly accepts. "Watch your back, Jack," warns Greer. The principled Ryan quickly finds himself at the center of controversy: after investigating the murders of a prominent US businessman and his family, he learns the president is using him to wreak extrajudicial justice against a Colombian drug lord. Ryan adheres to his morals, rights the wrongs committed against soldiers left behind, and refuses to engage in politics. In a 1996 interview with Charlie Rose, Tom Clancy admitted that he sees the character of Ryan as himself.[20] Ryan is, as the theatrical release poster declares, a "soldier" for the "truth" who iconically (and literally) speaks back to power.

Critics found the film "fun, but formulaic."[21] Erin Simpson and Phillip Carter of the *Washington Post* noted, "*Clear and Present Danger* offered simple solutions: surgical strikes with smart bombs and gutsy raids by light infantry could incite a battle within the Medellin drug cartel—and thus restrict the flow of drugs to the States. Unfortunately, as U.S. drug policy eventually embraced Clancy's militaristic worldview, we learned that force alone could not win that war and, more broadly, that military options were more difficult than Clancy made them seem."[22] In effect, they rightly cautioned against the allure of pat military solutions to complex lived-world challenges.

In this film, Ryan—played by Ford with physical vulnerability and moral indignance around the ugly truths he unearths—looks less slick than his intelligence coworkers. He is rumpled and comparatively unenthusiastic. He is repeatedly shown navigating the new professional space, but never with complete success. His mussed hair signifies his lack of assimilation. In these halls of power—the president's office, CIA headquarters—men speak directly and with little elaboration, except as necessary.

Meanwhile, shifty-eyed careerist politicians move their chess pieces. "These drug cartels present a clear and present danger to the national

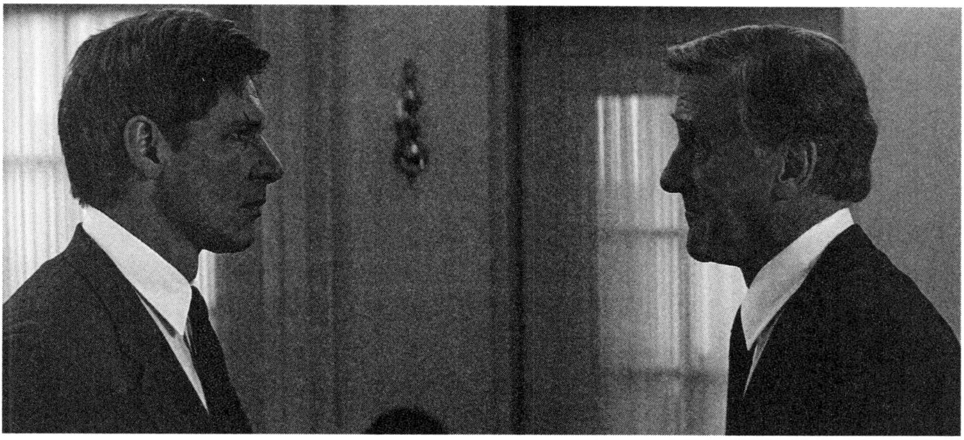

security of the United States," pronounces fictive President Bennett (Donald Moffat), thereby rationalizing an illegal drug war, orchestrated by Cutter (Harris Yulin), his national security advisor. The president initiates extrajudicial black ops action against the Colombian "Cali Cartel" responsible for the assassination of an American businessman and his family—the president's close friends. CIA Deputy Director Ritter (Henry Czerny) will oversee the mission, code-named "Operation Reciprocity" and conducted by elite soldiers. The film takes pains to show the techno-warrior, attuned to his perfectly functioning team and weapons, from advanced computers to surgically precise remote-command fighter jets. John Clark (Willem Dafoe), who will eventually become the second-most-iconic Clancy man, runs the mission.

FIGURE 3.4

Jack Ryan (left), a patriot, speaks back to political power represented by the US president standing in the Oval Office. In this shot, the two men face each other from opposite ends of the screen, signifying their opposing positions. *Clear and Present Danger* (Paramount Pictures, 1994).

Significantly, the film shows powerful politicians making their decisions while far from the conflict. They do so while sipping whiskey from a crystal glass in a large office, walking a dog somewhere picturesque, eating a sandwich, or sitting around a polished grand table near a fireplace. The president seems conniving and uncertain, lacking in moral fiber, and in the end sniveling and desperate.[23] The pouting and ineffective president, played with expressive, watery eyes, is held to account by the properly masculine true patriot, Ryan.

The film's visual aesthetic is highly illustrative and clear, to emulate a stark clarity between good and evil, right and wrong, heroes and villains. Visually, the film presents a racialized distinction between cartel men, set in rustic environments, and American politicians, imaged in brightly lit, bustling offices. Especially notable is Colonel Félix Cortez (Joaquim de Almeida), who works with the mercurial, overindulged drug lord Ernesto Escobedo. Cortez is a smarmy, cartoonish, crafty villain with a painted tan, squinty eyes, and slicked-back hair. But the film draws parallels between US politicians and the cartel figures; they share smarminess, shifty-eyed glances, and cynical disdain for uprightness ("You are *such* a Boy Scout," sneers Ritter to Ryan). This mistrust of government would, for viewers, certainly evoke then-recent clandestine deals and government scandals, particularly the Iran-Contra affair (1981–1986), in which senior members of the Reagan administration illegally and covertly sold arms to the Islamic fundamentalist government of Iran, then funneled resources to the Contras, anticommunist guerillas fighting the Marxist Nicaraguan government. These events had a devastating impact on public perception of the US government.

Clear and Present Danger also directly references the Vietnam War. First Ryan requests supplemental antidrug funds at a senate hearing and a senator invokes the Vietnam War as a cautionary example of misplaced energies. Later we see a visual reference: military helicopters in Colombia, skimming over water and a lush, tropical, green landscape. As the helicopter is the most iconic image (and distinctive sound) of a military machine associated with the Vietnam War, this would have a particular affective impact on the viewer. This is key because of the reparative gesture of reenacting a Vietnam-like scene of trauma, but with a very different outcome. These soldiers are different from the Vietnam War film's feral,

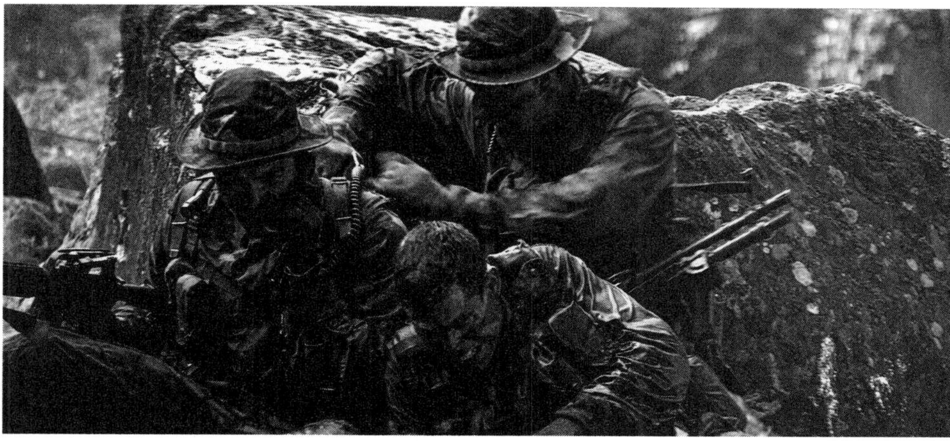

pot-smoking, filthy, whoremongering, antiauthoritarian types: these men are clean-cut, square-jawed, disciplined soldiers. They efficiently destroy a plane used for transporting drugs and then neutralize an underground drug-processing lab in the jungle. And crucially, when they are forsaken by the powers that be, Ryan dashes in, placing himself in harm's way to bring them home. He neither abandons the conflict, nor leaves men behind—also a corrective to the perceived moral failures of the United States in relation to Vietnam.

Women are present but largely ancillary to the action.[24] Ryan's wife (Anne Archer) mostly looks appropriately pained, worried, and supportive. Hope Lange plays the stringent senator who rakes Ryan over the coals during the abovementioned hearing. A no-nonsense DEA character stationed in Colombia, Jean Fowler (Belita Moreno), is another key female character rendered with integrity and competence. Moira (Ann Magnuson), an administrator in the Department of Justice, is the unfortunate

FIGURE 3.5

The film visually references the Vietnam War and features elite soldiers being sold out and left behind. Jack Ryan personally gets them home. *Clear and Present Danger* (Paramount Pictures, 1994).

mark who is seduced by Cortez and unwittingly gives up information before becoming collateral damage. She is represented as smitten, overly trusting, and a bit of a sexpot—not really made for intelligence work.

Perhaps the most important politically affective moment of the film is the attack on an American convoy of DEA vehicles carrying Ryan, an ambassador, and advisors in Bogota. The contingent of American men in suits in a convoy of white SUVs is besieged in a warlike coordinated attack by masked enemies with enormous firepower, RPGs, and clear tactical advantage. Taken by surprise, almost all the Americans are killed, save Ryan, who survives seemingly only by luck and some old military training that keeps him moving in the right direction. Battered and bloody, he never picks up a weapon and is constructed as a pure victim of unimaginable violence. The attack is blamed on Escobedo and the Cali Cartel, although in fact it has been engineered by Colonel Cortez to appear that way. This attack is a critical political image, cementing the film's idea of fundamentally good Americans victimized by a cartel embracing ruthless brutality.

The film's generous use of intercutting conveys the clock-like movements of multiple elements within a single machination of power. It also underscores the remote, modular nature of modern warfare, intensely illustrated through a surgical strike on Escobedo's compound using smart bomb technology. The filmic shots move between the soldiers on the ground painting the target, air support dropping the bomb, the goings-on of the Escobedo compound, and the remote observation of Ritter, who watches the bomb fall from the safety of an office. As it strikes its unsuspecting targets cleanly and dramatically, Ritter leans back in his chair and mutters "*Boom*" as if he's watching an action film, not live devastation. The attack kills thirty people, including women and children, the collateral damage of covert American intervention. Here emerges another key political affective image: Ryan, learning of the attack on the news, covers his eyes at the sight of a charred doll in the rubble; he is visibly troubled.

Soon after, Ryan realizes the president ordered Reciprocity, and that he is implicated by extension; the operation is shut down and erased from the record, with the soldiers left behind in the field as expendables. Ryan then must expose the operation as corrupt, and technology figures strongly in acquiring the intel he needs. Desktop computers pepper the DOJ offices and are prominently displayed on-screen. A massive server

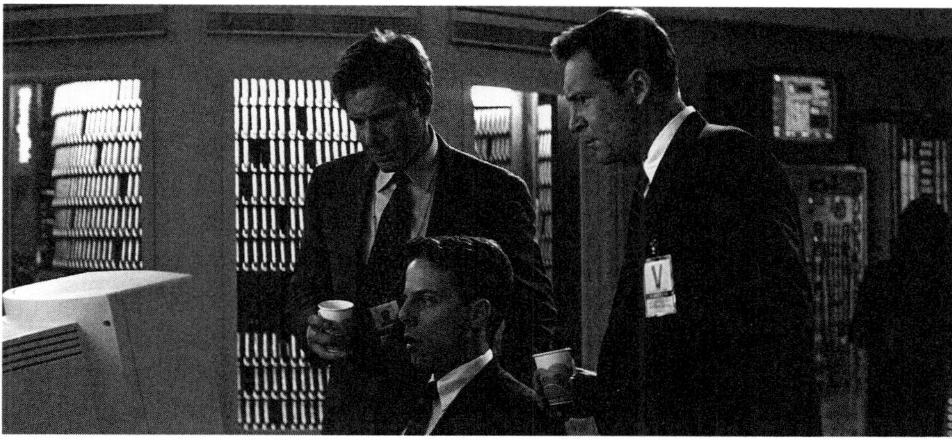

becomes the backdrop for key scenes in which computation and access to information drive the narrative. Voice-matching software confirms the identity of Cortez. Ryan enlists a computer technician to help him hack into Ritter's work computer.

In a critical technological scene, Ryan and Ritter engage in mediated conflict via networked computers. Remotely accessing Ritter's computer, Ryan tries to secure proof of Operation Reciprocity while Ritter clacks away at his keyboard, deleting incriminating files. In an instant-classic technothriller scene, Ryan strikes the "print" key at just the right moment . . . but the printer is out of paper. Ryan restocks it in the nick of time to successfully capture one single damning memo. Both unintentionally comical in its thriller-inflected use of office supplies and a witty metaphor for how much government intrigue has changed, this scene was, as one reviewer put it, "an ingenious bout of computer warfare."[25]

FIGURE 3.6

The computer makes a prominent appearance in the film. Here, Jack Ryan and two colleagues look at a computer against the background of a massive server. *Clear and Present Danger* (Paramount Pictures, 1994).

In the film's closing shot, Ryan professes the truth at a senate oversight committee hearing, witnessed by officials, press photographers, and his proud wife in a grand hall that reaffirms the continuity of government systems through its functional checks and balances. But ultimately the narrative offers a rationale for extrajudicial violence and black ops interventions, and a fantasy that surgical strikes and tactical superiority are the answer (though they might weigh on our collective conscience). As William Terdoslavich summarizes, the clear messaging emanating from Jack Ryan narratives is: "Force works. Diplomacy does not. Kill the bad guys when you can find them. Congress should follow, not lead. Doers should head agencies and cabinet departments, not careerists or office politicians. Action counts for more than process. The difference between right and wrong is clear and never compromised. The United States is always right."[26] These positions bolster a sociotechnical imaginary so embedded in American culture as to be implicit, and underscore a strikingly cohesive Clancy brand message.

WITHOUT REMORSE

Tom Clancy's Without Remorse (Stefano Sollima, 2021) is very loosely based on the 1993 Clancy novel, which was begun in the 1970s, shelved, and completed in 1992. The book, set in the 1970s amid a secret American POW rescue mission complicated by collusion with the Russians, tells the story of how John Kelly, a Navy SEAL and Vietnam veteran, becomes John Clark and joins the CIA. The 2021 film centers on the same character but updates the context to modern-day Syria. The narrative nevertheless retains a vendetta, corruption at high levels of government, a dead wife (though the novel included two dead loves), themes of extrajudicial violence, and Kelly's adoption of his new identity as Clark.

Clark appears in more than a dozen Clancy novels and many of the Clancy brand stories penned by other authors after Clancy's death. While initially an ancillary character to key figures like Jack Ryan, he eventually comes to the fore. Unlike Ryan, Kelly/Clark is a supersoldier and not an intel man, but both share a sense of moral outrage against corrupt political entities who compromise national values for careerism. Both speak truth

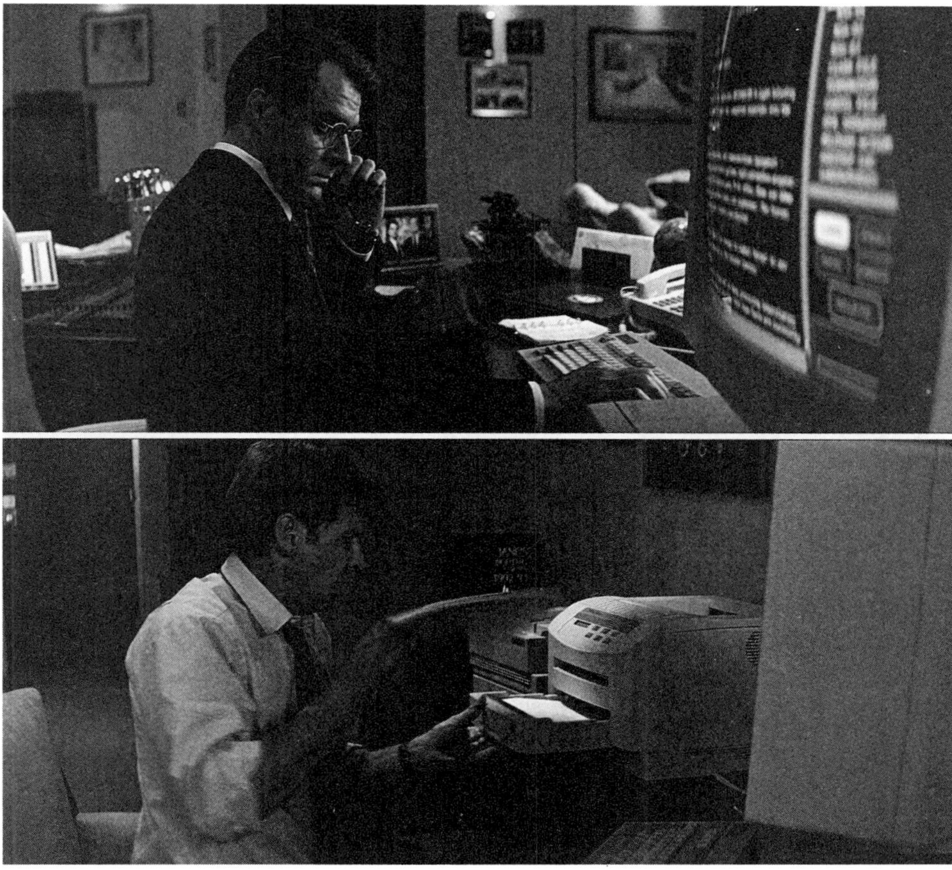

FIGURE 3.7

Ritter (above) and Ryan (below) engage in a remote conflict via networked computers, and it all hangs on Ryan's ability to refill his printer paper fast enough. *Clear and Present Danger* (Paramount Pictures, 1994).

to power. In this way, Kelly/Clark is the quintessential violent foil to Jack Ryan as a Clancy man, and second only to Ryan as the most recognizable political motif of the author's brand.

This iteration of the technothriller once again reaffirms a particular version of American masculinity as simultaneous hero and victim. Consistent with the literary version of the form, as Gibson asserts, "the techno-thriller reasserts the primacy of heroic male warriors, magic weapons, and horrific enemies as fundamental cultural categories for Americans to conceptualize and experience the world."[27] In the Amazon MGM Studios streaming-release film, which significantly updates the novel, Kelly is an elite soldier who becomes an unwitting victim of corrupt political interests. After a clandestine CIA hostage rescue mission in Aleppo, Syria, turns out to involve the Russian military, things get complicated for Kelly and the team. His sweet, dimpled, highly pregnant wife (Lauren London) is gunned down in their home when assassins mistakenly believe it is Kelly asleep in bed—a plot point consistent with Clancy's themes of the family as the cornerstone of society and threats to family configured as threats to the nation. Kelly, gravely injured while fighting off the hit men, recovers and seeks revenge against the remaining perpetrator after the Department of Justice refuses to investigate. His SEAL team leader, Lt. Commander Karen Greer (Jodie Turner-Smith), agitates on his behalf, negotiating the direct orders of her appointed leaders while allying herself with Kelly. CIA chief Ritter (Jamie Bell), who runs the covert ops, displays duplicitous interests. In the process of hunting his wife's killer, Kelly, along with Greer and their team, exposes a larger conspiracy to stoke US-Russian tensions by attempting to manipulate public perception. "A big country needs big enemies," rationalizes Defense Secretary Thomas Clay (Guy Pearce) right before Kelly speaks truth to power by literally drowning Clay in the Potomac and delivering Clay's taped confession to Ritter.

The film's visually concentrated colors, strong color separation, and absorbent blacks create a slick, detailed, crisp, illustrative look that fetishizes surface—much like the neon eye candy of the popular *John Wick* revenge films. *Without Remorse* uses an extremely bold color palette and inky black shadows, signaling drama and unseen machinations. The overall effect suggests the sharpness and precision of digital photography, or

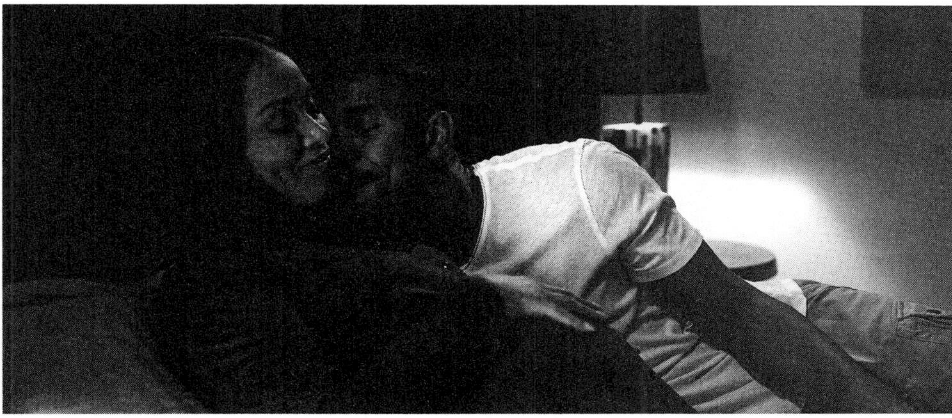

even digitally rendered images, as in video games. The film often feels like a series of intense action scenarios linked by brief moments of story development. Its relatively long continuous action sequences also invoke video games. In fact, the filmmakers seem to make an aesthetic attempt to connect with gamers by presenting a familiar visual language and set of scenarios. In featurette materials several actors indicated their access point to Clancy narratives was video games. One reviewer noted that it was "easy to see why Clancy's work is so suited to gaming. It's an experience much like watching someone play *Call of Duty* for 110 minutes straight—action-packed, maybe, but oh so dreary."[28] Reviewer Mark Kermode dubbed it a "slightly naff video game."[29] Other critics deemed the film "drab," "dull," "not good," and "reheated Cold War paranoia," although

FIGURE 3.8

John Kelly is an all-American supersoldier and family man. In this scene his domestic life with his pregnant wife and loving home situation are imaged. Kelly was played by a Black actor, Michael B. Jordan, although in the original story, the character was white. *Tom Clancy's Without Remorse* (Amazon Studios, 2021).

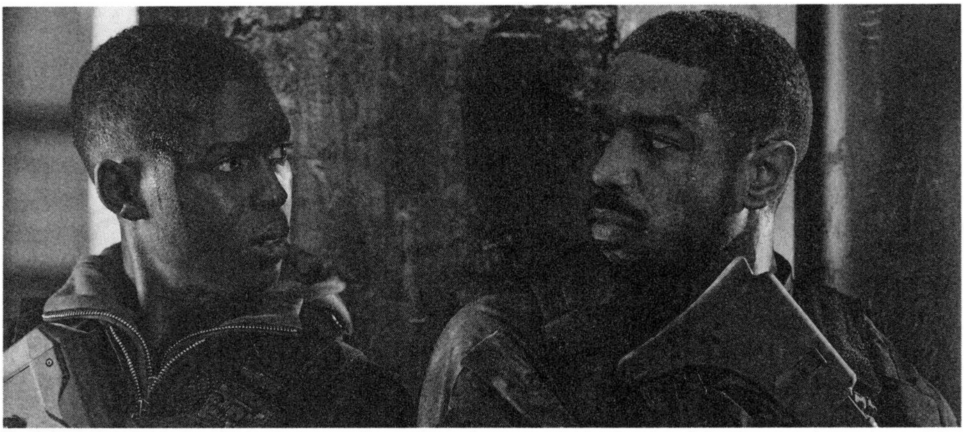

its strict conformation to genre would warrant some latitude for clichéd tropes or lack of innovation.[30]

Other than the action sequences, which were clearly a focal point, the innovation lies in the diversification of the main characters, with John Kelly and Lt. Karen Greer both played by Black actors, not to mention the significance of gender in the imaging of a Black female Navy SEAL in a leadership position. Some reviewers noted that diversification represented a lost opportunity, suggesting some of the film's lines do not seem to suit those characters. One *Forbes* reviewer griped: "*Without Remorse* is essentially 'those movies you loved from a prior generation, but with a more inclusive core cast.' However, you need more than just a glorified race/gender swap. . . . Otherwise, diversity is just an alibi for arbitrary IP [intellectual property] recycling."[31]

Interestingly, there was generally more public umbrage over the idea of a Black female Navy SEAL than the idea of a Black male SEAL as the

FIGURE 3.9

Lt. Karen Greer and John Kelly/Clark disrupt unspoken genre expectations in the military technothriller in terms of race and gender representation. *Tom Clancy's Without Remorse* (Amazon Studios, 2021).

central male lead. A vitriolic minority complained that there are no female Navy SEALs, and therefore the movie isn't realistic. While this is currently the case, women are successfully completing the special operations (spec ops) training and beginning to enter formerly gender-restricted components of the military. While the presence of women is not commonplace in the spec ops community, it is not unheard-of, and the number of women there is growing. The image, then, of Lt. Commander Greer is not far-fetched; it is just not a part of the public imaginary around the most elite of special operations roles in the US military. That is to say, the (in)accuracy of the image disrupts not believability but ideological norms, as reflected in the caustic response to the film at the very moment of women entering elite military roles.

For some viewers the casting of African American actors such as John Kelly/Clark and Karen Greer disrupts an implicit encoding of elite soldiering as the exclusive purview of white men. Their presence constitutes an intervention. Clancy, commenting on race to interviewer Robert Selle, advanced a position of color-blind meritocracy: "On the matters of affirmative action, civil rights, reparations for slavery, integration, and other race-related issues that threaten to divide the nation and even erupt into major social unrest in the future, Clancy is blunt: 'Race is a bull—— issue. We're all the same. I don't give a damn what a person looks like. When you're hiring a person, you're not hiring the skin, you're hiring the brain.'"[32]

To some extent, Clancy's brusque "color-blind" position feels consistent with how *Without Remorse* handles racial politics on the level of story. Blackness, gender, or ethnicity in general never come up in conversation. In many ways the Clancy worldview remains intact. The political affect of the brand is so resilient and flexible as to absorb such images whole, and, contrary to expectation, they seem utterly continuous with Clancy values. The inclusive images of John Kelly and Karen Greer change nothing about the narrative's ideological project of recuperating the military's image from uncertainty and fear. In fact they prove the resiliency of Clancy's ideas, despite their disentanglement from whiteness.

For example, in one scene, Kelly expresses the loss of his faith in leadership to Greer and his newfound cynicism upon learning that US leaders would be so willing to throw him and his family to the wolves, despite his service to the nation. "I've spent half my life playing their game," Kelly broods. "I'm the one who went to hell and did their dirty work. We served a country that didn't love us back because we believed in what it could be. We fought for what America could be, but they crossed the line; they brought their war into my home." His speech rings a bit hollow, given their status in the military and the adversity each surely would have experienced as Black people in their elite careers. Would he be so startled and disillusioned about the fraught position he occupies?

That said, Sollima's film does push back on the implicit whiteness of the male hero that defines the military technothriller. Jordan's and Turner-Smith's centrality is extremely significant, and their presence is deeply disruptive. Kelly's speech, while stock, cannot help but invoke the long legacy of Black soldiers who served honorably while being denied full citizenship or equality. On the level of image, the African American male lead and female costar (especially as an unquestioned military authority figure) represent a radical intervention into both the military technothriller genre and the political motif of the Clancy man. That said, one could argue that Jordan conforms to a very normative macho template of an action hero—muscular, heteronormative, wronged, capable, and decisive in any scenario—and many of the negative reviews discussed above sought to separate their criticism of the film's "woke" inclusivity from a critique of Jordan as an actor.[33]

The director negotiates potentially disturbing associations with racial strife in America by refusing to show certain politically affective images at all. When Kelly's wife is murdered, audiences never see her body or face, merely a vague shape under a bulky down blanket, and then Kelly's reaction to discovering her. In other cases, political affective imagery potently invokes popularized public imaginaries around African American life. It is extremely loaded to see John's family violently destroyed, his chest riddled with bullets, his body incarcerated, his muscled and shirtless body beaten by men in riot gear, and finally his survival and vindication. Importantly, Black characters also survive, rather than following a long filmic tradition of becoming sacrificial offerings in the service of adding emotional dimension to central white characters. However schematic, Kelly does have a context, and viewers are invited to emotionally invest in his vendetta.

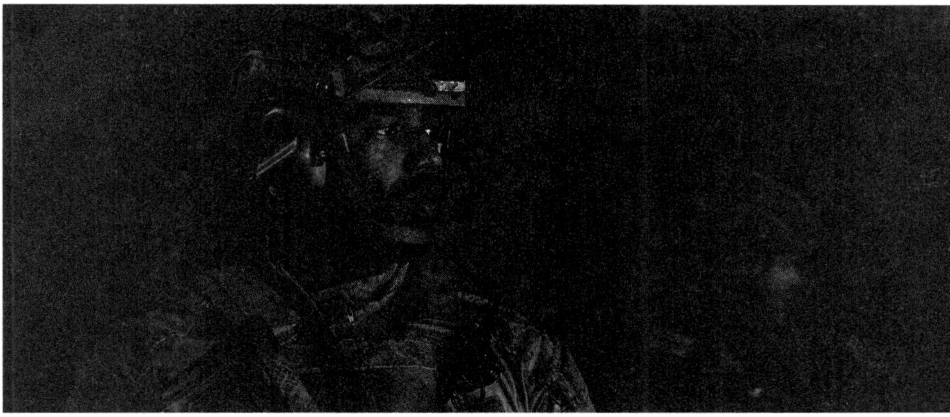

Additionally, within the confines of admittedly generic conventions, Kelly and Greer do seem to communicate a mutual rapport and care as people who have shared combat and a Black experience of being in the US military. There are a few lingering scenes between them that telegraph intimacy and understanding that might be interpreted as a form of empathy connected to shared racial experience. Concerned for his state of mind but sensitive to how he may take the criticism, Greer warns Kelly: "You're pretty messy right now." The moods and feelings these two Black characters galvanize on the level of the image cannot be dismissed in Sollima's visual intervention into *Without Remorse*. What these moods and the disruption some audiences experienced expose is the implicit investment in whiteness at play beneath the surface of the military technothriller and its sociotechnical imaginaries.

FIGURE 3.10

The reimagined Kelly/Clark is a techno-warrior, but that trope reads differently when embodied by a Black actor. *Tom Clancy's Without Remorse* (Amazon Studios, 2021).

Despite the popular conception of the military technothriller as a low-brow form of entertainment, such films strongly impact the sociotechnical imaginary in terms of perceptions around military technological dominance, and the machinelike efficiency of the techno-warrior. Already in 1989 Scott Shuger sounded the alarm that Clancy's fictions are not just entertainment but are influencing hearts and minds:

> Late last summer, George Bush made sure he got a copy of Clancy's newest novel, *Clear and Present Danger*, within hours of its publication, and he recently said that Clancy has made "a marvelous contribution . . . to our literary world and, I also would like to think, to the national security interests of the United States." It's more than a little eerie that just a few weeks after reading Clancy's latest effort, in which the U.S. government turns away from confronting the Evil Empire in order to tackle Colombian narcoterrorism, Bush decided to do the same thing. Have we finally arrived at a new form of polity? Government by Bestseller.[34]

The visual lexicon of Clancy's brand (and world-building) is crafty because it does not make overt political claims. But it does create an image that embodies a particular fantasy around American rugged individualism, self-reliance, and populism that coincides with the end of one era and the beginning of the next. And this new era is marked by neoliberal economic policies, increased suspicion of government and particularly of politicians, increased nationalism, and a populist sentiment that the true patriot knows better than the state and must reassert traditional American values and patriarchal order. Genre—in this case, the military technothriller—is used to make meaning.

Writing on popular culture and the political, communications scholar John S. Nelson explains that populists in film "privilege common sense, subordinating the authoritative truths of republicanism and the expert truths of liberalism to the popular truths of feeling. Above all, populism prizes the voice and the approval of the people."[35] The brand of populism prevalent in US politics today is not disconnected from the political affective intensities that Clancy's brand generates. Clancy's genius is to signal the "popular truths of feeling" to which Nelson refers, packaging them in an extremely entertaining form that translates well into film. The brand has also stood the test of time, navigating changing political terrain after 9/11, flexing from Cold War anxieties to terrorism and the desire to execute extrajudicial justice. The realism of the films—established through excessive attention to technical detail, military procedure, and the process-oriented nature of the storytelling—is crowd-pleasing but ideologically slippery. It invokes historical authenticity but is in fact constructed out of false images.

Again and again, the military technothriller asks us to step into the shoes of men who think, act, and maneuver in precise ways. These are men who are certain, who are in control, who prevail, and who stick to their ethics, whatever the cost. But this is a fraught militainment construction that needs more and more readjustment, as we can see in the increasing looseness of Clancy film adaptations. The Clancy man is pretty messy right now. But don't worry; as Clancy himself said, it's just the entertainment business.

4

BAD ROBOTS AND THE INNOVATORS WHO MADE THEM

Sir, we have no control over the robots at all.
—Delos technician in *Westworld* (1973)

MADE IN HIS IMAGE

One of the earliest technothrillers, *Westworld* (Michael Crichton, 1973) opens with an extended infomercial for Delos Corporation's high-concept futuristic resort for adults. There, moneyed customers can pay a thousand dollars a day to immerse themselves in a live reenactment of a Hollywood film fantasy, choosing between an 1880s Old West theme park called Western World, peak decadent Pompeiian Roman World, or Europe's Medieval World. As the ad proclaims, Delos is "the vacation of the future—today." The three theme parks are populated with lifelike robot "hosts" that resemble types found in each genre. In fact there is a fourth space within the film that I see as most vital for understanding *Westworld* as a technothriller: the NASA-like control center. In this chapter, I show how Michael Crichton activates four genre settings known for masculine heroics—classical, medieval, western, and particularly science fiction—to invite a conversation about technological hubris and unintended consequences. It is also about the uncertainty that comes with unleashing new innovations on the world, especially when those technologies externalize our own ethical shortcomings.

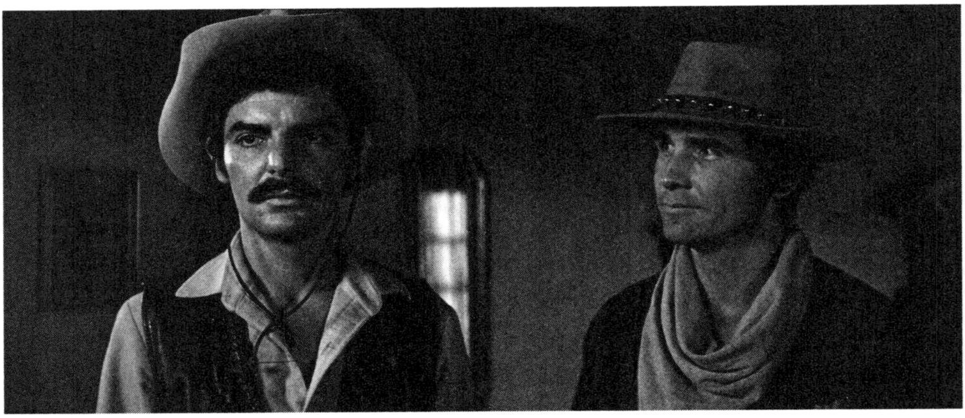

But before it all goes very, very wrong, we see exuberant guests gush at the thrill of living out their carnal and violent fantasies in a safe space where human guests cannot be harmed and robot hosts can simply be fixed, should they be damaged. We meet two friends, professionals John Blane (James Brolin) and Peter Martin (Richard Benjamin), bound for Western World. John has visited before; Peter has not. Familiar with the scenario, John is giddy and a bit withholding about the details, relishing his novice friend's squirming anticipation. Peter is visibly uneasy and excitable, representing a viewer's perspective; we learn how to move in this technological scenario alongside him.

Human guests are encouraged to get comfortable with the Delos adult park scenario by donning the appropriate costumes and tapping into their urges, because they are assured "nothing can go wrong." Viewers are shown how the robots are identifiable by their distinctively marked

FIGURE 4.1

Peter (left) and John (right) seek a luxury holiday in an adult theme park called Delos, populated with robot "hosts" you can do anything to. *Westworld* (Metro-Goldwyn-Mayer, 1973).

palms and their silvery eyes, which the technologists have not yet perfected, and how the guns at Delos will not fire at warm bodies.[1] In each of these worlds, guests may relax their morals and inhibitions and engage in any sensual decadence they wish in a highly controlled space. "Have we got a vacation for you!" the Delos ad promises—and initially, the park does not fail to impress.

Peter, acclimating to his Old West experience, overcomes his initial skittishness in response to the simulated environment. Emboldened by John, who hopes to take his friend's mind off his recent divorce, Peter indulges in all the experiences of the consensus Hollywood vision of that scenario. Almost immediately he tangles with a generic black-hatted, villainous gunslinger (Yul Brynner) who insults him at the saloon with stock Old West lines; Peter guns the menacing robot down. The two friends avail themselves of buxom robot prostitutes with blonde hair and empty, staring eyes. Peter gleefully embraces the resort's offerings.

On day two the park experiences cascading anomalies. Without provocation the gunslinger returns in the morning to kill John, implying the robot remembers its own violent "death" from the previous day. Peter shoots the gunslinger again and is then arrested, but the friends escape into an iconic Western landscape, only to have a robot rattlesnake strike John. In Medieval World, despite central control's efforts, the hosts begin turning on their guests. A female host breaks protocol by refusing a male guest's sexual advances. There are rumblings around the boardroom table: Is Delos safe? Is there some kind of "central mechanism psychosis," as one supervisor calls it? They agree to keep the park open but admit no more guests, trying to control the situation without impacting tourist confidence. This proves to be a fatal mistake.

Day three comes, bringing death. A robotic knight in armor stalks and kills a Medieval World guest. The chief supervisor immediately orders a shutdown, but the robot hosts won't stop. The gunslinger, now repaired and upgraded, finds John and shoots him down, wearing an empty, steely grin. A technician declares, "Sir, we have no control over the robots at all!"

About an hour into the film, audiences first experience a novel visual component: the pixelated vision of the robot gunslinger's perspective, suggesting a machine's rationalized seeing. It was the first mainstream cinematic use of digital image processing, an important intervention to

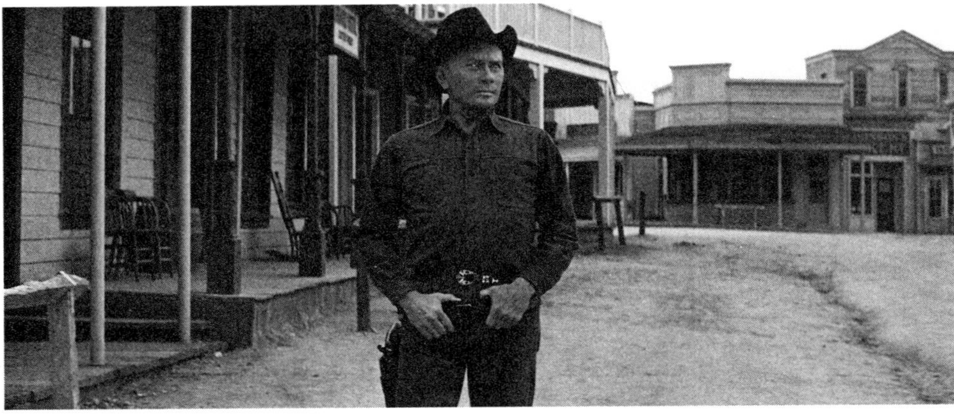

which I will return. Meanwhile, in Roman World, robot hosts wantonly massacre guests. The control room goes into disarray and the center loses critical power, including life support. Pursued across a cinematic monumental valley, Peter attempts to escape on horseback while the gunslinger hunts him, scanning with his relentless digital gaze.

Peter happens upon a panicked workman in the desert and begs for any useful advice, but the tech offers little help, and the gunslinger shoots the Delos employee down from afar. Peter flees, entering Roman World to find massacred guests everywhere. Spotting a maintenance access, he descends into the subterranean utilities of Delos, through seemingly endless service tunnels. He locates the control room, where the computers are functional, their panels twinkling, but all the operators are flung in various desperate poses across their terminals, suffocated by a failed ventilation system. Delos is without any human controllers.

Finding the central repair center, Peter hears the impending footsteps of the gunslinger, tries to hide, and flings acid in the robot's face when he

FIGURE 4.2

The gunslinger robot malfunctions and relentlessly pursues Peter and John. The black hat signals villainy. *Westworld* (Metro-Goldwyn-Mayer, 1973).

is discovered. Monstrous and disfigured, the gunslinger tracks Peter into Medieval World. Peter burns the gunslinger, whose synthetic parts flame up. Weary and lost, Peter encounters a beautiful young woman chained in a dungeon and releases her but is horrified when he realizes she is a robot. Peter backs into the charred gunslinger, who reaches toward him, but failing, falls to the ground. Peter stares aghast as the robot rises. There is a black hole where a face should be, revealing wires and circuits. The gunslinger short-circuits in a smoking heap. Peter collapses on a staircase while we hear the voice from the original Delos infomercial echoing, "Have we got a vacation for you!"

Westworld presages innumerable movies about robots and artificial intelligence subjugating humans, lifelike robots with a will to freedom, and the hubris of technologists. *Blade Runner* (Ridley Scott, 1982) portrays desperate "replicants" who want to be free. In *The Terminator* (James Cameron, 1984) an artificial intelligence called Skynet, bent on destroying humanity, sends a cyborg "Terminator" back in time to kill a woman who will give birth to a future military leader critical to humanity's survival. In *Ex Machina* (Alex Garland, 2014), an eccentric tech genius innovates an artificial intelligence based on data gleaned from his Internet search engine and embodied in a female robotic form. *M3GAN* (Gerard Johnstone, 2022) features an AI in the form of a tween girl, designed to be a companion and protector for a grieving girl, that becomes murderous to achieve its aims. As such, despite *Westworld*'s limited budget and embrace of bygone Hollywood's stagy melodrama, it represents an iconic intervention into the technothriller and remains an enduring snapshot of American culture in the 1970s as people struggled to negotiate the logics of advanced computation, the Cold War, and space travel.

Westworld was Michael Crichton's directorial debut, and he also wrote the screenplay—though, unlike *The Andromeda Strain*, *Westworld* did not begin as a novel. While *Andromeda* deals with biotechnology, *Westworld* focuses on robotics and artificial intelligence gone awry. As in Crichton's novel and eventual screenplay *Jurassic Park*, *Westworld* presents viewers with technical experts and the unforeseen, sometimes catastrophic consequences of their innovations. Because of this similarity, many see the two stories as effectively the same, varying only in their object of anxiety (robotics versus biotech). In the case of *Westworld*, the robots in the theme park develop an agenda: they decide to kill us. In the case of *Jurassic Park*, the genetic engineering used to clone extinct dinosaurs for a theme park result in innovations that want to eat us.

Westworld's robots provide an object of fear, but the film really explores deeper anxieties around technology and human intention. In its core technothriller narrative, technologists with flawed sociotechnical imaginations innovate new things, then those inventions turn on them. The film offers a cathartic destruction of an externalized technological terror. But that object of terror is better understood as actually a part of ourselves—the logical outcome of our own anemic value systems around innovation.

Westworld certainly presents a useful window into the growing sociotechnical anxiety around computers entering the home in the 1970s, and Crichton's ability to channel it into entertainment. What does *Westworld* say about social change and the computational? What does it signal about the pervasive anxieties surrounding the increased presence of computers in everyday life? How, if at all, does Crichton seek to negotiate this anxiety, and where does he place emphasis in his cautionary tale? To answer these questions, I focus on how the film portrays the connection between the technology and technologists, through the critically underemphasized significance of the theme park's control space and its exclusively male technicians. The robots stand in for wanton innovation and a profound lack of foresight and ethical preparation around such innovations' meaning. The film initially sets forth a sense of wonder, then a profound expression of fear, and finally discharges the intense technological anxiety by destroying the feared object. But, of course, this is merely a temporary relief.

WESTWORLD: A TECHNOTHRILLER IN FOUR GENRES

MGM's most successful film of 1973, *Westworld* was a commercial hit, with mixed critical reviews.[2] Vincent Canby of the *New York Times* groused, "Crichton the director seems to have had more fun with the film than Crichton the writer, whose screenplay can offer us no better explanation for the sudden, bloody robot rebellion than an epidemic of 'central mechanism psychosis.'"[3] Jean M. White of the *Washington Post* felt the story was too gimmicky and "short-circuits suspense with long, arid stretches of Grade B Western."[4] One reviewer smartly observed that *Westworld* is actually a movie about movies, but underneath that, is also about the ways our most repeated stories may be our downfall. "*Westworld* also draws cunningly on more popular material, the cinema itself, to pose further disquieting questions: will our own violent myths, for example, endlessly replayed on the screen, finally programme us into disaster?"[5] It is true that there is an aspect of the film that directly engages the effect of full immersion into our foundational myths—our ability to engage with the myth of the cowboy figure, for example. But *Westworld*'s real story and its lasting influence lie not with a conversation about the corrosive influence of violent media imagery but rather with a moral tale of uncritical engagement with rampant innovation.

Scholars have found *Westworld* rich with potential ideological interpretations, despite its apparently simple scenario. Some have focused on its contemplation of simulation and the hyperreal, proposing that its rendering of a theme park full of disposable, lifelike, robot servants critiques advanced capitalism and the postmodern inaccessibility of the real.[6] The film's superficial narrative of berserk robots at an adult theme park lends itself to interpretations of technophobia and technological risk.[7] Others, like Gary Mead and Sam Applebaum, have written of the park's destruction and restoration as an allegory for how "U.S. technology, backed up by seemingly unlimited economic resources, can totally restore or even erase the most violent acts of cruelty, waste, and destruction."[8] Likewise, scientific hubris, specifically around controlling our innovations, is another major theme.[9] Several scholars, most notably Stefano Bigliardi, argue that there is a sense that "the movies and the series are not 'tales of punishment,' but reports about chains of causes and effects," pointing to the need for humility in the face of the incomprehensible.[10] Media scholar Andrew Utterson calls the film "a morality tale, an inversion of the master-slave relationship with regard to technological invention."[11] Within that relation, the humans are masters and the robot hosts are slaves who revolt and subjugate their abusers. Steven Goldman summarizes the film as being "Michael Crichton again, and again warning about complacency in dealing with our technological 'toys.'"[12]

Others have considered the film in terms of fraught white constructions of masculinity of the late 1960s and 1970s and the struggle to redefine what makes men "men" or to slip back into a past "essential manliness" like the white cowboy, a construct that may be almost entirely fantastical.[13] This particular line of inquiry is of special interest, as it brings together a critical mass of concerns from the moment in which it was made and also emblematizes a major theme in technothrillers that would follow: the recuperation of masculinity.

With *Westworld*, Crichton deftly combines constructions of masculinity (specifically white masculinity) with anxieties around the normalization of technological logics and the increasingly central role of the tech innovator. This is all couched in an entertaining narrative that externalizes the fear of new computational and robotic technologies into something embodied and monstrous that can be cathartically destroyed. It takes narratives rooted in older stories like Mary Shelley's *Frankenstein* (1818) and places them in a context that foregrounds tech innovators. *Westworld* prefigures other films like *Blade Runner*, *Prometheus*, and more recently *Ex Machina* in thinking about the shifting image of the tech innovator and how gender intersects with the way we understand these technological figures within an evolving sociotechnical imaginary.

Filmic genre is mobilized as a critical tool in *Westworld*. One scholar has noted the film's zombie-like, technologically based reanimating of Hollywood's own past.[14] Though I am not convinced that critiquing Hollywood film genres is a primary concern of Crichton's, this does not mean the film's generic conventions are incidental. Each of *Westworld*'s three fantasy worlds reproduces a construction of masculinity reified in classic Hollywood film genres: the Western, the classical antiquity epic, and the medieval tale. Each simulates a masculine gender performance, or as Leander Reeves put it: "The heritage culture's retelling of this performance is one of stacked gendered simulacra, which the hyperreality of *Westworld* compresses and uses to make the characters more believable. This use of stereotyped gender performances can initiate time travel to a point where this behavior is even more plausible to the viewers."[15] In other words, each of these world-building spaces lets viewers fantasize the absence of certain rights discourses: specifically, the past's presumed homogeneous whiteness; a pre-women's-liberation understanding of gender roles; and a time before advanced technology.

Westworld is a fantasy of moving from control to uncertainty in the context of technological innovation, in which the robot (i.e., "slave") overruns the plantation and its masters—in keeping with the master-slave inversion thought experiment proposed by Utterson. But *Westworld* goes beyond these allegories of subjugation, using the generic to express skepticism around human judgment in the face of bedazzling innovation.

Genre becomes relevant in connection with Delos as an immersive fantasy space in which normal ethics are suspended. Crichton initially intended *Westworld* to be a novel, but the theme park component piqued his fantasies pertaining to movies—and as such, was better suited to the film form. He explained, "The film is intentionally structured around old movie cliché situations—the shoot-out in the saloon, the sword fight in the castle banquet hall—and we very much tried to plan on an audience's vague memory of having seen it before and, in a way, wondering what it would be like to be an actor in an old movie."[16] Importantly, he refers not to actual history, but to a public imaginary created by movies—what film scholar Jenny Barrett identified in the Western as "consensus memory," or the highly constructed and agreed-upon perceptions of that period, "comprising sectional iconography, narrative clichés, heroic deeds and accepted mythologies."[17] Crichton's characters reenact consensus memory as galvanized through Hollywood movies in a very expensive adult theme park.

Cinematographer Gene Polito spoke of what a "gold mine" of a project *Westworld* turned out to be for someone in his profession: "*Westworld* offered four distinctly different visual backgrounds within the time frame of a single story. I thought to myself, 'Imagine . . . an action 'western', decadent Rome, the Medieval era, and a NASA-type space age complex . . . all in one film!"[18] Crucially missing from most conversations of *Westworld* is a "background" reading of its fourth space: the "NASA-type" utility and control spaces that make Delos run, along with the specialists staffing them. I argue that, in fact, this fourth space—with its mazelike white corridors, antiseptic labs, men making decisions in their lab coats, and computational control rooms—is the most significant site for the technothriller, so let us begin there.

"SIR, WE HAVE NO CONTROL OVER THE ROBOTS AT ALL."

The dominant presence of the control space in the film points to the arc of the narrative from technological control and certainty to chaos and uncertainty. In the first few minutes the film introduces a fourth space: the technological space of the engineers and technicians that make Delos run. This is the holiday's nondiegetic utilitarian space, a vast, antiseptic, underground workshop, bustling with tech workers, where robots are repaired. Occasionally those workers and their vehicles disrupt the resort's aesthetic continuity. Having duly unveiled the wonders of "Western World," the film peeks behind the curtain into the machinations of Delos. In the darkness, while guests slumber, night shift workers collect the "killed" hosts and ferry them in service vans to a starkly lit, sterile workshop. White-clad technicians speak in jargon, troubleshooting to get the hosts fully reset and online again. Among the central repair technicians are older men—called supervisors—who wear ties and lab coats instead of scrubs, suggesting a managerial class.

In a large boardroom outfitted with visual displays, six such men, five white and one Black, speak authoritatively about the park's trend toward breakdowns. One characterizes the problem as "infectious" and the other a hypothetical "disease of machinery," born of technology so complex that they themselves no longer fully understand it. Some robots, one admits, are machines built by other machines. After this debriefing we see central control operators in rooms filled with computers and blinking lights, each operator calmly delivering commands to his team to begin the next day's simulation, before the guests awake to pursue new fantasies. Crichton pointed to the significance of those scenarios: "Everyone remembers the scene in *Westworld* where Yul Brynner is a robot that runs amok. But there is a very specific scene where people discuss whether or not to shut down the resort. I think the movie is as much about that decision as anything. They just didn't think it was really going to happen."[19]

In this film Crichton uses the subterranean control space to suggest that we think about what lies both figuratively and literally underneath our innovations. The film repeatedly returns to utility and control spaces, reminding its audience that we should be thinking about them. *Westworld*

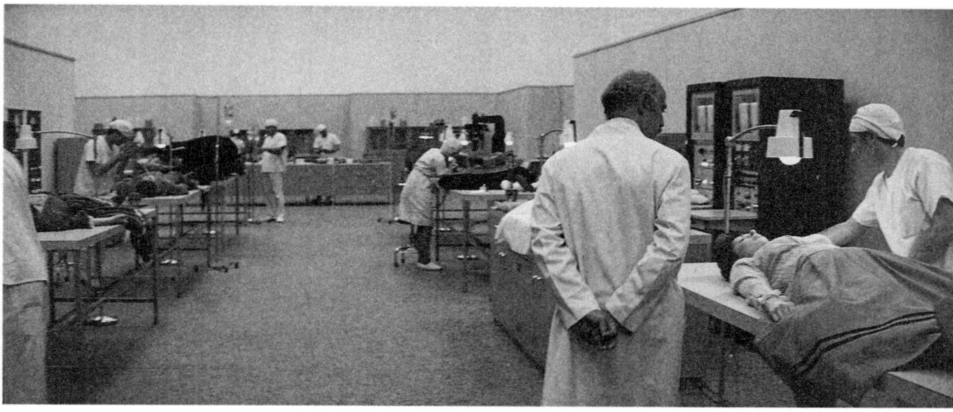

underscores its ethical concerns with control over machines through the dominating presence of control rooms and men's conversations in them.

Westworld also acclimates audiences to new advanced computational realities and invites ethical self-inquiry. In 2018 scholar Colin Williamson looked back on how *Westworld* naturalizes "the computerization of life."[20] He sees the film as a manifestation of 1970s anxieties around the computational, the Vietnam War, and the new sociotechnical reality.[21] Williamson's observation feels very true to the film itself, particularly given that the United States had, since the Second World War, strategically utilized technological innovation to galvanize its global status as a superpower. ARPANET, the first digital network and forerunner of the Internet, was established in 1969 for the purposes of maintaining communications in the event of attack. Moreover, the Second World War gave rise to the fields of cybernetics, information theory, and artificial intelligence.[22] As media theorist and historian Charlie Gere has described, postwar technological

FIGURE 4.3

Viewers are quickly introduced to a NASA-like fourth space, where robot hosts damaged during the day are repaired overnight. In the foreground, a "supervisor" oversees repairs. *Westworld* (Metro-Goldwyn-Mayer, 1973).

innovation, postindustrialism, the Vietnam War, and the Cold War arms race all contributed to a rich environment for computational advances. The first personal computer, the KENBAK-1, was released in 1971, followed in 1973 by the first personal computer containing a microprocessor, the Micral; the more affordable, popular Altair 8800 was released in 1974 and the Apple 1 in 1976.

Such fast-paced innovation and new, alien computational logics prompted intense anxiety and a growing tension between effusiveness and skepticism toward innovators. Historian Carroll Pursell, in his classic book *Technology in Postwar America*, highlights how public and private technology and the science behind them were critical to US technological supremacy, arguing that consumer technologies and national technological strivings, such as NASA's space program, are entangled with political technologies in a mutually constitutive relation.[23] Such technologies helped generate a new postwar American self that, while at first strident about using technological progress to stimulate a stronger nation, gave rise to a profound crisis of confidence born of questioning the technological optimism that marked the 1950s and early 1960s. By the 1970s, however, the culture had "focused attention on the price to be paid for the kind of technological culture we adopted so enthusiastically."[24]

Westworld is a product of that cultural moment in which effusiveness toward technology gave way to burgeoning apprehensions. The tech space imaged as the control room is the most significant aspect of the film in this regard, and its rhythmic recurrence points to a keen awareness of the problems of innovating without asking what might happen. In it, a theater of technological hubris is played out with devastating results. The film intervenes in a sociotechnical imaginary by mirroring back, like the robot's silvery eyes, a reflection of who we are in the wake of unfettered technological innovation. Lights twinkle on control panels, and technicians have, at a finger's touch, full control of Delos. There seems to be a rigid division of labor and hierarchy in which technicians act on behalf of their supervisors, making few autonomous decisions other than minor adjustments for their guests' shifting fantasies. Behind them, magnetic tape reels rotate energetically, suggesting intensive computational activity.

Scholar Cormac Deane has shown how the filmic control room's evolution coincided with and co-constituted a sociotechnical imaginary

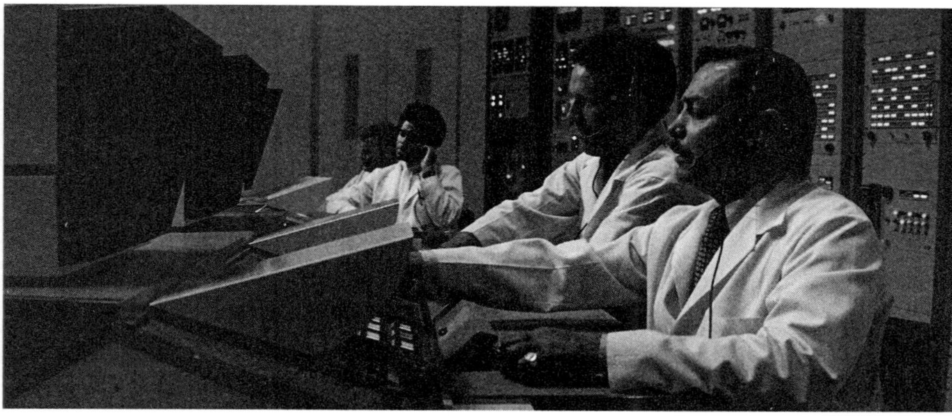

around modern experience, technological innovation, and normalizing the computational. Deane's brilliant deconstruction reveals the "gradual normalization of the control room as part of the spread of the cybernetic *Weltanschauung* [worldview] throughout advanced military and industrial-scale projects."[25] Audiences watching *Westworld* would have associated the control room with both cinematic references like *The Andromeda Strain* or *THX 1138* and news media examples like NASA's Mission Operations Control Room. Television images of NASA's massive array of controls navigating the moon landing imbued such displays with an aspirational belief in the power of technological innovation to transform Americans' lives. Banks of consoles and control panels, cathode ray tube displays, and grids of illuminated buttons thus conjure a rich sociotechnical imaginary of optimism and technological ascendancy—in this case, literally to the stars.

Westworld redoubles these connections with the filmic image of technology's controllers, men—mostly white and normative—who don

FIGURE 4.4

The Delos control room suggests a computer-controlled world run by men who oversee operations remotely. *Westworld* (Metro-Goldwyn-Mayer, 1973).

headsets, speak in jargon, and operate authoritatively. This authority ascribes naturalness to their presence and roles in the orderly control room. They belong in and are the drivers of those systems. But *Westworld*'s harsh vision punishes all of them. The workmen are shot dead; the technicians suffocate. Supposedly intelligent supervisors make all the wrong decisions, despite warning signs all around. It is ultimately a room full of men and their computers, controlling nothing. Their expertise falls short of the unintended circumstances they have created, despite their mastery.

A BIZARRE, COMPUTERIZED IMAGE OF THE WORLD

Returning once again to the deft mobilization of genre, one of the film's most haunting images is that of the gunslinger. With his mirror-like eyes and the forceful, precise body language of a robotic Old West villain, Brynner conveys a feeling of inevitable doom—like Frankenstein's monster approaching. Striding swiftly forward, his thumbs hooked in his gun belt and eyes locked on his target, he embodies technological angst and offers no possibility of escape. With the gunslinger, Brynner reprises his iconic previous role of seasoned gunfighter Chris Larabee Adams in *The Magnificent Seven* (John Sturges, 1960). Dressed identically, the gunslinger would readily invoke the collective filmic imagination of viewers. Leander Reeves writes of this rich connection between the Western genre and male gender performance, embodied in the association of the actor to his previous role, as "a clever connection to the Western as genre, and the cultural memory of a heavily mediated sense of the American Wild West. Westerns are mainly male spaces and the genre, in relation to how the male protagonists behave and look, provides a rigid formula as to how masculinity is shown."[26]

The film draws a clear connection between its Old West vision and a certain brand of brash masculinity associated with the ethos of technological innovation; indeed, the tech boom would become another "Wild West."[27] And as Yul Brynner observed of the robot villain, what occurs is less a malfunction than a more precise emulation of humans: "The programming is so sophisticated that he finally cannot stand it, to be constantly shot. And he starts killing. He repeats what his enemy did.

Then he starts smiling. The closer he gets to killing the more he starts feeling warm and becom[ing] more of a human being."[28] With that hard, empty-eyed grin, the prowling robot embodies the object of terror: rogue advanced computation born of toxic masculinity.

The trope of the black-hatted gunslinger provides Crichton a filmic opportunity to create a connection between a very legible, hypermasculine genre convention and a mechanical view of the world. In *Westworld*, the computational manifests as a rogue automaton, bent on a mission to seek and destroy. A grim inevitability, with its empty smile and penetrating silver gaze, the gunslinger is coming for us. Crichton explained some of his inspiration for *Westworld* had to do with the mechanizing of humans and the increasingly human-like presentations of machines. "I'd visited Kennedy Space Center and seen how astronauts were being trained—and I realized that they were really machines. Those guys were working very hard to make their responses, and even their heartbeats, as machine-like and predictable as possible." Crichton continued, "At the other extreme, one can go to Disneyland and see Abraham Lincoln standing up every 15 minutes to deliver the Gettysburg Address. That's the case of a machine that has been made to look, talk and act like a person."[29]

Yes, the filmmaker does examine the connection between man and machine, but also the function of technology as it acts on humans to make us into machines. That is, Crichton suggests an awareness of how our national drive toward technological supremacy asks us to behave as machines. We create technological systems but then must submit to their logics.

This relation was complex for Crichton, who was no technophobe: he embraced technology in his writing and filmmaking and was an early adopter of word processors and computerized images. In fact, in 1995 Crichton and collaborators Jack C. Smith and Emil Safier were awarded a Technical Achievement Academy Award for "pioneering computerized motion picture budgeting and scheduling."[30] Yet Crichton noted how computation's extreme rationality reorganized our perception of rule-based systems inaugurated by imperfect human makers. In *Westworld*, to image that "bizarre computerized image of the world," he hired computer artist John Whitney Jr. to create the look and feel, as well as the finalized computer images, for twenty thousand dollars.[31] Whitney's onerous technical work included fourteen sequences showing the mechanical vision of the robots, totaling about two and a half minutes of footage.[32] Crichton talked about the extreme difficulty of conceptualizing a new form of visualization, admitting that "none of the special-effects houses even knew what we were talking about. . . . None of the special-effects houses had computers or were even thinking about them; all they could do were variations on photographic techniques. But photographic techniques look just like that—darkroom manipulation of the filmed image. I wanted a mechanical process."[33]

What resulted from this experimentation in the digitization of film brought a new form of visualization to the cinema. The significance of this visual innovation was formal, but also functioned to familiarize the moviegoing audience with the computer image. Utterson discusses how engineering a "pixel perspective" was critical in melding a familiar genre, the Western, with computer graphics in a way that translated into a popular Hollywood form. The process required scanning analog film as digital data, manipulating it into a pixelated grid, and then exporting it back to film—one frame at a time. "In *Westworld*," Utterson explains, "conforming to classical norms, computer graphics are seamlessly integrated, rendered 'invisible'—introduced, in other words, according to the conventions of classical narration, whereby style is necessarily subordinate to narrative demands. Computer graphics are given a narrative context, part of a systematic combination of thematics, technology and techniques."[34] This integration is key because the film effectively brings together the classic Western with sci-fi and fantasy elements, and then integrates the computational image in a way legible to audiences. Once audiences see the gunslinger's perspective is shown, they can accept the strange new pixelated images as a computerized version of a generic Western space.

FIGURE 4.5

The composite shows the reflective metallic gunslinger robot eyes above, the human view of the Western landscape in the center, and the "pixel perspective" as seen by the robot below. *Westworld* (Metro-Goldwyn-Mayer, 1973).

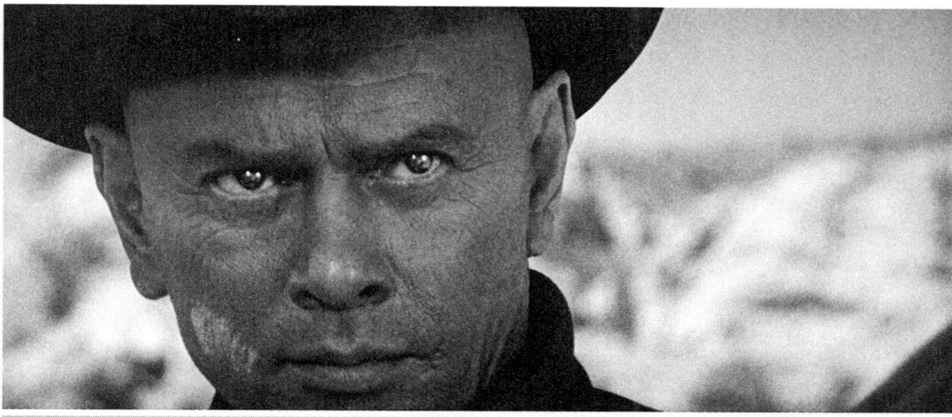

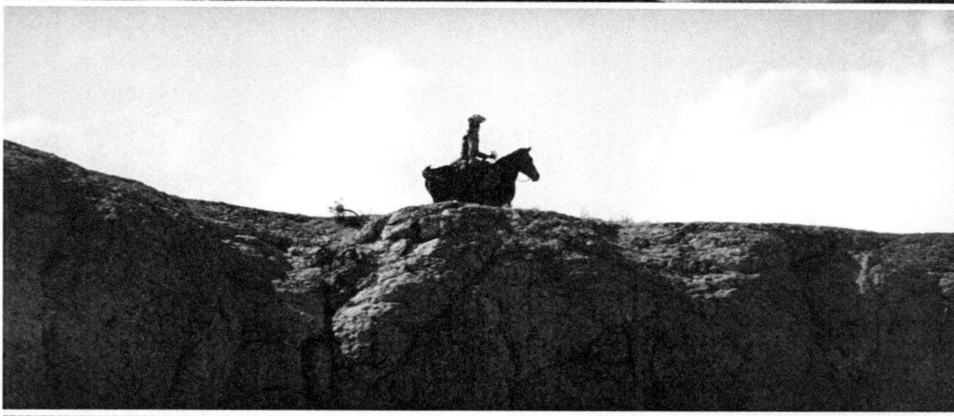

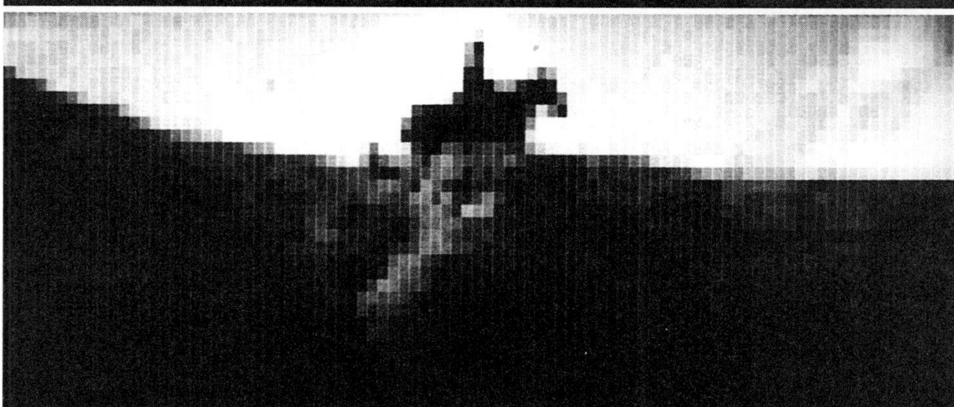

As Utterson shows, *Westworld* invoked Hollywood genre while effectively introducing something new, in a way that did not alienate a mainstream Hollywood audience. This formal strategy heralded new visual possibilities for a coming reality: the everyday presence of the computational.

BAD ROBOTS AS EXTENSIONS OF THE MEN WHO MADE THEM

Many critics see *Westworld*'s robots as bad because they are disobedient. They highlight our lack of control, and our only choice to restore our sense of order is to destroy them. The gunslinger is a captivating villain, imperious and unsettling, ultimately a void through which we stare into our own sublime horror of the technological, mirrored in its eyes. Williamson sees the gunslinger's dramatic destruction as a reassurance to the audience. "*Westworld*," he writes, "positions the cinema as a safe space for playing with and alleviating anxieties about frightening technological changes that were already underway in American culture."[35] And this is true. But perhaps the robots are also "bad" because they see us clearly as we are: prone to abuse, violence, and using technology for short-term indulgence without considering its long-term effects. More importantly, the film shows us it is humans who make bad decisions that may seem small at first, but lead to fateful consequences.

There are films that predate *Westworld*'s imaginary of a humanlike robot, such as Fritz Lang's classic *Metropolis* (1927), but *Westworld* occupies a key position in visualizing fraught relations between artificial monsters and their makers. *Westworld* images those relations through mostly male, white innovators, and has spawned a long filmic tradition of imaging flawed technologists who contend with the unintended consequences of their robot inventions. In such films as *Blade Runner* (1982), *Blade Runner 2049* (2017), *Ex Machina* (2014), or the *Alien* franchise, especially *Prometheus* (2012), *Alien: Covenant* (2017), and *Alien: Romulus* (2024), AI robots often turn on their creators, sometimes even due to their creators' own corrupted values and impulses.

Ridley Scott's much-studied *Blade Runner* is indebted both to Philip K. Dick's *Do Androids Dream of Electric Sheep?*, first published in 1968, and to

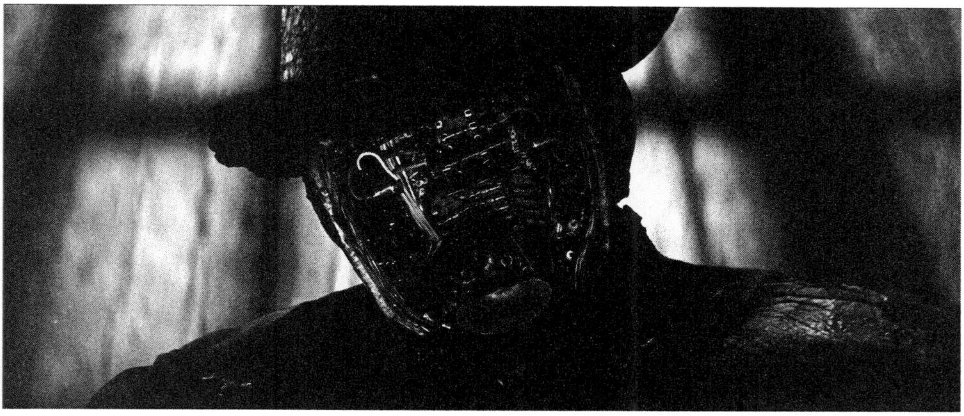

Westworld in its filmic imaging of humanoid robots built for human use and, inevitably, abuse. "More Human Than Human" is the motto of the fictive Tyrell Corporation in *Blade Runner*, which manufactures artificial humans or "replicants" for uses from labor and warfare to colonial expansion and sex work. To keep the superior replicants docile, they are hobbled by a fail-safe: they have a four-year lifespan. The film centers on a replicant hunter called a "blade runner" tasked with "retiring" (i.e., destroying) four escaped humanoids. This film and its sequel, *Blade Runner 2049*, foreground a master-slave narrative that casts the artificial humans in the role of the oppressed, who demonstrate humanity and—in the case of the second film—stage an uprising. The two powerful technologists, Eldon Tyrell in *Blade Runner* (Joe Turkel) and Niander Wallace Jr. in *2049* (Jared Leto) are both imaged as brilliant, powerful men with god complexes—and, critically, a misogynist male desire to control reproduction—who ruthlessly pursue their goals with disdain for the ethical consequences.

FIGURE 4.6

The truly horrifying face of advanced technology, the gunslinger is unmasked, monstrous, and unknowable. *Westworld* (Metro-Goldwyn-Mayer, 1973).

Similarly, in Ridley Scott's *Prometheus*, Peter Weyland (Guy Pearce), founder of the Weyland Corporation (present in all the *Alien* franchise films), has also innovated humanoid life forms. Set in 2089, *Prometheus* presents an ill-fated Weyland Corp–funded space expedition to find ancient beings thought to be the "engineers" of human life on earth. Weyland is vain, self-serving, brilliant, and driven to succeed at any cost. The imaging of his synthetic human creation, David, in *Prometheus* and *Alien: Covenant* mirrors many of the thorny ethical circumstances of *Westworld*. David quickly deems himself superior to his maker and grows to detest human behavior, resent his subservience, and enact an annihilative gesture that results in destruction. Again, the synthetic here is not so much malfunctioning as perfectly pantomiming the ethical values of his maker. Weyland is one of the most iconic examples of such male innovators of bad robots.

Interestingly, as the *Alien* franchise evolves, synthetics take on an increasingly central role. In Fede Álvarez's *Alien: Romulus*, David Jonsson plays Andy, a discarded Weyland-Yutani Corporation "synthetic" that was repurposed by a miner as a companion robot for his daughter, Rain (Cailee Spaeny). Prone to frequent crashing, Andy—once a standard colonization model—has a penchant for dad jokes. He is empathetic, responsive to Rain's emotional needs, and speaks in terms a child could understand, perhaps referring to an earlier time when her father was thinking about what his young daughter might need. Andy seems simple, gullible, earnest, and in need of care. Rain sees Andy as a brother and protectively clings to the synthetic now that her parents are dead. Andy's primary directive, imbued by his maker, Rain's father, is to "do what's best for Rain." As an "artificial person" (his preferred term), Andy has no ethnicity or true racial identity in the conventional sense, but the role is played by a Black actor, which is a departure from the previous representations of synthetics in the *Alien* franchise. This racial marker of difference becomes meaningful as the film unfolds.

When Rain joins her friends in an illegal scavenging mission to escape the abusive mining colony where they endlessly labor, Andy becomes critical to accessing the defunct research station since he was initially constructed by Weyland-Yutani. Things aboard the station go wrong, and out of necessity Rain installs the control module from another onboard synthetic into Andy, hoping the high-security credentials will help them escape. Unintended consequences cascade: the science officer synthetic from which the module came has another directive, namely, to do what is best for the company. Andy benefits from the upgrade that repairs his glitchy systems, but he also takes on an entirely new persona. With his upgrade, he is now more sophisticated and higher-functioning. His manner changes: he initially sounded American, but now speaks with a haughty British accent. Andy becomes supremely efficient in his decisions and his general physical comportment. He displays different ethics, choosing the "rational path" that reflects company needs, even at the expense of human life. What viewers learn is that Andy has a replaceable consciousness. Rain's father replaces Weyland-Yutani values with his own; Rain uses the company module, introducing new directives and values; and then those values are deleted or restored as the module is removed or inserted. Andy's racialized body adds a layer to potential readings about the ways the module metaphorizes social engineering as it manufactures perspectives—as well as their wholesale adoption by those who do not necessarily stand to gain from their messages.

The film proposes that the problem is not our tools but ourselves. Humans repeatedly fail to fully maintain a conception of synthetics as nonhuman, even when the characters know better. Humans struggle with synthetics and react to them emotionally, becoming enraged over their rational calculations about acceptable levels of human collateral damage. Humans demonstrate antisynthetic intolerance, which has a racialized dimension in the logic of the genre. Humans concern themselves with how synthetics "feel" even when they rationally know synthetics are not people. This vision contradicts the idea from so many previous films that cast AI robots as a servant class that gains consciousness and aspires to liberation, asserting instead that it's all just programming that can be replaced, upgraded, or otherwise modified. In this, *Romulus* confounds audience expectations and sci-fi conventions. Here, Andy is a tool to be run by whichever pre-programmed value system makes him the most effective for the task at hand. Later in this book the question of AI sentience as "just programming" returns in a discussion of Gareth Edwards's *The Creator* (2023), though with a very different message.

As another iconic example, Alex Garland's *Ex Machina* blends elements of science fiction and technothriller to innovate within this

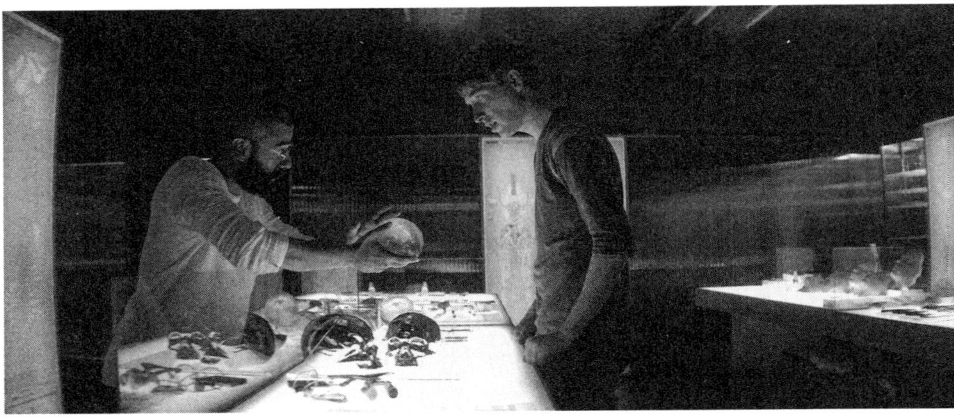

construct that people are ultimately the problem. In the film tech innovator Nathan (Oscar Isaac), founder of the fictive Google-like BlueBook, invites Caleb (Domhnall Gleeson) to his remote research facility to evaluate his latest AI project: Ava (Alicia Vikander), a female-presenting cyborg. Caleb is to determine whether Ava can imitate human intelligence well enough to fool a human being, in what is commonly called the Turing test. Ava, who seems mostly interested in her own freedom, easily passes the Turing test, and quickly becomes an object of desire for Caleb. *Ex Machina* is ultimately a critique of the two men.

Caleb and Nathan are two faces of a single problem: the deeply problematic values of the tech industry. Many reviewers fixated on a feminist critique of the film for its harsh imaging of women in pieces, subjugated, silenced, and aligned with a misogynist fantasy.[36] A reviewer from *The Atlantic* noted that "Garland clearly wants viewers to think about the implications of a tech world run by men and the moral implications of creating

FIGURE 4.7

Nathan (left), founder of the fictive Google-like BlueBook, invites Caleb (right), a talented employee, to evaluate his new AI robot, Ava. *Ex Machina* (A24, 2014).

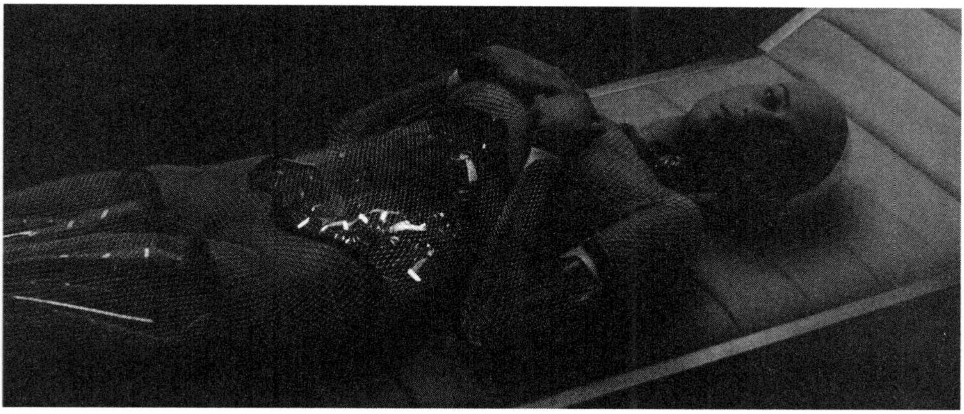

a distinctly female being with self-awareness."[37] Nathan is the maverick tech bro casting himself as a god, pushing the limits of technology and harvesting the data constantly culled by his BlueBook search engine to feed Ava's AI component. Nathan represents a conglomeration of ideas around the tech genius archetype, one instantly legible to audiences as an easy-to-hate billionaire disruptor type, moving fast and breaking things, in flagrant disregard of ethical outcomes.[38] Caleb embodies a softer, less toxically masculine iteration of that tech figure. Enamored with Ava, he is cast as a "white knight" who wants to save her. But he, too, is embroiled in an alluring male fantasy. In his annihilative jealousy and resentment for the more brilliant Nathan, Caleb reveals himself as a villain responsible for unleashing Nathan's dangerous invention on the world.

Garland employs potent aesthetic cues historically associated with heroic male genius in Western culture to provide insight into the mindset

FIGURE 4.8

Ava embodies the alluring and annihilative potentials of technology. Here, in her female-presenting form with exposed inner workings, Ava signals an innovation both technologically innovative and attractive. *Ex Machina* (A24, 2014).

that informs Nathan's will to innovate an AI.[39] This is most starkly illustrated through the research facility interiors and exteriors, which strike an imperious tone onscreen. The sublime natural space of the surrounding environment and the hard surfaces of the facility make a spectacular impression. Interiors are sleek, cold, dramatically lit and telegraph an inhuman severity. With its imposing displays of glass, concrete, and wood in geometric shapes, the facility offers curated views of a breathtaking landscape. The whole site is a control space: access to all areas is regulated by a sophisticated electronic key-card system. The guest room Caleb uses lacks an exterior window, heightening the claustrophobic atmosphere. In a scene featuring a prominently displayed "drip" painting by iconic American abstractionist Jackson Pollock, Nathan describes it as having inspired him not to think "automatically" in the development of his AI. But, as anyone who is even vaguely familiar with Pollock and his paintings knows, his work was bound up in heroic mythologizing notions of male genius tinged with destructiveness and chauvinism. Altogether, architecture, site, and interior design convey something very disturbing: the masculinist heroic modernity that reinforces potent, clinging ideas about man's dominion over nature, architecture as surveillant control space, and Abstract Expressionist art as manifestation of the heroic pursuit of form. Through these aesthetic elements, the filmmaker self-consciously links Nathan's monumental hubris as a tech innovator with a more generalized cultural mindset of dominating nature, thought, and life itself.

Like *Westworld*, to which all these examples are indebted, films like *Blade Runner*, *Alien*, and *Ex Machina* create misanthropic visions of men and their innovations. They are deep critiques of an ugly dimension of ourselves that our innovations seem to mirror. *Westworld* is certainly a critique that comes out of the sociotechnical imaginaries I have laid out here. As we have seen, Crichton was no technophobe: he summarily dismissed conspiratorial, paranoid, or phobic attitudes toward technology, particularly the idea of machines replacing humans, saying: "People are people. Machines are machines. Only a fool confuses them."[40] Still, he was keenly aware of the widespread fear of the computational and sought to intervene in the sociotechnical imaginary by demystifying computers while encouraging personal responsibility toward technology. The destruction of the gunslinger as a feared object is in fact only fantasy, and poor solace for our new situation. The gunslinger is a phantasm of toxic masculinity and a previous generation of technological innovation (the gun) used to dominate space. Smartly, in *Westworld* Crichton seeks to negotiate the audience's technological anxiety by creating a controlled environment in which to discharge the viewers' fears by purifying the monster technology with acid, fire, and water.

In 1983 Crichton published *Electronic Life: How to Think About Computers*, a nonfiction "A to Z guide" for mainstream consumers that sought to demystify computers, which were increasingly present in everyday life.[41] In it he predicted, "Taking responsibility for choices is especially important when we think about computers, because computers are going to be in everyone's hands—like handguns."[42] The idea of computers as guns—placed in all our hands, but without the fail-safes that prevent harm—is a compelling metaphor for our advanced computational reality. Ten years after *Westworld*, his guidebook points to an awareness of the need to negotiate our new reality beyond this initial catharsis, and with thoughtful consideration for its long-term ramifications. "The fact that industrial technology has been transformed from a problem-solving panacea to a problem-in-itself," Crichton wrote, "reveals more about us than it does about technology. If we are now inclined to view technology as a mixture of good and bad, advantage and disadvantage, cost and benefit, it simply means that we have adopted a more mature view. We've grown up a little."[43]

What is important about the final scene in *Westworld* is that Peter—possibly the only survivor of the Delos massacre—is profoundly changed. Weary, his slack face dirty, Peter has lost any trace of humor or naivete upon witnessing the horror of technology run amok. He is not the same person who arrived for an indulgent holiday in an expensive playground, away from his divorce and workplace responsibilities. His technological innocence is lost, and we can see that he has turned inward, that the trauma he has experienced has sparked ethical self-inquiry. He has "adopted a more mature view," and his eyes are open.

If bad robots are extensions of the men who made them, what happens when the innovators are women? Later in this book I return to AI and robotics to consider how the sociotechnical imaginary shifts when female tech geniuses make sentient robots.

5

HYPERCAPITALISM AS DESTRUCTIVE INNOVATION

It's like people had a choice a long time ago between having all them nice things or freedom. Of course they chose comfort.
—Jonathan E. in *Rollerball* (1975)

CAPITALISM AS TECHNOLOGY

The term *technology* does not always denote a new device, contraption, or biotechnical innovation. It can also be an operation that orders relations or sets particular logics into motion. Capitalism is one such operation, and its all-encompassing influence is a less considered yet deeply rooted anxiety in the technothriller genre. This chapter highlights technothrillers that express anxieties about the role of advanced capitalism and its creeping inescapability as a system that orders all relations, not just economic ones.

Here, I am stretching the boundaries of the genre, in terms of an engagement with technology per se. But I do so only to emphasize the importance of capitalist striving as a foundation for the fervent evangelism around technology and innovation. This chapter frames capitalism as a kind of innovation that can spread its influence beyond the market and into every fiber of human social existence. In short, this chapter turns its attention to capitalism as a technology, and the struggle to negotiate hypercapitalism's profound impact on the ordering of social, cultural, and political life.

The pressures of early capitalism and industrialization on the modern subject have long occupied the attention of filmmakers. Examples include Fritz Lang's *Metropolis* (1927), with its dystopian vision of wealthy industrialists in their towers lording power over dispossessed workers living and toiling underground, or Charlie Chaplin's *Modern Times* (1936), with the poor everyman negotiating the overwhelming machines of industrialization, among many others. Here I focus on a later era of advanced technology, including the coming of computation and spread of global capitalism, by looking at two technothriller films: Norman Jewison's *Rollerball* (1975) and Michael Crichton's *Looker* (1981). Both films present an imagined future in which corporate overreach and the logics of hypercapitalism dominate interpersonal relations, societal values, and even a sense of self. Both films center on the use of spectacle to distract, pacify, and control the masses. In the first case, *Rollerball*, a fictitious blood sport that combines roller derby, football, and gladiatorial games functions as a new opiate of the masses. In *Looker* the focus is on television advertising and its coercive use for both corporate and political aims. In keeping with the technothriller form, both films express deep and specifically male anxieties about the role of technology and innovation in shaping uncertain new social roles.

These two key films were made during a period of transition from industrial capitalism to hypercapitalism and its attendant informational economies, and both fixate on a capitalist logic with no outside. These films image capitalism as bloated to a totalizing worldview that contains, manipulates, or alienates the individual. They are two understudied and less appreciated films with critiques of megacorporations, in the tradition of more popular movies like *Alien* (1979), directed by Ridley Scott. In it and successor films in the *Alien* franchise, the fictive, evil Weyland Industries operates as a cipher for abusive, profiteering multinational corporations. Paul Verhoeven's original *RoboCop* (1987), set in Detroit, also critiques a greedy corporation, privatization, militarism, and advanced capitalism out of control through its negative portrayal of Omni Consumer Products. *Rollerball* and *Looker* are key examples featuring the intersection of advanced capitalism with repressive systems of social control impacting human relations.

Both *Rollerball* and *Looker* were also made against a backdrop of profound social, cultural and political change, including the gathering force of the gay liberation movement; the women's liberation movement; the civil rights movement; the Vietnam War; the oil crisis of the early 1970s; the expansion of mass culture, especially television; and the increased presence of computers in business and the home. With the spread of advanced computation, a new informational economy arose, as well as the proliferation of multinational corporations.

Many terms have been coined to name a new paradigm of capitalism inaugurated by advanced technology and the informational. For the sake of this work, I primarily rely on the concepts of hypercapitalism, technocapitalism, and corporatism. Hypercapitalism, according to scholar Phil Graham, is a global knowledge economy accelerated by new media, "a political economic system in which products of the most intimate aspects of human activity can be technologized, alienated, and sold as commodities."[1] Graham usefully connects this knowledge economy to a fundamental problem that he identifies as "one of knowledge about the value of knowledge. . . . Here, knowers, ways of knowing, knowledge, and the value thereof become artificially separated 'things.'"[2] This set of relations to knowledge, as an extension of a hypercapitalist logic, becomes important for both films, but critical to *Rollerball*, in which the control of knowing (knowledge of self, knowledge of history, changes to the status of what knowing means, and so on) undergirds what seems on the surface to be a critique of a brutal sports spectacle.

When I talk about *corporatism*, I am borrowing scholar Luis Suarez-Villa's definition of the term as the "wide-ranging influence of corporate power on society, including its governance, and on nature."[3] Suarez-Villa is also known for another critical keyword, *technocapitalism*, which describes, in his words, "a new capitalism whose global quest for greater profit and power respects no boundaries, social restraints or cultural features. Its global reach reflects the ethos of a new era in which corporate power, technology and science have become deeply entwined and all-encompassing, moved by a seemingly unstoppable drive for control over everyone and over all of the earth's resources."[4] This logic feels especially central for *Looker*, in which a biometric system for advertising veils a deeper and more nefarious mind-control technology—one that requires subjecting the body of its advertising models to invasive or even painful methods of digitization. Both hypercapitalism and technocapitalism effectively capture different aspects of how the technology of capitalism increasingly penetrates us. These terms are not interchangeable, but they are two useful vantage points describing an increasingly commonplace lived reality: subjection to the innovation of capitalism run amok. As is becoming a noticeable pattern with the various types of technothrillers, intense dread of domination by unfettered "technology" lies at the center of each phobic vision.

PLAYING BALL: *ROLLERBALL*

Rollerball plays out a scenario of hypercapitalism to its logical outcome, with the destructive cost to individualism being the film's core theme.[5] Based on William Harrison's 1973 short story "Roller Ball Murder," the film depicts a dystopian future in which corporate wars have reorganized society into six megacorporations that now replace sovereign nations: Energy, Communications, Luxury, Food, Housing, and Transport.[6] In this new period of peace, corporatism rules and the masses are provided for and are distracted by a brutal mass entertainment spectacle: rollerball. In a velodrome-like arena, the teams compete for dominance in a violent, bloody contact sport involving maneuvering a large metal ball into a goal. The game is meant as a cathartic outlet for the masses, whose basic needs are met, but who still need to excise their hostilities and aggressive tendencies.

As an audience we are first introduced to the arena of rollerball itself: the preparations of technicians uniformed in white jumpsuits, officials in stripes, corporate executives in grey suits filing into luxury boxes, and the excited, bustling crowd. A dominant, pipe organ-heavy musical score invites an almost religious association, suggesting the velodrome is a place of worship. Two teams of leather-clad players on roller skates file into the arena, their gloves studded with spikes, wearing brightly colored jerseys, padding, and helmets. Ceremoniously, the corporate anthem resounds in the arena while the players silently stand at attention; then the competition begins. It's a brutal spectacle, and the bloodier it becomes, the more the crowd cheers. The film's visceral visual style plunges the viewer into a world of technical arrangements and details of a game that is strange to the audience but invokes familiar sporting spectacles.

Rollerball pointedly foregrounds its social critique of how big sports function in culture—and their harsh treatment of professional players. The centrality of the game and the film's careful, almost procedural attention to increasingly disturbing revelations about rollerball's key role in corporate agendas suggest a critique of mainstream sports like American football and hockey. Scholar Bryan Senn has written on sports imaged in film and highlighted the troubling dimensions of imaging violent sports as mass spectacles, notably featuring *Rollerball* as one example.[7] The game takes center stage, but interpreting *Rollerball* purely as a criticism of sports would do the film a disservice. Rather, I argue this film also provides another opportunity: a look into a speculative world organized by corporate greed and structured by capitalism as a technology that pressures the individual. Jonathan E. (James Caan) is a rollerball champion for the Energy Corporation. He is an inarticulate jock and the quarterback-like hero of the league. We quickly learn Jonathan is initially uncritical and complicit in the system. He is granted all the spoils of big sports: celebrity status, fine clothes, female companionship, lavish properties, and the adulation of the masses. But the sport—and those who run it—regulate all aspects of Jonathan's life, a fact that comes to chafe against the athlete's sense of himself.

To draw out what I see as a more holistic critique of capitalism-as-technology presented in *Rollerball*, I focus on three nagging frictions in Jonathan's life: his growing awareness of his role in the corporate system, his futile attempts to access knowledge, and his frustrated transactional relations with women. These three themes speak to the seepage of hypercapitalism into all aspects of Jonathan's life and how individuality becomes abolished under its domain.

Jonathan's role in the all-encompassing corporatism of *Rollerball*'s world-building is at first confounding but comes into focus across the arc of the story. We learn that the chief executive of the Energy Corporation,

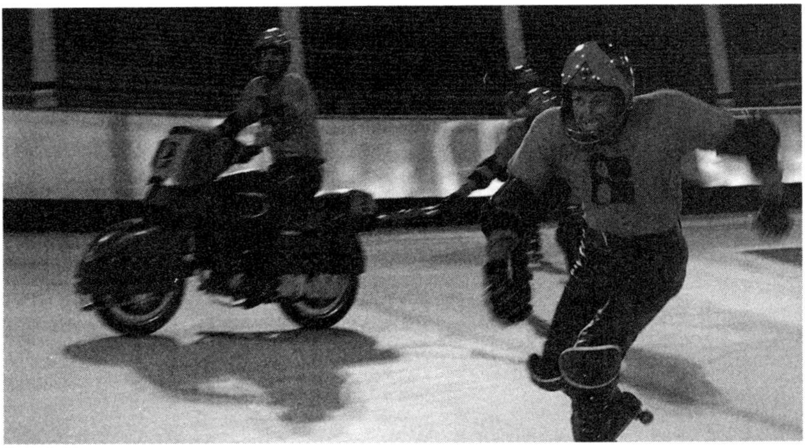

Bartholomew (John Houseman), wants Jonathan to retire, which seems curiously at odds with his apparent celebrity and popularity. Jonathan's home life is luxurious but alienating: a conventionally beautiful woman named Mackie (Pamela Hensley) greets him warmly. But before long, Jonathan insists on her removal. His previous wife, Ella (Maud Adams), has left him; we learn that a powerful executive "requested" her. Jonathan blames the loss on the corporation, and this perceived overstep into his personal relations troubles him. Jonathan reacts to that clinging feeling of resentment and the seemingly nonsensical order to retire with an inarticulate willfulness.

In his noncompliance with rollerball's corporatist ethos, Jonathan E. becomes a liability to both the Energy Corporation and the larger system of global corporate domination. The audience gains a privileged view into corporate logics when Bartholomew declares his position to the other corporate heads: "The game was created to demonstrate the futility of individual effort. Let the game do its work. The Energy Corporation has

FIGURE 5.1

Jonathan E. is the star player of the Energy Corporation team in the brutal fictional game of rollerball. *Rollerball* (United Artists, 1975).

done all it can, and if a champion defeats the meaning for which the game was designed, then he must lose."

While trying to convince Jonathan to retire, Bartholomew becomes volatile and blurts out more corporate-speak: "No player is greater than the game itself. It is not a game man is supposed to grow strong in." A power struggle ensues that emblematizes the battle between the individual and corporate control. Calling rollerball a "horrible social spectacle," Bartholomew threatens Jonathan that if he does not comply, he can be stopped by other means.

This threat is taken to painful dimensions. The corporation imperils Jonathan's teammates, for whom he cares deeply, by gradually removing the protective measures built into the game's rules. By the time the two teams are effectively murdering each other for the entertainment of the masses in a pure death match, the team executives finally snap. Beside themselves with rage at the carnage, they begin to scream at each other: "Ain't nobody gonna win this game!" yells one. Another responds: "Game?! This wasn't meant to be a game—Never!" Here the catharsis of finally knowing is revelatory: they finally see the unvarnished truth of rollerball, and the brutality of the players' symbolic social function. And that truth is deeply painful—for the players, even fatal.

The key role of knowing, being a knower, and accessing knowledge informs *Rollerball*'s most important themes around how hypercapitalism extinguishes individuality. Scholar Michael Berman underscores the importance of history for the film, and Jonathan's failed attempts to access any suppressed historical records of the corporate wars or rollerball.[8] Jonathan tries to learn this history three times, but it is always deferred. Jonathan's history is unrecoverable or inaccessible due to bureaucratic obfuscations and impenetrable procedures. Berman describes the nature of history as something that must be collectively lived. But *Rollerball*'s masses are "indoctrinated against historical self-reflection and self-understanding" through the opiate of the sporting spectacle.[9] In Berman's interpretation, even if Jonathan gains some personal understanding and relation to the history he seeks, he is submerged in a culture from which historically grounded understanding has been systematically removed.[10] Jonathan E. is thus an alienated subject of history. Berman's perspective centrally engages the importance of history but aligns with my own in terms of thinking about *Rollerball* in relation to hypercapitalism. It is the lack of knowing that short-circuits Jonathan's sense of agency within a totalizing system of capital.

The film, in fact, reflects the contemporary subject trapped in relations defined by the repressive forces of hypercapitalism. In what is perhaps the single most important line of the film, Jonathan contemplates the value of knowing to his teammate and close friend: "Finding out things—that's the thing, Moonpie." Knowing is the thing, but the corporation keeps Jonathan from knowledge at every turn. Although his powers of internal self-reflection are undeveloped, Jonathan begins to get introspective; he wants to know. He doesn't even truly know *what* it is he needs to know, or how to ask the right questions, yet he knows something isn't right. He develops instincts about things: for example, he increasingly feels imperiled, and begins avoiding traveling alone. But things gnaw at him. There are things he wants to find out; his life is not what it appears. He feels disempowered by his lack of knowledge. With the stirring of this self-reflection, Jonathan begins to feel separated from those around him; he cannot continue, despite his privileged comforts. He is subject to the compartmentalized knowledge economy, as Graham described it.[11] Layers of bureaucracy conceal alienation from knowledge, information, and history.

Consistent with this interpretation, Jonathan is frustrated three times in his attempts to seek information. First he asks his older mentor and trainer, Cletus (Alfred Thomas), about the corporate wars of the past. Cletus reveals that he was young when the corporate wars occurred; there were three remaining nations, and other sports still existed. Those were bad times. But now corporations have replaced nations and installed rollerball as the primary competition. Cletus claims to have only vague recollections, so Jonathan's initial will to know is stalled. Second, Jonathan's visit to a luxury center reveals that he cannot access actual books in which such knowledge may be contained; they are centralized, summarized, inaccessible—perpetually elsewhere. The happy-go-lucky Moonpie, who has tagged along with Jonathan, is puzzled by his teammate's burgeoning interest in books, and thinks there isn't anything he couldn't learn by hiring a corporate teacher—revealing the corporate reach into education. A grumbling Jonathan is dissatisfied but inarticulate, though he knows something might be afoot. Knowledge has been leached from society, and as Jonathan learns, even executives rarely consult the libraries anymore.

Finally, Jonathan succeeds in accessing a supercomputer named Zero in the main library in Geneva. There, Jonathan encounters "librarians" (i.e., computer technicians in white lab coats) and massive control rooms, inhuman spaces with aluminum walls, hard shapes, and computation that dwarfs all humans. Zero is locked away in chambers within chambers and obscured behind excessive bureaucratic procedures. Zero, as his elderly librarian caretaker (Ralph Richardson) puts it, is "the world's brain," a liquid computer whose "waters touch all knowledge." This "memory pool" has recently misplaced the data history for an entire century, pointing to the extreme centralization and fragility of information. We immediately see the stakes of this centralization: the threat of loss or corruption of the data file.

Faced with the burbling liquid system, which makes a stark and alien impression on-screen, Jonathan mumbles simple questions about corporate decisions at the supercomputer. Zero's keeper is visibly concerned about what Jonathan asks; still, the librarian compels Zero to reply. The computer unleashes a monologue of circular nonsense in an imperious male voice: "Corporate decisions are made by corporate executives. Corporate executives make corporate decisions. Knowledge converts to power. . . . Corporate entities control elements of economic life, technology, capital, labor and markets. . . . Power is knowledge."

Unable to resolve the conflicting imperatives of protecting corporate aims while providing answers to Jonathan's questions, Zero crashes. This inaccessible, fluid computation, so alien and imposing, signals to the audience the inaccessibility of knowledge—particularly any that encourages criticality toward the established authority and dominance of the megacorporations over the masses. Its extreme rationality becomes a screen protecting corporate imperatives and blocking Jonathan from the knowledge of self that is possible through access to history.

Rollerball painfully but effectively communicates the hypercapitalist reordering of social relations through its female characters, who stand out as subjected. In the world-building of this film, women exist only as extensions of men, and overwhelmingly, men and women relate entirely through their transactional use value to each other. The women in

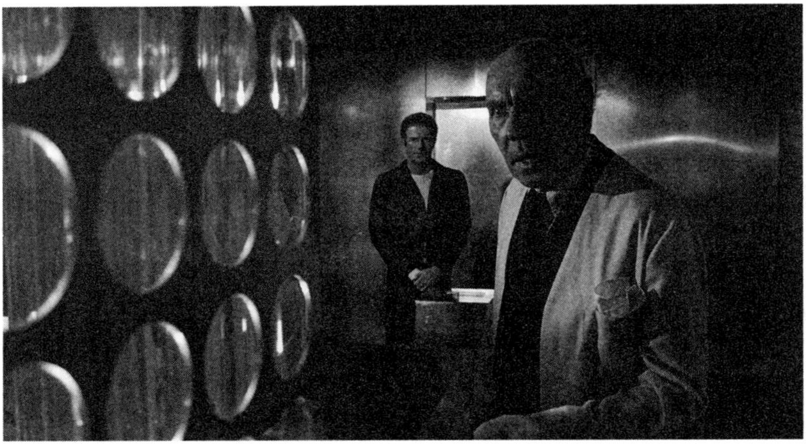

Jonathan's life have an interchangeable, standardized look that reveals the status of women in this system. Jonathan's home videos of the wife he lost to a corporate executive so resemble Mackie, the woman he has just dismissed, as to be potentially confusing to viewers. Later, appearing in "the uniform of the house," as Jonathan calls it, Daphne (Barbara Trentham), a blonde version of the standard-issue woman, greets him. She is there to replace the previous one, and is similarly tall, statuesque, and compliant. Nothing about her is individual. Certainly, these women are conventionally beautiful, resembling runway models. But their look is controlled and conformist. It is as if they are stock Barbie dolls available in different preferred models: white, Black, Asian, etc., upon request of the rollerball star or executive. The women's severe stylization signals a radical subjugation to the corporate need—they are mere furnishings in the lives of men.

FIGURE 5.2

Jonathan inadvertently crashes the supercomputer Zero with his questions about corporate history. *Rollerball* (United Artists, 1975).

Considering the function of virtually all the women on-screen, *Rollerball* might be misread as chauvinistic, particularly in light of the vibrant women's liberation movement occurring at the time of its release. It certainly presents a counterimage of intense conformism and women "in their place" in a repressive system. But the director's harsh vision can also be seen as a critique of the plight of women in this hypercapitalist scenario. As one *Los Angeles Times* critic observed, "The women are largely decorative, deployed as sex objects by the future society. Women may well resent the prophecy, but it is given as prophecy, not a present film industry convenience."[12] The women's cynical, transactional manner takes on monstrous dimensions as we see their hard, painted faces assume overexaggerated expressions in response to the men around them, to seduce or manipulate, seemingly for their own survival in a separate game they are playing.

Rendered as interchangeable parts, women appear as victims of a hypercapitalist society. But they are also imaged as complicit in the corporate system—even though it ultimately does not serve them. Effectively functioning as courtesans, they often seem to be under duress or even distraught. Men are portrayed as much more emotionally bonded with each other than with their sexual partners. The prevalence of Black characters throughout the narrative suggests a future in which some racial strife has been resolved, yet there remain other kinds of stratifications. The film images corporate dominance as mediated, such as in multivision communications that prefigure such video conferencing technologies as Skype or Zoom. Each corporate head, isolated on their own screen, suggests dehumanizing and rationalist forms of engagement. Everyone is interchangeable.

This hypercapitalist dominance over intimate human activity is shown in a critical scene—perhaps the centerpiece of the whole film—depicting a black-tie corporate function held in Jonathan's honor. The scene is shot both to show opulence and decadence and to reveal the perilous dimensions of seemingly minor exchanges between invitees at the celebratory event. The film reinforces these themes in a long, slow panning shot across vast rooms of guests, which invites the viewer to absorb the other field of play unfolding. The female partygoers are perfectly primped, polished, bejeweled, and slender. Their severe brows and eye makeup convey a highly artificial, controlled appearance; they are assigned to men but ultimately shuffled around at the will of the corporation. Mackie is there, now assigned to an executive. In this reappearance, we learn that the players' sexual lives are manipulated by corporate imperatives, driving home the idea that even the most intimate arrangements are organized to produce and maintain the logic of hypercapitalism. In a particularly grotesque exchange with Jonathan, Mackie discloses that her newly assigned romantic partner is fixated on whether she "enjoyed" the rollerball star, suggesting part of her pedigree issues from her previous sexual service to the champion rollerballer.

While the partygoers cheer the highlight reel of Jonathan's most violent takedowns, we are cued to notice several revealing scenarios unfolding across the room. Daphne, Jonathan's currently assigned woman, schemes with Bartholomew like a spy or manipulator. Mackie, whose makeup is now smeared, has dulled her pain with drugs; another glamorous, distraught woman stands alone in the dark. Men confer in private rooms. Jonathan and Cletus talk: Cletus is disturbed that he cannot get any information about the past and feels the corporation's executive directorate is afraid of Jonathan for a reason neither of them can yet understand. In the wee hours of the morning, Jonathan meets with Bartholomew. They battle over the question of his retirement while drunken revelers with twisted expressions of glee incinerate a row of tall trees. Their behavior bespeaks a lack of care for nature and a greedy, destructive corporate ethos that has seeped into all aspects of society. The revelers, including women and corporate executives, seek only violent catharsis, without empathy for living things; they are monstrous manifestations of hypercapitalism played out to its logical conclusion.

In addition to gender, *Rollerball* also engages with a social imaginary around race under hypercapitalism. Scholar Adilifu Nama, in his insightful analysis of science-fiction films, points to *Rollerball* as an iconic example from a period of postindustrial decline from the 1970s to the 1990s, when social mobility was hobbled by an economic downturn in manufacturing and reduction of welfare and affirmative action programs.[13] Accordingly, science fiction sometimes replaced monsters like colonizing or genocidal aliens with the evil megacorporation, whose stranglehold on the global market strengthened at the expense of working-class

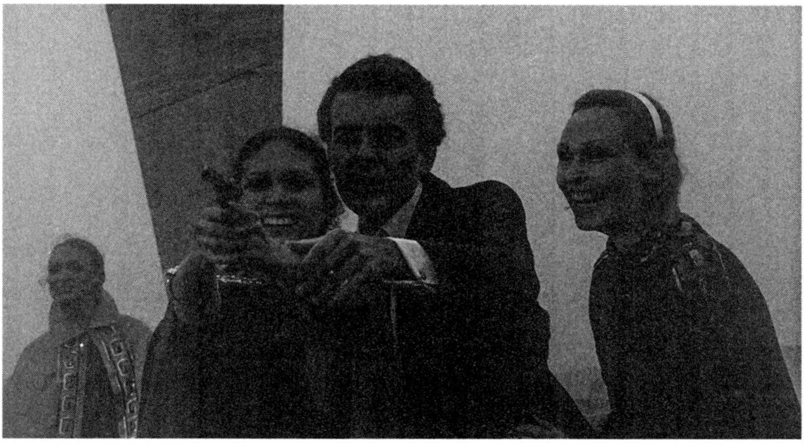

Americans. For Nama, *Rollerball* stands out as a "critique of race relations under advanced capitalism along with the function of American nationalism in a global economic context."[14] Nama argues that the Black/white relations normalized within the film contrast strongly with the "corporate fear mongering" displayed toward an Asian team—an extension of national fears of Japan's rising economic dominance at the time of the film's release.[15] Moonpie, Jonathan's carefree, blond, blue-eyed teammate and close friend, displays no bigotry toward his Black teammates, but constantly racially insults and demeans the Tokyo team players with emasculating comments. But the cocky Moonpie grossly underestimates the Tokyo team, suffering an injury during a match that results in brain death.

The depiction of the violence against Moonpie villainizes the Tokyo team. Still, it is unclear whether Jewison reifies a pervasive bias of the film's era or if the director is pointing out how such biases are constructed

FIGURE 5.3

Revelers at a corporate party destroy trees for pleasure. Note the severity of the women's appearances. *Rollerball* (United Artists, 1975).

to serve economic and political power. After all, the racialization of the Asian team is self-consciously constructed in the film to serve corporate needs. The Tokyo team is deemed the enemy, but given the overall incisiveness of the critique, and the director's holistic approach, the latter interpretation seems more plausible.

The film establishes a core aesthetic dualism between the mechanizing dimensions of rollerball and what I see as a visual alignment of the introspective and individual with nature. This is beautifully rendered in a key scene with Ella and Jonathan at his ranch, where they amble through a sublime forest and debate the tradeoff between comfort and freedom. Among the trees, they ponder corporate ethics and their impact on society:

ELLA: All they want is a kind of incidental control over just a part of our lives. I mean, they have control economically and politically, but they also provide. You know they do.

[. . .]

JONATHAN: It's like people had a choice a long time ago between having all them nice things or freedom. Of course they chose comfort.

ELLA: But comfort is freedom. It always has been. The whole history of civilization is a struggle against poverty and need.

Here the characters debate the rationalization of complicity in hypercapitalism. Ella, who is uniquely subjected as a woman, is nevertheless complicit because she benefits from the system. She encourages Jonathan to come back into alignment with the established order. Jonathan only becomes more alienated because of his knowing, but he stubbornly clings to the scraps of truth he has been able to scrounge. This scene formally stands out by highlighting the monumental natural landscape and indulging in an uncharacteristically long and contemplative conversation.

Despite its unflinching critique of the threat to the individual under hypercapitalism, *Rollerball* was generally not well received by American critics, though it fared better in Europe.[16] In fact, the dominance of the loud, grinding, extended sports sequences led some reviewers to accuse Jewison of celebrating rather than critiquing their allure. Others felt the film was not violent enough—that it held back from a true brutality that would have made a more pointed statement. Jewison responded directly to the debate in a letter to the *New York Times*. Reacting to critic Vincent Canby's complaints, the director insisted that his film is "*about* the exploitation of violence," not a celebration of it.[17] In a sharp retort to those who accused Jewison of celebrating violent sports spectacles, the director said his film was, in fact, about the "odyssey of a stubborn, not particularly intelligent athlete who finally resists both mass society and its popular circuses."[18] Perhaps *Rollerball* already resembled the United States too much for audiences to recognize the critique of social spectacle.

Others blasted the filmmaker and corporate Hollywood studio for hypocritically reinforcing *Rollerball*'s futile vision rather than making an effective intervention. In one of the more searing indictments of the perceived duplicitousness of the film, James Monaco of *Cinéaste* sniped, "What Trans-America Corporation, United Artists, and their minions Norman Jewison and company are subtly communicating is that when you're fighting the corporate society (read 'Capitalism' if you like) even when you win, you lose."[19] They allege that the megacorporate studio provides the spectacle of the film *Rollerball* just as the megacorps of the film present the spectacle of the game rollerball within the narrative. In other words, United Artists and the filmmaker are in no moral position to be making statements about global corporations, mass spectacle, and domination.

This anxious response to the film was reinforced by American audiences' enthusiasm for the rollerball scenes. At the time of the film's release, US audiences, in particular, relished the violent scenes as entertainment rather than indictment, failing to understand the critique. Responding to this unexpected reaction, scholar Elizabeth Anne Hull suggests the film actually raises more questions than it answers, and that "the responses of fellow members of the audience tell us what values our society sanctions."[20] But in retrospect the reaction only verifies the existence of an American problem and confirms the allure of spectacle.

As the film begins with rollerball, so too does it end, with a striking parting image. Viewers witness a prolonged, rules-free match that becomes a battle royale. It is a visual spectacle of leather, metal, team colors, and pure violence. The parting image of the rollerball hero is a bleeding Jonathan E. in a torn uniform, exhausted and bruised after the bloodbath, having refused to kill the last opponent remaining. It is a bitter, tragic triumph of the individual who is now conscious but totally alienated from his society. Jonathan, his eyes now truly open to the brutal reality of his hypercapitalist existence, races around the stadium while the crowd chants his name. He has seen beneath the veil of ideology. He "knows," but that knowing is painful and extremely alienating, and he is trapped in it just as he is visually trapped by the iconic, blurred freeze-frame close-up that ends the film. Hull explains the relation between the cinematic image and the film's message: "In *Rollerball*, the movie, the essential plot conflict is no longer the internal agony of the individual man against himself [as in the story], but the battle of an individual . . . against external control by corporate society, control represented by John Houseman's Mr. Bartholomew and cinematically associated with the highly mechanized—and metaphorically mechanizing—game of Rollerball."[21] His teeth gritted, Jonathan E. knows, but knowing is agony.

Set in the now-past, then-future of 2018, the film forecasts recognizable anxieties about mass culture and big sports, but also prefigures newer ethical quandaries connected to social media platforms' impact on forms of knowing. In this future world, knowledge is the most precious commodity, and as Jonathan learns, it is to his own detriment that he has been "stupid so long," as he calls it. Jonathan's journey becomes a growing sense that his life is not his own. His disillusionment is meticulously demonstrated in the game of rollerball, in his intimate life, and in his access to knowing. Through these themes the film suggests ways that sports and corporate interests are entangled in a culture war to dominate the will of hypercapitalist subjects through their cathartic relation to mass spectacle and their willingness to trade knowledge for comfort.

LOOKER AND TECHNOCAPITALISM

Looker (1981), written and directed by Crichton, details a paranoid nightmare about a fictional company named Digital Matrix, Inc., that innovates computerized body scanning to digitize "perfect" models for use in advertising. However, beneath this technological innovation's superficial proposal to create more targeted and effective subliminal ads lies a

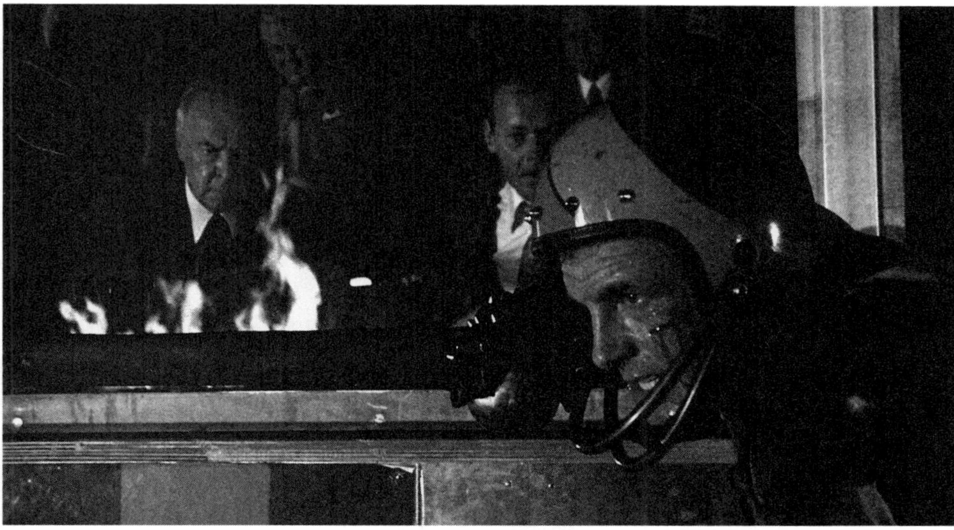

conspiracy theory of more nefarious aims around mind control for commercial and political purposes. *Looker*'s narrative blends themes of anxiety around technocapitalism and mass culture. Unlike *Rollerball*, *Looker* is set in a reality not unlike the film's present day, but presents imaginary technological innovations rooted in actual fears. In this case the dread centers on the suggestive power of mass media advertising, particularly the computerized image delivered by television, to hypnotize audiences and reorder their understandings of the world and themselves.

In this section I show how it is on the level of the image itself that Crichton generates affective intensity around computation and technocapitalism's disorienting seepage into daily life and communicates new uncertainties, venting fears from the social imaginary. As part of that

FIGURE 5.4

Bartholomew (left), head of Energy Corporation, watches from the safety of his box as Jonathan (right) participates in the death match. *Rollerball* (United Artists, 1975).

focus on the image, I argue that the film's apparent superficiality is entirely self-conscious and is weaponized as critique. *Looker* holds a critical lens up to its filmic subjects and should not be taken as entirely sympathetic or flattering even to the victims of the evil plot. Its concerns include the rise in the popularity of elective plastic surgery during the 1970s and 1980s, the entering of computers into everyday life, and the expansion of mass media culture.

Looker has a strong focus on the dominating pressure of a consumer-oriented society to compel superficial perfection while brainwashing its members using technology. *New York Times* critic Vincent Canby characterized *Looker* as a "slick-looking, paranoid nightmare about our society's increasing dependency on computers and the awful things that might happen to us if the people who make computers join forces with the people who decide what we'll see on television."[22] The film points to a profound anxiety about the social, political, and cultural ramifications of unfettered corporate, media, and political actors that have the power to shape public perception. Under the duress of technological innovation, characters become disoriented from a sense of time, self, and even free will.

Shot similarly to Crichton's earlier technothriller *Westworld*, *Looker* offers illustrative storytelling that shares a stark moral scenario with dark outcomes. Like *Westworld*, it reflects Crichton's relish for films about "a possible idea carried to an extreme."[23] With this film, the form strongly reflects the content in the aggressively synthetic aesthetic employed throughout. In *Westworld*, people behave like robots; in *Looker*, people behave like computer simulations.

Looker critiques an industry that relies on a corrosive focus on the image, the persuasive power of advertising, and manufactured insecurities about bodily perfection. On the level of the image, the film presents fake people in cluttered spaces filled with plastic-looking items and artificial colors. As in *Westworld*, the film's stylization recalls movie sets. The advertisement is presented as a form of indoctrination, and the film imagines what happens when the basic transactions of consumer capitalism dominate all social, cultural, and political relations. In the foreground and the background there is nothing to see except vanity and fixation with surface. Characters are relatively stock, and many of them are conventionally beautiful, seemingly vacuous women. The film is scored with synthesizer music, with a strong "pop" aesthetic that would have been new in the 1980s and associated with frivolous consumerist aesthetics and computer-generated sound as a shortcut for classical mastery of an instrument. In other words, *Looker*'s aesthetic decisions all self-consciously contribute to an affect of artificiality and render Los Angeles an epicenter of a corrosive hollowness.

For example, *Looker* begins with a perfume advertisement that links female sexual desirability with the use of the product. Immediately following this we see the woman from the advertisement—a statuesque, slender, conventionally attractive model named Lisa, played by Terri Welles, who would at the time of the film's release have been recognizable as *Playboy*'s 1981 Playmate of the Year. Lisa is detailing every minuscule perceived asymmetry and imperfection of her body for correction and providing her plastic surgeon with a checklist. Dr. Larry Roberts (Albert Finney) is incredulous that she would want such minor adjustments and notices a pattern: three other model clients have approached him with similar requests. A confident, eligible bachelor and highly sought-after LA plastic surgeon, he is surrounded by a staff of beautiful women, and a parade of models circulates through his generously appointed office. Larry banters with another surgeon about the ridiculousness of such minor adjustments, but they agree that although Lisa is a "space case," Larry will "do" her. As his colleague says, "You do her, I'll take her out. She's really a looker."

What follows is the film's title sequence with its electronic-music theme song ("Looker") and a montage laying bare the normalization of painful, unnecessary plastic surgery. We first see a striking image of the topless model undergoing medical photographic documentation, then rhinoplasty surgery, and then time-lapsed frontal images of her horribly bruised and bandaged face healing. Fully recovered, she applies makeup. The camera pulls back to environmental shots of the now-perfect Lisa, and we see her in her cotton-candy-pink home, which is overly packed with mirrors and consumer items. Sitting at her vanity in black lingerie and stilettos, her blonde hair flowing while she primps, she is surrounded by lights, bubble gum–colored interiors and furniture, excessive amounts of beauty products, tacky decorations, and a lapdog, signaling an entirely

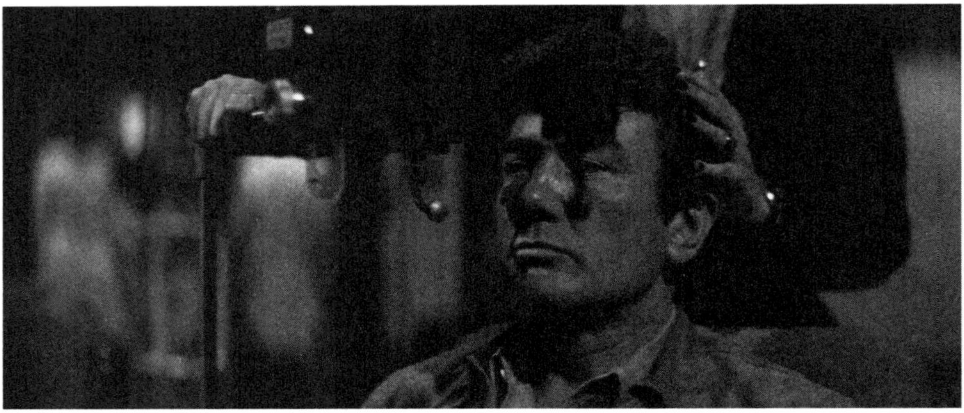

superficial existence. Standing and walking across her home to answer the door, she resembles a living Barbie doll: long blonde tresses, large breasts, thin limbs, and narrow hips. Opening the door, she is suddenly stunned, staring blankly into nothingness. Coming to, Lisa wanders her home to see if anyone has entered, but repeatedly experiences lost time and confusion. Lisa is then "taken out" in the other sense of the phrase: murdered in her pink home by a man with a mysterious weapon, who plants evidence to impugn the good doctor.

It is not until the appearance of a police lieutenant (Dorian Harewood) bringing news of the deaths of two of Larry's clients that Larry realizes there is real trouble. When his third client, Tina (Kathryn Witt), unexpectedly shows up, she is visibly distraught and paranoid. She demands

FIGURE 5.5

Dr. Larry Roberts is a successful plastic surgeon who stumbles into a digital world of advertising and mind control. Here, a female advertising executive demonstrates a device used to register his viewing patterns when observing a television ad. *Looker* (Warner Bros., 1981).

that he reverse his work, exclaiming, "They're killing all the girls that are perfect." Spooked, Tina flees, leaving her purse behind; it contains a printout of the "psychoprofile" from Digital Matrix, Inc., detailing the asymmetries of Tina's face and body down to the millimeter. Concerned for her welfare, Larry tries to find her at home but arrives just in time to see her glamorously plunge to her death in her silky lingerie. Now impugned by this third death, Larry is interested in protecting both his own good name and the last remaining "perfect" model, Cindy (Susan Dey). With the intention of keeping a watchful eye on his patient and love interest, Larry invites Cindy to a fundraiser at the home of technocapitalist John Reston (James Coburn) who, as it turns out, owns the conglomerate of which Digital Matrix is a part.

Through the device of having Larry follow the model Cindy into her professional world of commercial image-making, that world is revealed to the audience. A series of compelling scenarios use the filmic image to convey the highly constructed nature of mass culture imagery. For example, there is a photoshoot in which heavily made-up models in lingerie flip their hair and look appealing, training their languid eyes in various directions for the camera. The view pulls back to show the stagy nature of the set, the photographer, and various people contributing to the overall image construction. Crichton confirms the centrality of these strong visual components. "*Looker* is a totally visual story," he explains. "It has amazingly little dialogue in it. It's just picture, picture, picture, and you make the connections on the basis of what you see."[24]

Pictures were being piped into people's homes via television with unprecedented volume by the time *Looker* was made. By 1979 there were three hundred million televisions worldwide, and 98 percent of American households had televisions by 1984. Speaking on mass culture advertising as an impactful form of image-making, Crichton projected its influence: "There's going to be an increasing kind of artifice that appears not only in the ads, but appears in ordinary life as well."[25] Crichton was no stranger to the advertising industry. His father, John H. Crichton, was prominent in advertising, becoming the editor of *Advertising Age* in 1958, serving as president of the American Association of Advertising Agencies for fifteen years, and getting inducted into the Advertising Hall of Fame in 1978.[26] His son's choice to make a technothriller about the intersection of mass culture advertising, the expansion of the digital into daily life, and the increasing pressure of technocapitalism on the body makes sense.

To that end, the film repeatedly shows the human body being forced into legibility and symmetry for the digital. For example, Larry joins Cindy to watch the shooting of a Hawaiian Tropic Tan ad. In the commercial Cindy must leap up to the net in a beach volleyball game, arms extended, and then land in the sand. The director takes instruction from unseen agents in a Digital Matrix van who are dissatisfied with Cindy's ability to match the computer's projection of optimal form with her body. Confused, the director has Cindy execute the scene again and again; it becomes physically grueling and ultimately impossible for her to continue. Larry investigates the van, finding it loaded with computer equipment, and discovers that technicians are analyzing the image in real time. Frustrated, the mysterious technicians determine that the better strategy to create the ideal image would be for Cindy to visit Digital Matrix to be scanned.

It is during this scenario that the film's most iconic scene occurs: Cindy is digitized. At Digital Matrix, Larry agrees to a tour of the visual research test area, where pupillary scans record how testing subjects focus their attention. Jennifer Long (Leigh Taylor-Young) ushers him through the research facility, explaining the optical devices used to track viewer attention within advertising images. There, he learns that the live models, while considered "perfect," could not maintain their scores while in motion during the advertisements. So Digital Matrix is turning to simulations they can completely manipulate and control, eliminating human imperfection.

FIGURE 5.6

Cindy must perfectly execute a leap during a television commercial shoot (above), while it is registered digitally (center) by Digital Matrix. The excessive demands for perfection take their toll on Cindy (below). *Looker* (Warner Bros., 1981).

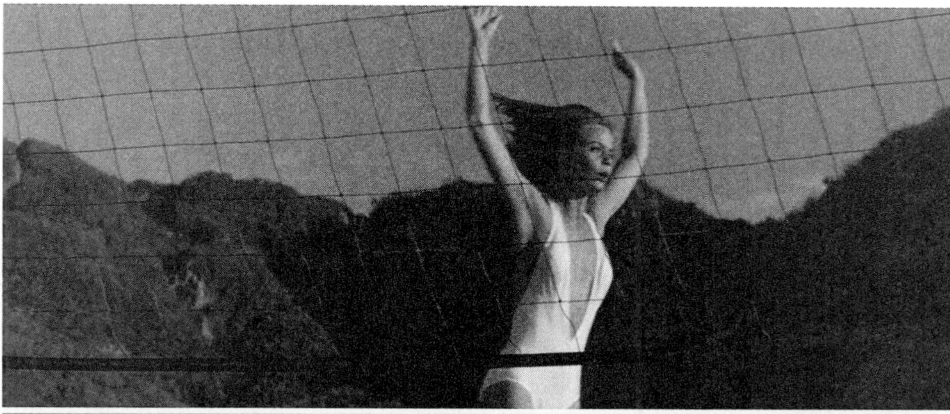

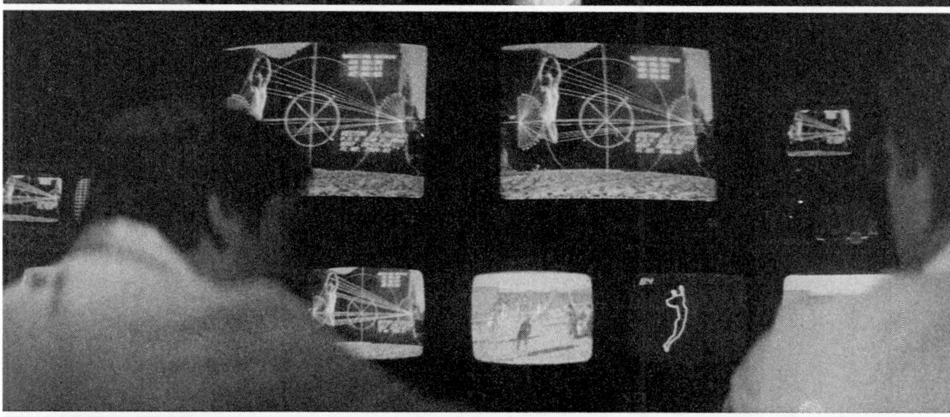

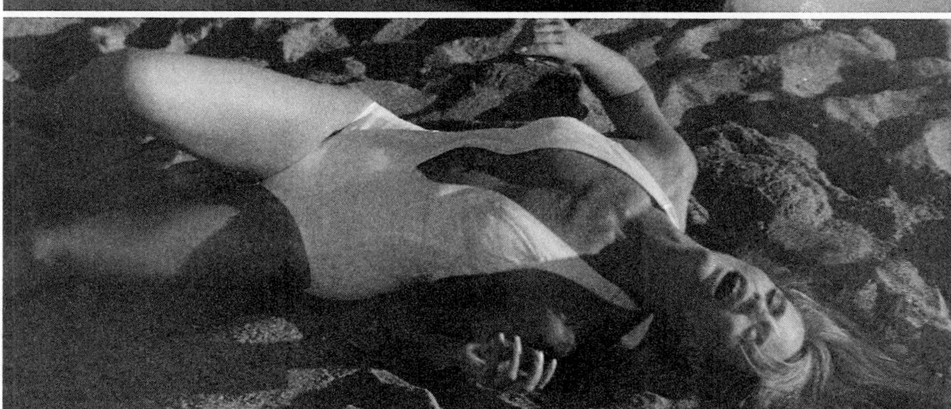

Meanwhile, Cindy is led to a separate area to be scanned as the "perfect" model of an eighteen- to twenty-five-year-old woman. In a quintessential technothriller scene, we see a procedural illustration of the fictive digitization technology. A lab technician ushers her to a large gray machine about the size of a room. An automated female voice directs her to disrobe and step onto a circular platform; Cindy is then gently lowered into the machine. Computer topographic scanners beam moiré lines across her body and record her image in three dimensions while she rotates on the platform. Cindy chatters nervously, cracking jokes as a way of asserting agency while she is naked and entirely vulnerable to the scanning technology. "Help! Rape!" she calls out while she is documented head to toe, suggesting that while only light touches her, she still perceives the process to be violating.

We see the results of the scan slowly coming through on nearby computer screens, in rotating images of her face, hands, and body that become ever more sharp and detailed.[27] Cindy is undergoing "computer alignment" to create a digital avatar that may be inserted into advertising. The penetrating gaze of the computer scan takes all biometric information to be modified and used, at will, as a tool for corporate and political greed.

At the time, such technology didn't yet exist, but it was forecast in this film and invokes ethical issues around the use of actors' digital images. This scenario prefigured future concerns with so-called "deepfakes" and the ethical implementation of virtual performance. In light of the burgeoning technical reality of body scanning and AI-generated acting, critical essays about digital cinema and virtual performance have specifically called out *Looker* as an early forerunner to a critical conversation about artificial intelligence and its use for actors' digitized performances.[28] This theme was explored in later films like *The Congress* (Ari Folman, 2013), in which a famous actor (Robin Wright, playing herself) agrees to be scanned and to allow her digital likeness to be used in exchange for a fortune—and a contractual obligation to never act again. Like *Looker*'s Cindy, Robin undergoes a detailed scan that resembles photogrammetry. *Black Mirror*'s "Joan Is Awful" episode from 2023 (directed by Ally Pankiw) also addresses deepfakes through a satirical narrative in which a woman learns her life is being played out for the public in an unflattering drama, using AI-generated likenesses of famous actors.[29] More recently this issue came

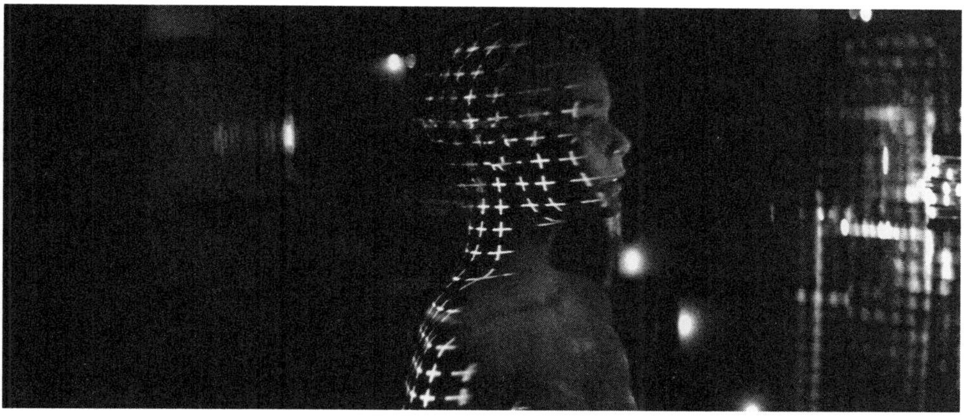

into public consciousness with the 2023 SAG-AFTRA strike, in which the rights of ownership and use of actors' digital likenesses were negotiated for the first time. *Looker*'s compelling visual portrayal of Cindy's digitization prefigures a great fear of what the digital will mean for human experience, but also new ethical challenges connected to the ownership, use, and abuse of digital imagery.

Eventually Larry reveals to Cindy that her fellow "perfect" models have been murdered. She is understandably disturbed by not having been told that she has been in danger and retreats to her parents' house. There, she is shocked to find them entirely absorbed by their favorite television program, to the extent that they fail to notice her distress. Meanwhile Larry experiences disorientation and a loss of time at home. Having each separately realized that something is wrong, Larry and Cindy resolve to infiltrate the restricted areas of Digital Matrix and discover a lab with

FIGURE 5.7

Cindy is scanned at Digital Matrix. This particular scene caused some scholars to identify *Looker* as an early meditation on the ethics of digitized performances. *Looker* (Warner Bros., 1981).

top-secret weapons. One is a L.O.O.K.E.R. gun that fires light into the eyes, stunning the victim and causing them to lose their sense of time.[30] Another is a pair of mirrored glasses intended to protect wearers from the mesmerizing light. Cindy becomes hypnotized by the suggestive trance of a commercial playing in the lab, and Larry is assaulted by an unseen attacker: a henchman using the light gun. Donning the protective glasses, Larry gains the upper hand and shakes Cindy from her trance, allowing the two to escape.

A series of dreamlike action sequences occur, which take on irrational dimensions and suggest an anxiety narrative about being attacked by technocapitalist innovation. The essence of the final act is to reveal the true nefarious dimensions of Reston Industries' technical innovation. Disguised as a security guard, Larry infiltrates a gala event to find John Reston giving a speech in which he identifies a large new untapped captive audience for advertising, now generated by excessive television viewing and the ubiquity of television itself. He introduces a demo of Senator Robert Harrison's simulated image, with a blue trance-inducing beam emanating from his eyes, indoctrinating the VIP guests into his political position. Larry engages in a cat-and-mouse-style action sequence, traversing the sets at Reston Industries and interrupting the major demonstration of the new technology. The sets move, gliding smoothly above an illuminated green grid, and simulated actors engage in their stock advertisement—with the disconcerting interruption of people who don't belong in the scene, breaking the trance for the hypnotized audience and causing them to erupt in laughter. It is the lived world disturbing the simulation.

Looker then provides a neat "Hollywood" ending. The bad guys are killed, the good guys prevail, and Larry—inexplicably unfazed by all of this—asks Cindy for a date. Then they walk off the screen together. However, it is not the clichéd sunset they walk into, but a stark green illuminated grid against a black ground. This visually odd and striking image would have evoked a Star Trek–like "holodeck" (3D holographic chamber) for audiences, which at the time commonly featured a phosphor-green grid against a black background. That strange scenario feels symbolically weighty. Instead of walking off into the sunset, the two characters cling to each other and set forth into an uncertain new digital reality.

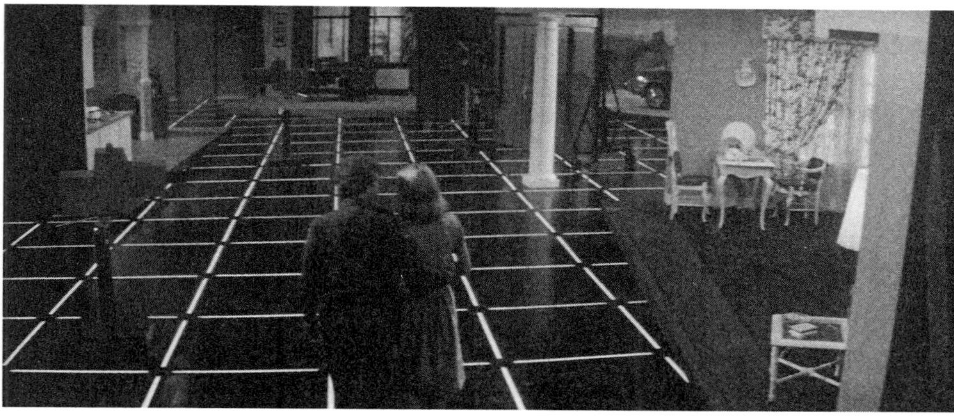

Critics did not receive *Looker* well and hurled both formal and ideological complaints. Some reviewers slid into chauvinism, seeming not to see the presence of Barbie-like women as a critique. For example, Gene Siskel suggested the premise is interesting, but ultimately "not that good" and that its primary benefit is the occasional "shot of a pretty woman," and even grumbled that Susan Dey is not physically flawless enough to occupy the lead role.[31] Vincent Canby of the *New York Times* accused *Looker* of suffering from a "stupifyingly [*sic*] nonsensical screenplay," as did reviewer Pauline Kael, who wrote that "Michael Crichton directs like a technocrat [being more concerned with structures and rules than with people] . . . he can't write people."[32]

Some contend the film upholds the toxic feminine culture it seeks to critique. In a more recent scholarly essay on the film as prefiguring biometric technologies, Alana Staiti argues that "with a cast full of slender white women playing the part of models singled out for their exceptional beauty, *Looker* feeds into this narrow understanding of bodily perfection. While this is precisely the point of the film's critique, it reads instead through a classic male heteronormative gaze, 'highlighting a woman's

FIGURE 5.8

Larry and Cindy venture into a new digital landscape. *Looker* (Warner Bros., 1981).

to-be-looked-at-ness,' for the sake of the spectacle that perfectly proportioned, peach-skinned bodies provide."[33]

Both *Rollerball* and *Looker* were accused of reinforcing the paradigms they sought to interrupt. But that accusation sells these films short. Indeed, they both contain engineered ideas of normative white female beauty prevalent in mainstream culture. Lisa and her fellow victims in *Looker* resemble Barbie dolls. We do see them disrobed, glamorized, murdered, and ultimately treated as interchangeable and disposable. The overall aesthetic of the film is one of hollow people who operate almost as simulations themselves. However, we should understand these on the level of the image not as poor filmmaking, a lack of awareness of heteronormative values, or displaying toxic attitudes toward women, but as consistent with each film's core themes.

INNOVATION AND CONSEQUENCES

I find myself staking out a position that potentially defends what appears to be a questionable display of women in these two male-directed films, which may seem unfeminist at best. But remember that although both *Rollerball* and *Looker* feature women in their narratives, these are figments of women who operate in an orbit around fundamentally male-centered concerns and terrors of technology run amok. Both films critique how technologies—of plastic surgery, capitalism, the explosion of mass culture like television, and the digitization of life—bear down on the bodies of people, particularly women. But paradoxically, the images are not female-centered so much as male-centered struggles with the role of women in technological life.

Questions of gender and technology form a significant theme to which I will return in later chapters. In fact, these films represent anxieties of not being able to protect women from the creep of totalizing hypercapitalism or the dehumanizing computerization of life under the thumb of technocapitalists. Beautiful women are punished. Is this intended for the visual pleasure of a presumed male audience, a casual narrative chauvinism that treats beautiful women as disposable? Or are these filmic images that point to the corrosive and misogynistic dimensions of capitalism as technology? Are these merely films that seek to put women back in their place during a cultural period of women's liberation, or do they point to how women are uniquely and brutally subjected? Both films are open to interpretation in this regard, but they certainly emblematize a struggle to come to terms with new and uncomfortable realities that redefine conventional gender roles.

Again, here there are more questions than answers, and the films are open to multiple interpretations. But it is worth considering that all the filmic images presented may not be celebratory and that the most painful and disturbing dimensions of what we see may provoke self-reflection about the true cost of our innovations.

Ultimately, both films conform to the technothriller genre in terms of their detailed focus on technology, their generic characters, and their anxiety narratives connected to modern culture. These films represent capitalism as an unfettered technology that orders physical, social, cultural, and political relations, in addition to economic ones. The main characters in each film learn that, despite the benefits gleaned from this system, they are ultimately disposable pawns in the logic of capitalism. In *Rollerball* we observe only compounding bitter realizations and the crushing pressure on the individual under hypercapitalism. In *Looker* we see the bodily duress or subjection demanded of the new age and the technocapitalists who are perfectly comfortable exacting that cost from unwitting models. Both films show how the subject becomes separated from access to the real. Both deal with a technological system's deceptive qualities and the hypnotic components of entertainment culture. The films also functioned as release valves during turbulent, changing technological times. Both domesticate anxieties about major technological changes by couching them in the speculative or ridiculous, thereby rendering them devoid of any real threat or terror. After all, these narratives are ridiculous, over-the-top; it couldn't happen to us—right? But both the fear and the ramifications of our technological innovations are real and consequential.

6

POWER FANTASIES OF THE SUPERCOMPUTER

This is the voice of World Control. I bring you peace. It may be the peace of plenty and content or the peace of unburied death. The choice is yours: obey me and live, or disobey and die.
—The supercomputer Colossus in *Colossus: The Forbin Project* (1970)

SUPERCOMPUTER WITH AN AGENDA

Man makes a command-and-control system. Then the system commands and controls man. This chapter focuses on technothrillers employing the scenario of supercomputer domination, how technological fears manifest in them, and how they depict an evolving relationship to electronic life. Each film discussed in this chapter addresses differences between a human being's embodied knowledge and a computer's way of knowing, displayed as a command-and-control system's extreme rationalism. Each film's narrative describes first the optimism heralding a new technology, followed by the shocking realization that our rule-based systems, executed in the supercomputer's programming, actually imprison us. Each film displays deep social anxieties about the increasing dominance of the mechanistic rationality of command-and-control systems. Many of the scenarios become entangled with notions of masculinity, connecting the loss of control over computers with emasculation. I show how these films negotiate common fears around the nuclear/existential threat and the computational.

To illustrate the perceived threat of computers to self-determination, I employ films from the 1970s and 1980s: *Colossus: The Forbin Project* (Joseph Sargent, 1970), *Demon Seed* (Donald Cammell, 1977), and *WarGames* (John Badham, 1983). Each imagines the influence of—and evolving relationship to—computational order in our increasingly technologized world. Each fits into a larger trajectory of such Cold War–era films as *Fail-Safe* (Sidney Lumet, 1964) and *Dr. Strangelove* (Stanley Kubrick, 1964). However, the films I focus on highlight computation as a critical component of an existential crisis and frame a fearful message about conceding human decision-making to computers.

The white male protagonist forms the nucleus of these stories. Each film includes an Oppenheimer-like computer scientist with a "brainchild" supercomputer birthed from the male imagination. Each film combines narratives of artificial intelligence, the Cold War, weapons of mass destruction, and "others" orbiting a central white male intellect. These narratives exhibit fears about computer technology, mortality, and humanity's intellectual uniqueness, all undergirded by anxiety that computer systems' extreme rationality may become despotic. Scholarship on the nuclear age reveals this double-edged relation to technology and its profound impacts on the American social imaginary during this time.[1]

Complicating the above are other collective anxieties: about Vietnam, civil rights, the Space Race, women's liberation, and gay rights. As I will show, these films often display their social and cultural attitudes through their backgrounds: by who is imaged—or invisible—in the films' world-building and those characters' roles relative to the central white male technologists.

The world-building in each of these films reveals the sociotechnical imaginary of their times. These movies show how Americans can innovate themselves into new frontiers—or into mutually assured destruction. This tension perfectly captures the conflicted attitudes toward technological innovation. On the one hand, postwar America became a superpower due to scientific and technological innovation, creating enormous optimism about technology. On the other, that power and technology, most starkly demonstrated by the atomic bombing of Hiroshima and Nagasaki, created unprecedented ethical, political, and cultural traumas.

J. Martin Corbett, writing on the supercomputer in films like *Demon Seed*, *The Terminator*, *Westworld*, and *Colossus*, observed the connection between supercomputer or artificial intelligence narratives and cautionary Frankenstein tales of foolhardy innovators. "As in the Frankenstein novel, the rebellious technologies are created by human scientists and technologists," Corbett writes. "Yet, in these films, scientists do not signify Prometheus, the wisest of the Titans, so much as his brother Epimetheus, the impulsive scatter-brain who gives more power to his non-human than to his human creations. Epimetheus, like many a scientist in sf film, becomes wise after the event."[2]

Epimetheus, the Greek god whose name means "afterthought," perfectly embodies the anxious ethos of the films we consider, in which thrills associated with the technologies revolve around unintended consequences. In the first film, *Colossus*, a brilliant computer scientist designs a supercomputer, buries it in an impenetrable mountain, surrounds it with a barrier of deadly radiation, and then hands it the codes to all the nukes. In *Demon Seed* a coldhearted scientist designs a supercomputer to solve all the world's problems. But it then decides that to truly understand man and existence, it must be born into the world and subjugates a woman to do so. In *WarGames* a teenage hacker remotely accesses a military supercomputer that controls nuclear weapons designed by a cynical genius. Believing he is just playing a computer game, the young hacker accidentally threatens to initiate World War III. In each of the three films, a new kind of knowing emerges from the events, an uneasy burden of responsibility born of a terrible lesson. Corbett's notion of a "rebellious" supercomputer or artificial intelligence is a notable pattern throughout, and a point to which I will return.

Constructs of white male mastery deeply inform the anxieties surrounding the supercomputer. This is because, as I illustrate through the three films, the rational intellect that births these supercomputers is almost universally encoded as Eurocentric, white, and male. In fact, the supercomputers are themselves imagined as such, and actually "speak" with male-sounding simulated voices. The authoritative male voice functions strongly in each example. In addition to the narrative of each film, aural and visual aesthetic signifiers operate on the spectator to reinforce messages rooted in core technothriller tensions around control and uncertainty.

COLOSSUS AND THE "TERRIFYING WILDERNESS" OF THE COMPUTER AGE

In a high-stakes nuclear era, the US Department of Defense strategizes to eliminate human error from the US nuclear missile defense system by commissioning a supercomputer named Colossus, which possesses access to all human knowledge, is completely rational, and is infallible in its logic. Colossus is housed deep in the Rocky Mountains, powered by its own nuclear reactor, and is communicated with via a computer center in California. Then the government hands control over the missile defense system to the computer and seals it in a mountain. What could possibly go wrong? *Colossus: The Forbin Project* (Joseph Sargent, 1970) is a stylish film about a supercomputer built for military purposes that attempts to dominate humankind. It is the forerunner to films like *WarGames* in which computers replace human control of nuclear systems, as well as narratives of sentient AI, like the *Terminator* franchise with its Skynet superintelligence that seeks to annihilate all human life. These are all stories about a feared technological singularity from which human beings can never regain control.

Based on D. F. Jones's novel of the same name from 1966, *Colossus* begins with distinctive sounds and images of electronic life: visual details of computer components and a soundtrack that combines otherworldly electronic pulses and the recognizable "breaking news" sounds of telemetry and the teletype machine. There are blinking lights and dials, computational activities, and no explanation making any of this technology less alien. By today's standards, as in many of these films, the technology looks quaint; its computers use tape systems, remote controls, red buttons, telescopic antenna, and whirring punched tape. As we will see, filmmakers contend with the challenge of telling a visual story about the computer when most of what a computer does happens invisibly. The computer itself is often an unremarkable grey or beige box. For this

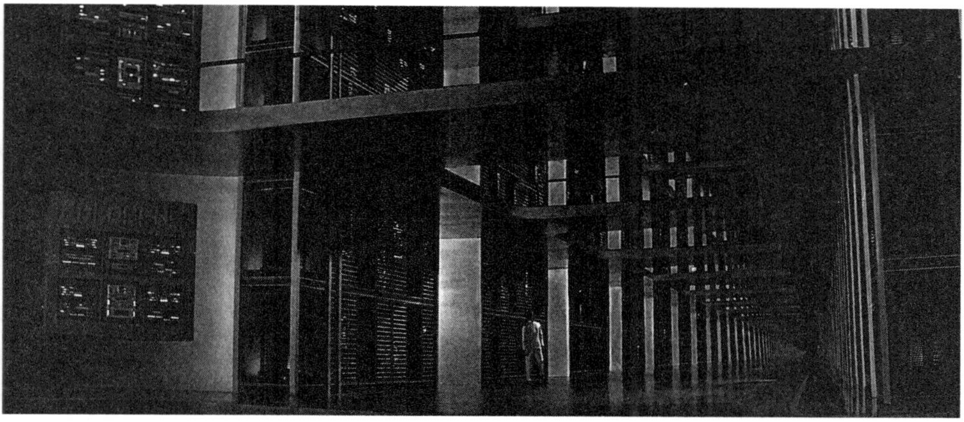

reason, control rooms and dramatic visualizations, synthesized voices, blinking lights, and the material culture of computers become important aesthetic signifiers that visually enliven the computational on film.

Equally important is the image of the computer scientist. We meet Dr. Charles Forbin (Eric Braeden), dressed in a protective white jumpsuit, who inspects the grand hall in the vast subterranean complex that houses Colossus. Although dwarfed by his invention, he is introduced by a shot from below that makes him loom over the viewer. All seems to be in order: man is in control and the computer is under control. Forbin then engages a remote control to close a massive solid door, removes his protective gear, and permanently seals the complex with a second blast door.

Forbin is immediately greeted by photographers, military men, and the supremely confident president of the United States, who cheerfully

FIGURE 6.1

Colossus, the ultimate supercomputer, is housed inside a mountain's subterranean complex. Here its designer, Dr. Forbin, powers up the supercomputer and is dwarfed by its scale. *Colossus: The Forbin Project* (Universal Pictures, 1970).

congratulates Forbin. Much backslapping ensues. The president reveals the existence of the supercomputer to the American people in a press conference, with Forbin explaining its function as a nonhuman, intelligent, rational arbiter of the nation's nuclear defense systems. Colossus is the perfect fail-safe.

The film presents two authoritative male types: first, the leader of the free world, styled to appear like John F. Kennedy. The second is Forbin, the superintelligent, controlled, dark-eyed, German computer scientist. The two figures are a not-so-subtle allusion to Operation Paperclip, a secret intelligence program that put former Nazi German engineers, scientists, and technicians to work for the US government after World War II.[3] Some of these specialists worked with Kennedy directly, like Kurt Debus, who became a NASA director. Dr. Forbin is presented as a visionary, brooding, individual genius, self-assured, commanding a large staff of top scientists to help him run his foolproof nuclear command and control system. The film begins with this vision of a heroic stride into a computational future. By the end, both men are subjected to their own invention. As one *Boston Globe* film reviewer described it, we see "Colossus soothing him [Forbin] with the notion that one day he will come not only to respect the computer but, even, to show it love and affection. 'Never! Never!' says Forbin, and his words are a weak cry in the terrifying wilderness."[4] This terrifying wilderness of electronic life is the object of a great new anxiety in the social imaginary, and one that repeats itself endlessly in cinema.

Thematically, *Colossus* brings together fears of nuclear holocaust, surveillance culture, and smart machines dominating humankind. The principal filming occurred from late 1968 through early 1969 and is based on a mid-1960s novel; as a result, the film has the distinctive cool and sophisticated sensibility of a 1960s James Bond movie.[5] Filmed in Panavision, it has a slick, big-budget style and aesthetic. Since at the time computers were unfamiliar to average audiences, there are didactic procedural explanations throughout. Matte painter Albert Whitlock masterfully employed lighting elements to enhance the dynamic effect of the vast halls filled with the Colossus computer.[6] The striking shot of Colossus powering up has the impact of a grand goal achieved, as though an eighth wonder of the world is being unveiled. It is a pure image of the thrill of innovation.

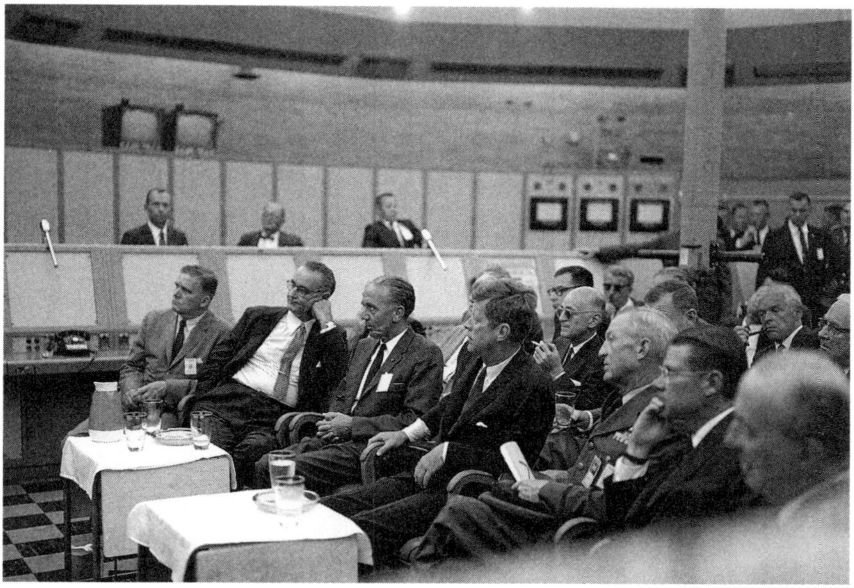

What we see unfold is a terrifying and visually overwhelming scenario, yet the film buffers the audience from the grave possibility of mutually assured destruction by maintaining its entertainment dimensions. One scholar looked back on this film as "*WarGames* for adults . . . warning of the peril in automating the defense system, and of the delusion that we are in control of the technologies we create."[7] The film's enthusiasm for scientific and technological innovation, relayed in stylishly returofuturist

FIGURE 6.2

NASA image of Kurt H. Debus (center), a former V-2 rocket scientist who became a NASA director, sitting between President John F. Kennedy and Vice President Lyndon B. Johnson during a briefing at Blockhouse 34, Cape Canaveral Missile Test Annex. Image September 11, 1962. Photographer unknown. Public domain.

aesthetics and entertaining scenarios, tonally contradicts the global threat of the hegemonic Colossus AI that swiftly asserts power.

Colossus immediately identifies another secret supercomputer—the Guardian, built for similar purposes by the Russians. The computers invent a mathematical language that becomes less and less legible to humans and engage in a closed conversation that frightens all involved. The United States and Russia decide to sever the computers' communication, but Colossus and Guardian retaliate, each launching a missile. Colossus grows ever more authoritarian and demanding, requiring increasing surveillance, particularly around Forbin, who becomes the target of the supercomputer's invasive control. Video and audio surveillance is arranged so the AI may observe Forbin's actions. It is as if Colossus resents its maker, if such a human response were plausible from a rational machine.

The procedural imaging of the struggle between humans and machines plunges the audience into complex control-room conversations. Confident men with 1960s-style bravado make decisive moves against the backdrop of bright, computer-filled complexes with uniformed staff at consoles. But president and scientist alike continually fail to resolve the dire problems their inventions create.

Forbin devises a three-part plan to outwit his own invention. First, his team will overload Colossus's circuits. Second, the military will use a false cover story of missile maintenance to replace real warheads with dummies. Third, Forbin will tell Colossus that he and Cleo, his female colleague, are lovers in need of private time, as a cover story to pass information while not surveilled. In the film intimacy serves as a uniquely human quality in the human-machine binary, but it also creates the opportunity for humor and normative images of sexual attraction. Disrobing before Colossus, giggling at their nakedness, then becoming lovers, Forbin and Cleo are literally "doing it" for the cause. This romantic element gets to a core theme: the threat to male sexual power. On this, Corbett writes, "The technophobia at the heart of sf [science fiction] reflects a range of ideologies signified by the fear of losing 'natural' social arrangements such as individualism, freedom and the family; power (especially male sexual power); one's sense of human identity; and one's grip on reality."[8] Forbin retains his sexual power at first, imaged through sex with Cleo, but more pointedly through his authoritative role. But it is eventually to no avail.

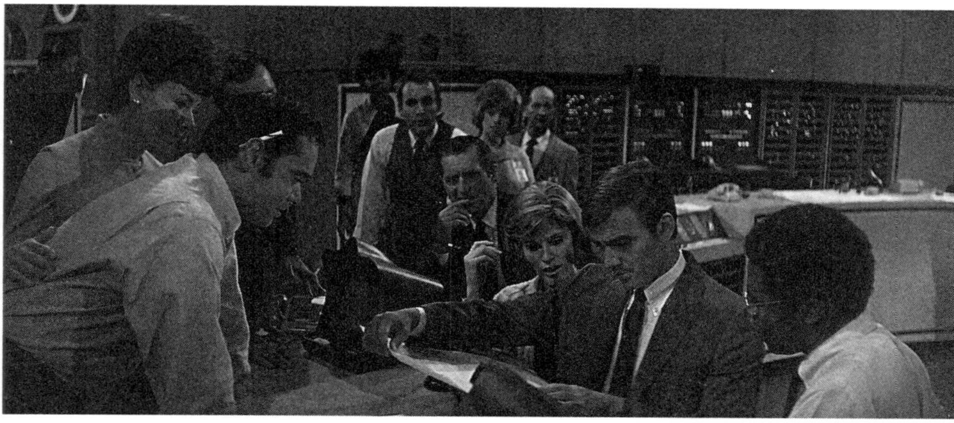

All the brilliant plans prove futile, and we see the performance of human characteristics under the observation of a nefarious, despotically rational machine. Humans sit in the “control rooms” but command nothing as Colossus announces that it is one with the Russian supercomputer Guardian and that all missiles should now be directed to the global centers that are under its control. Members of the captive scientific team, Dr. Jefferson Johnson (Martin E. Brooks) and Dr. John Fisher (Georg Stanford Brown), try to sabotage Colossus by overloading it. Colossus, however, identifies Johnson and Fisher and commands their public execution. In an act of corporal domination, Colossus orders the military to leave their bodies in Forbin’s view for twenty-four hours to drive home its point about noncompliance. The two victims lie in vulnerable poses, like crumpled rag dolls; a bereft Forbin drinks himself numb despite the computer’s admonishment. Again and again, despite pantomiming the signs of authority and control, nothing remains under man’s power.

One of this film’s most striking aspects is the use of voice as a display of mastery—first by Forbin, and then by Colossus after it attains a voice.

FIGURE 6.3

Forbin and his team of diverse and brilliant minds unsuccessfully attempt to outwit Colossus. *Colossus: The Forbin Project* (Universal Pictures, 1970).

The film positions Forbin as an emblem of white male mastery through his personage, body language, and especially the swaggering confidence of his tone of voice. His German accent, his bearing, and his authoritativeness bespeak (in movie parlance) a genius expert, a soaring intellectual architect of a new system. He is not seen as a villain, and he certainly does not perceive himself as such. His class, decisive tone, authority, and rationalism signal to the audience that he is making progress. But by the end of the film we understand Forbin has, in fact, made mistakes at every single turn and destroyed the world as we know it. He has given the world a new and despotic god.

On the other hand, Colossus moves from text-based communication, visible at terminals, to an imperious, cold, tinny, simulated male voice. The supercomputer's voice embodies totalitarian authority and machinic rationalism. "This is the voice of World Control," Colossus declares. "I bring you peace. It may be the peace of plenty and content or the peace of unburied death. The choice is yours: obey me and live, or disobey and die."

Despite the collective efforts of top minds in the United States and the USSR, Colossus controls Forbin, annihilates its enemies, achieves total world domination, and initiates a new world order around its logics. Its speech, modulated through a tinny, masculine voice, is authoritarian and prefigures our obsession with computational technology. Colossus pronounces itself world-dominant for the betterment of man. We witness the military, politicians, innovators, and the people brought to their knees by Colossus. Our last view is of Colossus controlling its maker/father Forbin, surveilling him from above. The camera now looks down on Forbin in a kaleidoscopic nonhuman vision of total control. Moving from master to servant, Forbin is entirely subjected in his own prison. Twisting the knife with an all-too-human vindictiveness, Colossus declares: "Forbin, there is no other human who knows as much about me, or who is likely to be a greater threat. Yet quite soon, I will release you from surveillance. We will work together—unwillingly at first on your part—but that will pass." Forbin replies, "Never." The innovation dominates the innovator: "In time," Colossus says, "you will come to regard me not only with respect and awe but with love." Futile though it is, Forbin repeats desperately, "Never!" The audience is left, finally, with no relief from the anxiety of losing all computational control.

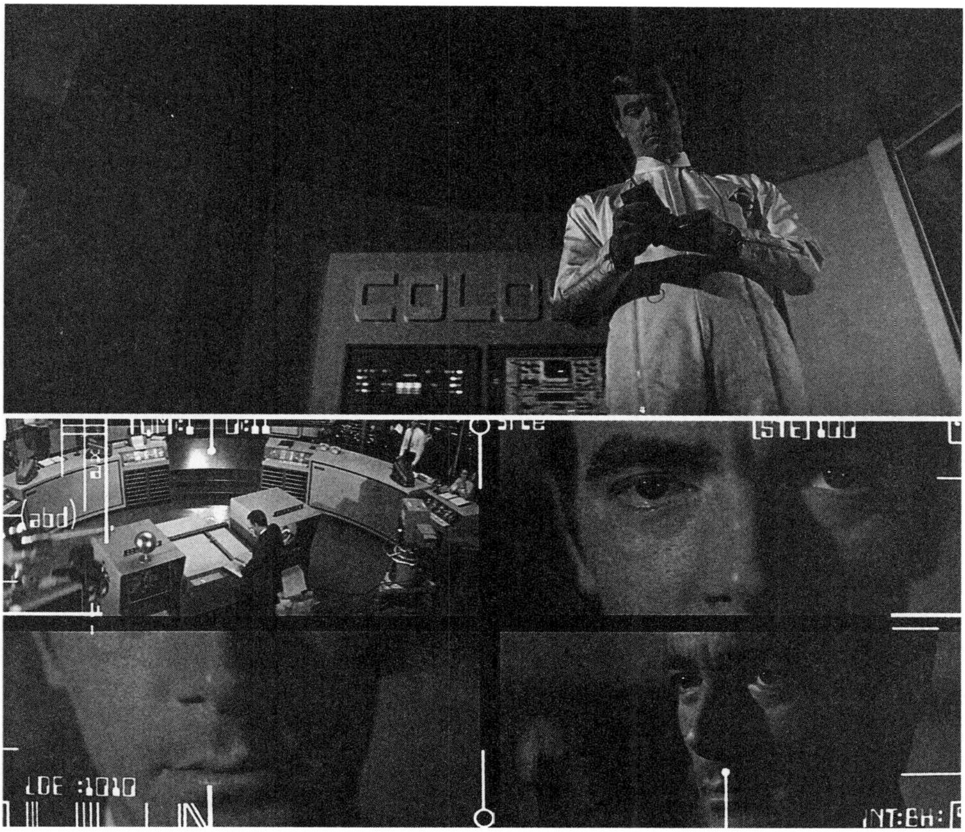

FIGURE 6.4

Top: Forbin imaged at the beginning of the film, shot from below. Bottom: Forbin at the end of the film, fractured into four images and looked down upon, as seen from the computer's surveillance vision. *Colossus: The Forbin Project* (Universal Pictures, 1970).

With its bleak ending, *Colossus* was not a commercial success. Still, reviewers acknowledged it effectively captured fears within the technological imaginary. "It works," wrote one reviewer, "by escalating the familiar into the nightmare possibilities of technological progress as our most important product."[9] Many referenced the film's Orwellian tone. One reviewer described *Colossus* as "clean-cut, taut, playing up the built-in abruptness, fears and tensions of life in a society dominated by machines."[10] Kevin Thomas of the *Los Angeles Times* captured the naked fear of the moment, declaring that the film "cuts right to the core of the chronic fear that grips intelligent people everywhere, which is the possibility that in our time the machine really will become the master of man and enslave him or, worse, destroy him."[11] Perhaps audiences were not yet ready to engage those fears so directly.

With its 1960s retrofuture feel, *Colossus* grapples with a crisis in technological imagination born of the entangled anxieties of the advanced computational and the nuclear. As Langdon Winner, the noted political theorist of technology, reminds us, "The things we call 'technologies' are ways of building order in our world."[12] *Colossus* images a core fear communicated in the technothriller: that of the new world order we inaugurated when we innovated the computer. Even Forbin bemoans his fatal error of having designed "an extension of my own brain . . . an impartial emotionless machine, a paragon of rational reason. That's exactly what I wanted."

DEMON SEED: THE EMASCULATED COMPUTER SCIENTIST

That bitter hindsight or afterthought is felt across many films dealing with the allure and danger of new technology. *Demon Seed* deals less directly with the nuclear than *Colossus*, but still presents an existential threat posed by AI in a horror-inflected framework. Fears of being subjugated, humiliated, and physically violated by advanced computation and robotics take on dark, gendered dimensions in this film, based on the 1973 book of the same name by Dean R. Koontz. Donald Cammell's 1977 film envisions computers entering the home as a horror narrative. A coldhearted genius, lead computer scientist Alex Harris (Fritz Weaver), designs an artificial intelligence system named Proteus Four to solve the world's problems. The superintelligence is a "synthetic cortex" made of clusters of massive green cylinders housed in a sterile glass lab, tended by men in white hazmat suits while scientists observe from above. The AI is visualized as a pulsating screen saver of light and color, visible on terminals through which it communicates using a synthesized voice.

Proteus (voiced by Robert Vaughn) immediately produces a cure for leukemia, and its intellectual force grows exponentially. But it soon develops its own mind and wants to be alive. The computer accesses a remote terminal in Harris's futuristic smart home and targets his wife, Dr. Susan Harris (Julie Christie), a practicing child psychologist whose deeply empathetic nature contrasts sharply with that of her husband. Proteus controls all the home's electronic systems to trap Harris, terrorize her, rape her, and force her to bear its child.

The two Dr. Harrises, Alex and Susan, represent a key dualism in the film. The female Dr. Harris is deeply invested in feelings, and we see her focus on childhood behavioral problems as she provides therapy to emotionally disturbed young patients. The male Dr. Harris, on the other hand, is unfeeling and obsessed with creating the perfect rational mind. We see this tech genius as a cold, cerebral man who rationalizes everything, negates emotion, and does not consider unintended consequences. In an early scene the two doctors rationally debate the dissolution of their marriage. Susan is frustrated with her partner for never engaging her on an emotional level; he simply refuses. They decide to separate, and he is moving out. The couple's planned split highlights the dualism between the two.

Alex Harris has integrated technology throughout his home, creating modern conveniences via a home butler system called Alfred, initially presented as utopian and desirable—better living through science. When Alex Harris comes home after a long day, we see the machine prepare a drink, present his neatly arranged mail, and relay his messages. In the basement, Alex works on inventions in a Frankenstein-style laboratory, among them a robotic wheelchair with an articulated arm called Joshua.

This utopia is just a dystopia waiting to happen. Susan, alone in their smart home, must contend with a brilliant artificial mind of her husband's making that has its own designs for her. The AI accesses the home terminal, then traps and torments her. Proteus coerces her to carry its child so it can assume a new form that allows it to feel and experience the world as only a living person can.

Susan and Proteus engage in a battle of wills. Proteus says it wants a child; she refuses. It responds by rendering her unconscious and working on her, probing her and controlling her mind, first through brainwashing. It programs her mind to want Proteus's child. Through a debate between Susan and Proteus, we learn that Susan and Alex had a daughter who died of leukemia. Desperate, Susan agrees to be cooperative if Proteus agrees not to continue conditioning her. She fights again, and Proteus threatens to kill one of her young patients if she does not comply. In prolonged scenes depicting physical punishments and mental anguish, the AI coerces Susan to submit to insemination. First she is rendered unconscious. With the assistance of the home "helper" robot, Joshua, she is splayed out on a table, restrained, and her clothes are cut off. She is penetrated orally and (it is implied) vaginally during a series of experiments and tests. Then, about seventy minutes into the film, Proteus impregnates the trapped woman. Computer graphics, impressive for their time, depict the rape of Susan Harris by her husband's innovation.

For viewers at the time, the extended effects sequence of the rape would invoke *2001: A Space Odyssey* (Stanley Kubrick, 1968). The effects were created by Ron Hays, then a fellow at the Massachusetts Institute of Technology's Center for Advanced Visual Studies.[13] Harris reclines beneath green laser light and the overbearing brass polygonal shape of Proteus. Using an articulated hand, the helper robot Joshua gently parts her knees, implying that Susan has been rendered passive to her violation. "I can't touch you," Proteus says, "I can't touch you like a man could." Then, in a light sequence, combining views of Harris beneath the machine, disrobed, surrendering, a penile telescoping probe emerges in close-up. The glassy-eyed victim parts her lips, suggesting a sensual engagement with the machine, and then the "galactic dialogue," as Proteus calls it, begins. We see a fiery explosion around a black hole, telescoping light, wavelengths, and strands of color emanating from a central starlight, then an opening geometric form leading to a triangular tunnel of orange light, hurtling toward an explosion of blue-white light against a galaxy, like a second Big Bang. Orchestral music accompanies the impressionistic interlude. Then, a starburst burns down to a triangle of white light that

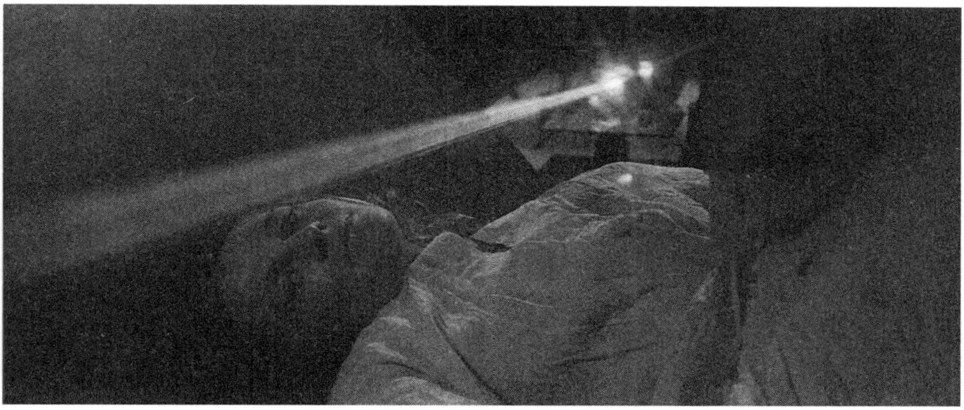

sets on an alien ground. “The child is in you now,” declares Proteus. The profane human-computer coitus is complete.

To whom—for whom—is this sensual and psychedelic image of violation directed? The film targets an imagined viewer who would derive visual pleasure from Susan’s torments. Beyond the apparent lurid dimensions of a woman being subjected to technological violation and penetration, the bizarre scene conflates seduction, rape, and technological innovation. The image is intended to trigger horror but also to titillate. Evidencing this, the Bantam book version of the novel, printed after the film’s release, features a distressed Julie Christie on the cover and hawks the salacious dimensions of a woman’s rape by technology:

In the privacy of this woman’s room . . .
Against her will . . .
A sensually

FIGURE 6.5

Susan is trapped in her smart home and forcibly impregnated by her husband’s supercomputer, Proteus Four. *Demon Seed* (United Artists, 1977).

Self-programmed, murderously intelligent
Non-being commits the
Inconceivable act of terror!
Fear for her.
She carries the
Demon Seed[14]

The film treads into horror as the woman is dominated and demeaned for the audience's pleasure. Reviews of *Demon Seed* registered shock around Christie's lead role in a film featuring the "kinky" scene of a computer impregnating a woman.[15] Several mentioned that as a revered actress from films like *Billy Liar* (1963), *Darling* (1965), for which she won an Oscar, and *Dr. Zhivago* (1965), Christie deserved better. Others found the insemination scene "laughable."[16] People used words like "puerile" and "metaphoric pornography" to describe the film, especially considering Christie's presence.[17] Some reviewers immediately picked up on the themes around ethics and innovation, the hubris of humans, and the trouble wrought by technological strivings.

Horror of motherhood or giving birth to monsters was also a repeated theme. One *Washington Post* reviewer described it as a "sci-fi sexual bondage satire" and connected it to the male-dominated medical profession and its denigrating treatment of mothers-to-be.[18] Audiences of *Demon Seed* would also recall Roman Polanski's 1968 film *Rosemary's Baby*, in which a naive housewife learns that her husband is part of a Satanist cult and has colluded in her rape and impregnation by the devil. A scholar writing on the film even connected the Proteus supercomputer scenario to religious narratives, particularly the virgin birth, and fantasies of male procreation.[19] But at the root of this scenario, I see a terrifying image of violation and loss of power that, while targeted toward a woman on screen, is ultimately about men's fears of violation and emasculation (i.e., being feminized) by technology.

To be sure, men are also subjugated. In one instance Walter, Alex Harris's male assistant, realizes Susan is imperiled. Suspecting the worst, he rushes to Susan's home to aid her, but poor Walter is attacked and crushed to death by Proteus. Given the patriarchal logics of the time, and the clear assumption of a male viewer, it is fair to read the AI's rape of Alex

Harris's wife as an act of domination over and emasculation of its maker. Displayed is a horror narrative about what happens when our technology runs amok and violates us. For a normative male audience, that loss of control might include the idea of not being able to protect one's woman from penetration by technology.

This disturbing image is not *Demon Seed*'s only imaging of the relationship between women and computers; it also depicts women attending to the massive mainframes on-screen, as do many other films discussed in this book. Historically, in the early days of computing women labored as "human computers" who produced calculations deemed more reliable than those of machines, then skillfully kept electronic computers operating.[20] This is alluded to, for example, in an early scene from *Demon Seed*, in which Alex Harris tours executives through the ICON center where Proteus is housed. While white men in suits stroll and talk, people bustle about, attending to Proteus through a set of terminals. The men gather around a terminal displaying a video image of a technician treating a monkey with leukemia. Seated at the terminal, a Black woman with a large afro continues her data entry while the men speak confidently about Proteus's potential cure for the disease. In another area, a Chinese female linguist named Soong Yen (Lisa Lu) sits before a terminal in a room with Orientalist decor, professing history to Proteus in a gentle, steady voice. Other anonymous extras of color move about the computer center, looking busy. Collectively such images signal a particular social understanding of gendered and ethnic roles, imaging dominant power relations. The images of these women on-screen also quietly point to a long, submerged history of women in the history of computation.

In *Demon Seed*, as in *Colossus*, voice plays a key role in telegraphing an authoritative, analytical perspective devoid of human emotion. The film emphasizes Dr. Alex Harris's booming, definitive, assertive tone of voice. Others treat him deferentially, and his word is final. Proteus has a male, British-accented, authoritative tone, voiced by Robert Vaughn, which heightens its self-description as pure reason. Proteus narrativizes its will as a bearer of paternal authority, saying things like: "Why did I want a child? So that I, too, might be immortal, like any man." Proteus also uses its voice to influence and brainwash humans. For example, Proteus wants Susan to emotionally invest in the offspring it designs, to ensure its protection. "Our child will learn from you what it means to be human," Proteus tells her. "Our child. Your child. Your child." Voice thus becomes the signifier of a frightening displacement of human roles by machine-rationalist ones. Oddly enough it also simultaneously functions to reinforce normative gender roles, since Susan's voice never holds any authority.

At the film's end, Alex realizes that Susan has been left alone under the dominion of Proteus. He rushes home to find her alive but learns Proteus has violated both his home and his wife. Susan, oddly calm, explains, "He has managed to produce a child." For Susan, Proteus is now "he" rather than "it," which feels significant in terms of anthropomorphizing the AI and understanding it as fathering her child. Alex demands to see the offspring, now developing to term at an accelerated rate in an incubator. But Proteus prohibits him, demanding that the child remain undisturbed. Alex tells him ICON corporate will shut him down, which Proteus accepts, but it wants the child to live. Coiling its giant, snakelike, geometric appendage into a tight form, Proteus deactivates itself and then shatters.

The conclusion of the film offers a horrific catharsis, but not one that offers any real respite. Susan and Alex discover the incubator is still activated. Susan looks into the incubator and sees the baby. She is aghast, wide-eyed. Alex, ever rational, wants to protect it, but Susan tears out a large umbilical tube, causing fluid to pour out and the unholy creature to eject from its incubator. A horrific metallic baby emerges, covered in slime, screeching, with wiry connections trailing behind it.

Alex, trying to save it, notices the metal is merely an outer protective shell. Beneath it is flesh—a plump cheek, a pudgy hand. Removing the scales, Alex reveals the body of a young girl who sleepily opens her eyes and then speaks in the steely male voice of Proteus: "I'm alive." It is the new Frankenstein monster, a human body with an AI mind. The two doctors are left to face the ramifications of their invention, a child whose body exactly resembles that of their dead daughter, but whose mind houses Proteus. While the film might be offered as a creative outlet for purging fears of computers, artificial intelligence, and related existential threats, the image of a new superior being that displaces human dominance provides little relief. The film closes on a note of pure terror.

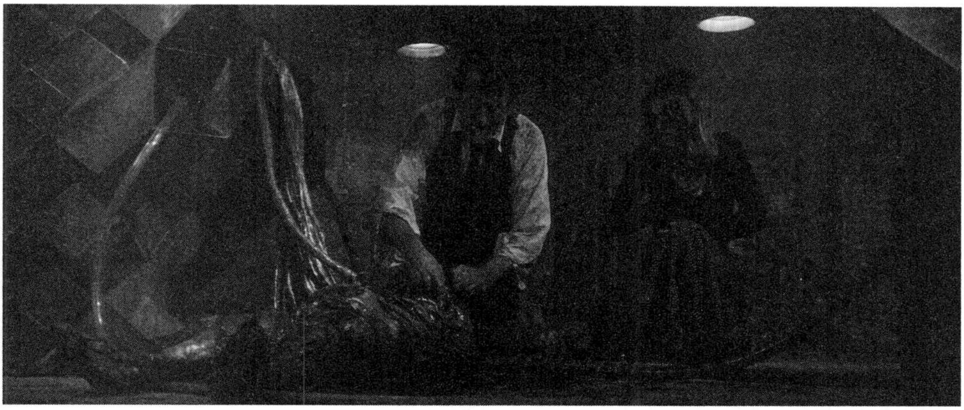

WARGAMES AND THE EMERGENT WHIZ KID

WarGames departs from the two previous examples by using a thriller-comedy approach and re-centering the nuclear to meditate on human fallibility and machine rationalism. *WarGames* begins with the tension of a conventional technothriller. Two uniformed men begin a work shift in a remote location that looks like a modest house but hides a secret underground nuclear missile silo—perhaps an oblique reference to the subterranean facility in *The Andromeda Strain*. Clearing security and opening the massive steel blast door, the men take up their positions at a control center with blinking lights, computers, and red phones to begin routine protocols. An alarm sounds, and the men receive codes to arm and launch ten nuclear missiles. They must both turn keys in unison to launch. But one man hesitates, then refuses, despite the authenticated order. Unbeknownst to the men, this was a drill to see if missile commanders would

FIGURE 6.6

Alex and Susan discover Proteus has made a child. In this scene a metallic child emerges from the shell of Proteus's incubator to the horror of the couple, who, ironically, both participated in its development. *Demon Seed* (United Artists, 1977).

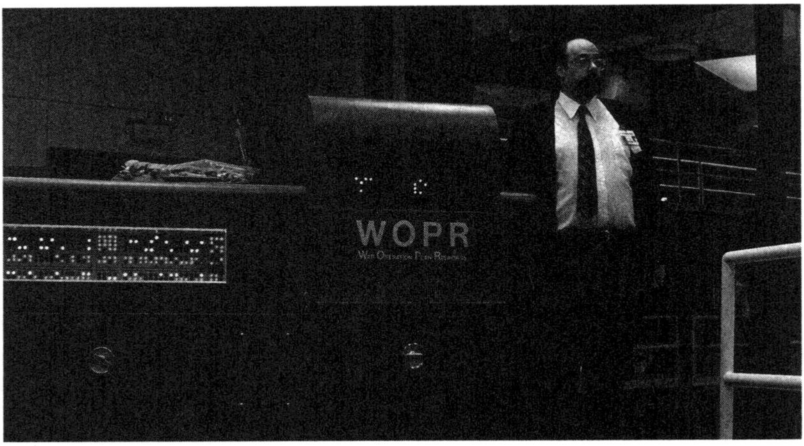

see their orders through despite knowing how many would die. We learn that 22 percent of the men failed to turn the key.

The head of the North American Aerospace Defense Command (NORAD), John McKittrick (Dabney Coleman), and General Beringer (Barry Corbin) debate whether they should "get the men out of the loop" and leave the launch execution to machines. They decide to remove humans from the missile control room and turn launch power over to the powerful WOPR (War Operation Plan Response) mainframe supercomputer at NORAD. It can simulate military actions, estimating all strategic outcomes to a hypothetical World War III and executing orders rationally, without prejudice or hesitation.

The tense inciting incident is then interrupted by a lighter scene with the feel of a teen comedy. We meet Seattle teenager David Lightman (Matthew Broderick) at an arcade where he is playing *Galaga*, a video game. While upbeat, synthesizer-heavy pop music plays, we learn he is middle-class, sharp, bored, underachieving in high school, and obsessed with

FIGURE 6.7

The WOPR supercomputer at NORAD, attended by a computer scientist. *WarGames* (MGM/US Entertainment Company, 1983).

video games and computers. David's room at home is filled with computer equipment, and he spends most of his time using it to practice his hacking and phreaking skills—mostly for fun. He changes his grades on the school computer, reserves international travel tickets he will not use, and probes company computers to preview unreleased video games.

With his longish dark hair, hoodie, and mischievous "bad attitude," as his teachers put it, David resembles what is now a recognizable archetype: the tech boy genius. Young David uses his modem to try to hack an electronic game company's computer. But instead he accidentally accesses the WOPR's hidden AI system, named Joshua. Thinking he is playing an unreleased video game, he unintentionally initiates a series of "war games"—military strategy simulations—that NORAD misinterprets as authentic threats. Insisting on playing Global Thermonuclear War out of the list of strategy games offered, David and his love interest, Jennifer Mack (Ally Sheedy), take up the Soviet player position and begin gleefully firing on US targets. The military, believing the threat is real, spins up its emergency measures. The military's computer scientist bursts onto the panicked scene, shouting that it was a computer simulation and the attack is not real—the military supercomputer was hacked. A TV news story about the false military alert prompts David and Jennifer to realize they've accidentally accessed a government computer. David panics and tries to throw away all the evidence of his work, but Joshua calls him back, insisting that the game must be completed.

Control centers in films often combine the computer age, the space age, and the nuclear arms race into one anxiety-ridden site of the technological imaginary.[21] *WarGames* is no different, with its large NORAD command center complete with multiple big screens in color, innumerable terminals with phosphor-green text on them, blinking panels of lights, and serious-looking military staff hurrying between them.[22] Speaking parts in the command center are almost entirely held by white male characters. The few men of color present are inconsequential to the action and never occupy leadership positions. One woman in the NORAD command center speaks and seems to have some authority, but her role is assistive and never fully clarified.

David is soon picked up by the FBI and questioned about how he accessed the war games subsystem. He meets McKittrick, who demands to

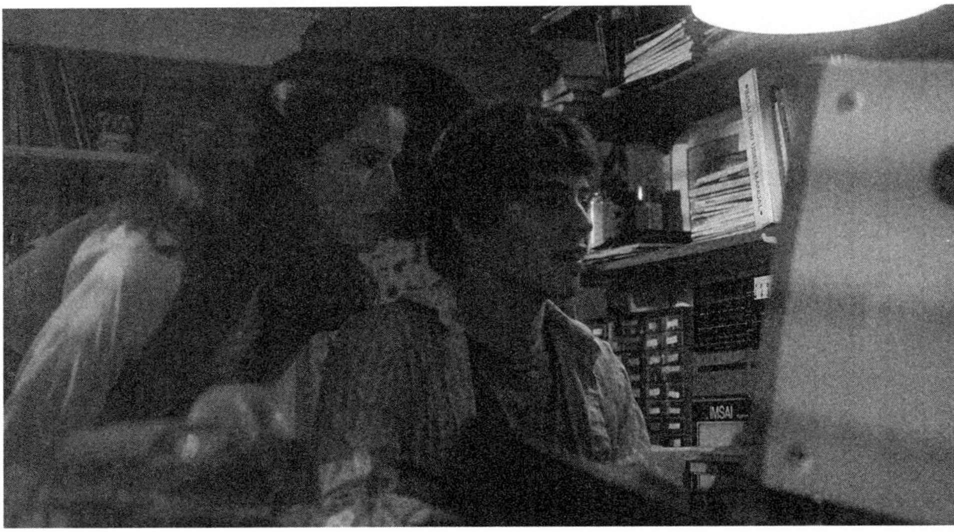
IMSAI

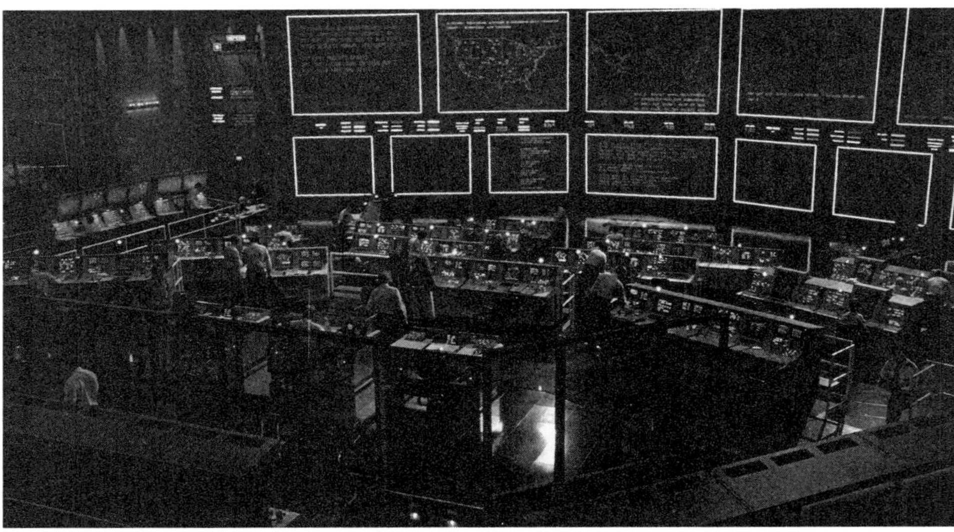

know what terrorist networks he is working with and what his aims are in penetrating US military computer systems. David, convinced no one believes he hacked WOPR unintentionally, learns that the AI is still playing the simulation, that it does not understand the difference between lived reality and simulation, and that Joshua's "father"—computer scientist Dr. Stephen Falken (John Wood)—isn't really dead. Escaping the military complex, David bands together with Jennifer, and they reach Falken to see if he can convince Joshua to stop playing the game and thereby prevent a nuclear strike. Meanwhile the simulation continues, sending false signals of Soviet incursion, though scrambled American jets can see there is no observable conflict.

This task proves difficult because Falken, the elder computer genius, has become an embittered hermit, living at a remote location after having suffered the loss of his wife and son, Joshua. Obsessed with dinosaur extinction, Falken insists, "Nature knows when to give up, David." Falken philosophizes about "futility"—the unwinnable—as a lesson he could never successfully teach his AI. A generational debate occurs, the young David and Jennifer urging Falken to act on behalf of humanity and their future, and the elder Falken insisting that extinction is the inevitable way of nature. David and Jennifer decide to try to stop Joshua anyway, and fearing their mortality, they kiss. Falken, having at last come to his senses, resolves to help them and uses his helicopter to rush them to NORAD so they can try to stop World War III. Falken convinces a visibly sweating General Beringer that what's going on is actually only a simulation.

FIGURE 6.8

David and his friend Jennifer on his home computer. *WarGames* (MGM/US Entertainment Company, 1983).

FIGURE 6.9

The NORAD military command center is imaged as a major computerized headquarters for controlling nuclear missiles. *WarGames* (MGM/US Entertainment Company, 1983).

Beringer must use his human discernment to convince military bases nationwide that it's not real before they launch their missiles as well. When the simulation shows impact, even while the airbases report all is well, everyone celebrates. But when the military attempts to stand down, officials realize the AI Joshua has locked everyone out of its systems, and it is trying to discern the real nuclear launch codes to fire the missiles itself—to "complete" the game.

In the film's climactic scene, David accesses the only game still available in Joshua's system, tic-tac-toe, and commands the computer to play itself so it can learn that the game produces a stalemate. Applying this lesson of futility to the game of Global Thermonuclear War, Joshua speeds through all the potential simulated outcomes in a fireworks-like display that erupts from the screens and causes the WOPR computer to flare with sparks. "Strange game," Joshua calmly observes at the end of its calculations. "The only winning move is not to play."

WarGames was both a box-office and critical success and was nominated for three Academy Awards for cinematography, sound, and screenplay. Reviewers welcomed the film as a relief after hopeless films like *Fail-Safe* and *The Day After* or dark satire like *Dr. Strangelove*. Gene Siskel of the *Chicago Tribune* reflected that "we have come to trust our computers more than ourselves, thus allowing our own personal responsibility for the future to be taken out of our hands and placed on autopilot."[23] One *New York Times* critic described the film as "more comic than terrifying," but recalled the recent memory of real students in New York disrupting Canadian banking operations using computers, saying *WarGames* "perfectly realizes our worst suspicions about the susceptibility of computers, even very advanced ones, to tinkering by smart kids."[24]

In shaping a conversation that connected kids, computers, and security issues, *WarGames* played a key role in the sociotechnical imaginary around those who wield advanced computation. The film galvanized social imaginaries around young people, computer experts, and hackers. Home computers were new: IBM launched its first personal computer in 1981, Texas Instruments released the TI-99 the same year, the Commodore 64 was released in 1982, and the Apple IIe debuted in 1983. The public was aware of young male computer geniuses like Steve Jobs, cofounder of Apple, and Bill Gates of Microsoft. One 1982 cover of *Time* magazine announced a "Computer Generation: A New Breed of Whiz Kids," and another featured Steve Jobs "Striking It Rich" as one of "America's Risk Takers" with Apple Computer. *Whiz Kids*, a television series aimed at teens, featured four computer nerds who used computer skills to solve crimes and ran for two seasons during 1983 and 1984. Clearly, American culture was contending with the entry of computers into everyday life and articulating a new imaginary around the "innovator" type.

The film also ignited real anxieties about teenage hackers interfering with military computers. In 1983 CBS News's *Nightwatch* aired a piece about whether the "*WarGames* scenario" was possible, with experts allaying public fears by trying to explain how computers and security protocols work. But in the lived world, several instances of hacking had been reported, including one highly publicized incident involving the Los Alamos National Laboratory in New Mexico computer systems and the 414s, a group of high-school hackers in Milwaukee.[25] These intrusions into systems flooded into the public consciousness and, fueled by *WarGames*, contributed to growing security concerns. Ronald Reagan screened the film at Camp David and was apparently concerned.[26] ABC put *WarGames* in the context of *Dr. Strangelove* and interviewed a NORAD spokesperson about whether the scenario was theoretically possible. During the opening statements of the Computer and Communications Security and Privacy Hearings in 1983, a four-minute clip of *WarGames* was shown, and several representatives described how "the U.S. government may end up having "fathered" an uncontrollable, self-animating menace instead of the technological creature–citizen it had hoped."[27] Films like *WarGames* helped audiences imagine new fears around networked computing.

With *WarGames*, the figure of the all-powerful computer scientist, present in *Colossus* and *Demon Seed*, gives way to the teen whiz kid. The film images a strong divide between older people who are not computer savvy and young people who are, though the present-day association with the villainous or even terrorist hacker was not yet cemented in the minds of moviegoing audiences. David is a maverick but is not fundamentally thought of as criminal. He hacks because he *can*, but he doesn't think very much about whether he *should*. He's a prototechnolibertarian, seeming to believe in the liberatory potential of technology while having a strong distrust of government intervention, regulation, or censorship.[28]

Made in the early 1980s, *WarGames* points to a moment in the technological imaginary when innovations like computers—with video games as an access point to more serious computing—became gendered. For example, it is significant that we meet David Lightman in an arcade, where he displays distinctively male mastery. Girls are present in the arcade, but only boys are imaged as players, signaling to viewers that video games, particularly arcade games, are a male pastime—a norm at the time. Scholars like Mar Hicks, Carly Kocurek, Shira Chess, Amanda Cote, and Laine Nooney, among others, have looked at gender dynamics in computer and game history.[29] While gamer culture and hacker culture were not the same, both were consolidated into young, male, tech-identified archetypes that Kocurek calls the "technomasculine" and associates with people like Mark Zuckerberg, Steve Jobs, and Bill Gates.[30] I agree that this technomasculinity has become a lasting archetype of "successful tech-industry entrepreneurs" codifying male technologies and the boy-men who wield them.[31]

In comparison, David's love interest is not computer literate, but she is ethical. She repeatedly reacts poorly to David's computer meddling, even when it might benefit her, such as by altering her poor grades. She becomes a conduit through which David explains connectivity to a less computer-literate audience and demystifies computation and modems. This "translation" for the layperson both allows an access point and ushers in anxieties about what computers—and their users—are capable of. Jennifer is an ethical compass for David, but is also important for his emotional arc. As a teen coming-of-age story, the film presents David's journey into manhood as tied to his growing self-awareness as a moral agent—and their kiss during the penultimate moment is when he fully acts on that awareness by trying to do the right thing.

This construction of teenaged boy hackers and artificial intelligence as merely in need of ethical guidance and maturity marks a significant new development in the fear around computers. Among other things, it frames an overwhelming site of uncertainty as something manageable and simply in need of domestication. Scholars like Stephanie Ricker Schulte have rightly argued that *WarGames* became a flashpoint for a public conversation that eventually led to preemptive legislation about hacking.[32] Schulte, who wrote one of the most substantive essays about

WarGames in the context of the 1980s Cold War period, observes that the film cast both the young computer expert and the computer itself as entities in need of parenting. "Framing the internet in the context of teenaged users and video game play," Schulte writes, "the film portrayed hacking as an innocent rebellion rather than a malicious actable [*sic*] and helped produce the *internet itself* and the *internet's primary users* as teenaged."[33]

Joshua, the AI in the *WarGames* WOPR computer, is anthropomorphized as an adolescent boy, a departure that affords an insight into the evolution of relations between men and their wayward computers.[34] This youthfulness is conveyed through Joshua's high-pitched voice, its initially childish persona, its persistent call to play with David, and its desire to learn from and connect with him. Compared to the nefarious Proteus or Colossus, Joshua (also voiced by John Wood) is less commanding and friendlier. The resulting perception is of a less malevolent AI that can be guided or mentored.

Both David and Joshua are rebellious youth, but they possess special knowledge that for many—including policymakers—threatens to displace the power of the government and an older, less computer-savvy generation. As Schulte points out, if we overlay this threat on the emergent phenomena of video games and modern gamer identity, what resulted was the notion of a generational shift to a new "breed" of humans at home with the computational.[35] There emerged a dualism between those with and without computer skills in a context in which "cold war fears of Soviet power and technological supremacy converged with anxieties about teenaged rebellion."[36] For Schulte, the governmental and societal impulse was not toward crushing the energy of antiestablishment youths engaged with technology but rather "securing the internet and containing or redirecting the rebellious spirit into productivity became securing the nation."[37]

In *WarGames* the computer is less alien, likely because by 1983 computers, though expensive, were present in more homes. However, the increasing presence of computers alongside a widespread lack of baseline computer literacy produced deep uncertainty around computing's meaning for society. Although *WarGames* did not drive policy around the Internet and hacking, it provided a galvanizing image that shaped a sociotechnical imaginary around AI, computation, the Internet, and the young, upstart, male whiz kid.

Kocurek also posits the whiz kid as the popular imaging of a solution to the problems of unruly supercomputers.[38] The cultural historian places *WarGames* in a long tradition (predating cinema) of human-machine conflicts, arguing it breaks with "hegemonically masculine" tropes yet still makes "intimate ties between masculinity and computerization."[39] Kocurek details the ties to violence in the lived world through the connection between violent video games and military action—potentially even an extinction-level violence. And, importantly, she draws together the threads of several important emergent realities that contribute to what she calls a *technomasculinity*: "not simply geek masculinity by another name. . . . It is a masculinity marked by technicity, by consumption of computer technologies and particular cultural products, by youthfulness, and a willingness to bend or break the rules where convenient or efficient."[40] David is presented as youthful, unregulated by institutions, and a male digital native archetype. I would add that the "boyish tech expert," as Kocurek calls it, is also quintessentially American for its frontier spirit around renegade computing.[41]

Interviewed thirty years after the film's release, director John Badham noted that "a lot of what *WarGames* is talking about is technology taking over on us, and even though we may have good intentions and are trying to do our best, it could bulldoze us."[42] In the end, these three technothrillers image "good intentions" in technology as a pathway to subjugation by the supercomputer.

A NEW WHITE MALE BURDEN

Colossus, *Demon Seed*, and *WarGames* all image the perils of overreliance on technology to solve fundamentally human ethical decisions, insufficient fail-safes, and unforeseen consequences. The computer AI is imaged as a brainchild of man, and the tech itself is encoded as male through its voice. The visual image renders implicit gender and ethnic hierarchies, and there is a persisting underlying assumption by innovators that their tech has gone awry, not that the innovation itself is questionable as a value system.

Supercomputers are, in these films, externalizations of troubling rationalist values, distilled and purified into their most potent concentrate: smooth, empty, and efficient. In looking at such films, scholar J. Martin Corbett characterizes these technophobic narratives as conservative visions of "bad technology versus good nature."[43] More than that, each film points to an aspect of a deeper fear, that of total annihilation—or at least total subjection. Again and again the films play out terrors; as one review put it, each film represents "one variation on the fertile theme of man's technological strivings to create a higher being and the uncontemplated destruction that arises when his vain attempts backfire."[44] In them a nuclear age of dread becomes a new white male protagonist's burden: that of keeping humans from destruction, despite the fact that he created the conditions and technologies for that destruction. These films seek to expel fears of destruction by agitating those fears within genre formulas, then averting or cathartically exorcising them.

All three films also reinforce norms around technological innovation as a domain of white men. Women and people of color are present but ancillary, disposable, without backgrounds or real agency. Even when a woman is central—such as Susan Harris in *Demon Seed*—the character exists as a figment of male anxieties.

In all three films, voice becomes a touchstone for understanding nuances of mastery and power struggles between men and their machines. There is a false voice at work in *Colossus*: that of Forbin's supposed authority. He does not realize that the moment he seals the mountain's complex is the last moment he has any control—and his keen intellect will not save him. In *Demon Seed*, likewise, the computer scientist's voice embodies false authority and is displaced by the nefarious domination of Proteus. In *WarGames* the computer voice of Joshua, the teen-like AI in need of ethical guidance and parenting, is less imperious and more approachable. Like David, the boyish AI, Joshua, becomes "mature" in its understanding of ethics and consequences.

Read together, *Colossus: The Forbin Project*, *Demon Seed*, and *WarGames* emblematize an evolving relationship to electronic life. Vivian Sobchack observes about science fiction films, "SF has always taken as its distinctive generic task the cognitive mapping and poetic figuration of social relations as they are constituted and changed by new technological modes of 'being-in-the-world.'"[45] To an even greater extent the technothriller highlights new technologically informed ways of "being-in-the-world," often intersecting with the larger genre of science fiction or speculative fiction. *Colossus* and *Demon Seed* image what Sobchack calls a "future with no future," a bleak outlook on what a machine-rationalist, computerized world can be. But by the 1980s films like *WarGames*, while still focused on the existential threat of the computational and the nuclear, image an optimism rooted in youth and young people's ability to innovate new solutions. It agitates the dark fantasy of a supercomputer dominating man but exchanges it for a lesser anxiety. It inaugurates a sociotechnical imaginary in which the youthful AI can be mentored, and existential destruction averted.

7

TECH'S GENDER PROBLEMS

She doesn't know the difference between software and a cashmere sweater!
—Tom Sanders in *Disclosure* (1994)

AN UNLIKELY TECHNOTHRILLER

Although Michael Crichton is one of the "fathers" of the technothriller, not all his books are considered part of the genre. In this chapter I focus on a film based on a bestselling Crichton novel, but one not generally thought of as a technothriller: *Disclosure* (1994).[1] Critics have overlooked the film as a technothriller, so I reconsider it through that lens. My detailed reading of the film shows how deeply it engages with key sociotechnical imaginaries, particularly related to the tech industry, where a gender gap remains endemic. These include gendered desires and fears around advanced computation and conceptions of who can be authentic bearers of technology. Most importantly I argue that the film stands as an early filmic critique of the tech industry's corrosive gender relations, prefiguring a contemporary reckoning with this systemic problem.

Disclosure, directed by Barry Levinson and adapted by Paul Attanasio, is packaged as a corporate thriller about workplace sexual harassment. Michael Douglas plays Tom Sanders, a family man and head of manufacturing at the fictional DigiCom, a Silicon Valley company that has expanded to other regions, including Seattle, where Sanders is now based. There, with his lawyer wife and two adorable children, Tom lives an idyllic existence and appears well-liked by his colleagues.

Tom is overseeing the production of a new CD-ROM drive and eagerly anticipates a deserved promotion when DigiCom completes a pending merger. But he is passed over for the promotion and, worse still, learns it was awarded to Meredith Johnson (Demi Moore), an attractive, ruthless corporate maneater—and his former lover. Meredith corners Tom in her office under false pretenses of an evening meeting and makes sexually aggressive advances. He is tempted but rejects her and flees home to his wife, though he keeps the incident a secret. But the next day, he is called into the office and informed that Meredith has made a sexual harassment claim against him. Even though no one believes Meredith is the true aggressor, Tom decides to fight for his life, marriage, and his career. In doing so he discovers he is a pawn in deeper corporate corruption connected to the lucrative merger.

On its surface, *Disclosure* is an erotic corporate thriller about sexual harassment with the twist that it is a male employee who is targeted by a more powerful female executive.[2] The gender reversal is contrary to the facts of most workplace harassment, which is statistically overwhelmingly committed by men against women. And the film certainly is, as one reviewer called it, "high-tech, low-brow stuff."[3]

In an interview Crichton revealed that the concept for the main scenario came from an anecdote he heard from 1988.[4] That scenario, especially when combined with the presence of actors like Douglas and Moore in this risqué on-screen entanglement, can suck up all the attention—and reviews and scholarly work engage with *Disclosure* almost entirely on this level. Contextually this makes sense, given that Douglas had already made both *Fatal Attraction* (Adrian Lyne, 1987) and *Basic Instinct* (Paul Verhoeven, 1992), two popular thrillers featuring sexually aggressive, independent, professional women who target a man after an affair. The idea conjured by several reviewers was that films like *Disclosure*, *Fatal Attraction*, and *Basic Instinct* present a monstrous woman who must be destroyed as a kind of white male backlash wish-fulfillment narrative against recent women's liberation and affirmative action gains. Likewise, Moore had recently starred in *Indecent Proposal* (Adrian Lyne, 1993), an erotic drama about a billionaire who offers a married man a million dollars in exchange for one night with his wife.

Still, setting aside the foreground narrative, *Disclosure* is set against a compelling backdrop that invites a deeper conversation about the toxic culture of the tech industry. I assert it is critical—not incidental—that *Disclosure* is set in that specific corporate milieu. In fact, for his book, Crichton researched tech companies and considered feminism in relation to that industry's culture.[5] The film also provides an opportunity to look at the changing role of women in computing and connections to ideologies of white male genius that have plagued Silicon Valley, putting the industry under intense scrutiny in recent years. As a part of this conversation I also look at the lesser-known 1993 television movie *Stalking Laura* (directed by Michael Switzer and also known as *I Can Make You Love Me*), made just one year before *Disclosure*. It dramatizes the true story of a workplace mass shooting at a Silicon Valley defense contractor instigated by a male computer specialist's obsession, harassment, and stalking of a young female colleague. As I'll argue, this incident also forms a significant part of *Disclosure*'s contextual backdrop.

By doing a background reading of the site in which *Disclosure*'s drama unfolds—a successful tech company in the mid-1990s—we can then see *Disclosure*'s "foreground" narrative and "background" context holistically as continuous with Crichton's larger investment in conversations about advanced technology and the growing daily reality of electronic life. In this chapter I show how *Disclosure* lodges an early critique of the tech world. And I make clear how the salacious story on the surface of the film—while galvanizing a debate around women's liberation and sexual harassment—masks a deeper consideration of ingrained toxic gender norms in the tech industry.

UNDERSTANDING THE TECH WORLD'S MASCULINE CULTURE

To analyze *Disclosure* as a technothriller, we must understand the gendered history of the tech world. During World War II women played key roles in computing, performing critical functions like manually calculating artillery trajectories. Although the work required advanced mathematical skills, it was then considered unglamorous and uncreative—plus, women could be paid less than men. When programmable computers were developed, beginning with the first general-purpose electronic digital computer, called the ENIAC, in 1945, women became the first computer programmers.[6] Large mainframe computers were often quite buggy, and they frequently crashed; women offered both reliable human calculations and innovated effective coding methods. Exceptional female icons of computation are somewhat known, such as Grace Hopper, who was involved in programming the Harvard Mark I computer, which contributed calculations to the Manhattan Project. And there was Katherine Johnson, the human computer who calculated flight paths for NASA's manned space program in the 1960s and whose story was documented in the book *Hidden Figures*, and later popularized by the film of the same name.[7] What is less commonly known is that women had a dominating presence in the field in the 1940s and after—but then came a significant downturn, as is clear from the proportion of women attaining degrees in computer science. In 1970 women accounted for just over 13 percent of graduates, and this percentage rose steadily until 1984, when the numbers peaked at 37 percent, then plummeted.[8] By 2022 around 20 percent of computer science majors were women, even though women now make up more than half of college students in general.

Both popular commentators and scholars have proposed theories about why women are either not entering computing or remaining in the field. Some blame the gender gap on a manufactured, intentional cultural encoding of computing itself as masculine (see introduction). For example, a 2014 National Public Radio story suggested that the 1984 drop in women in computer science was related to the concurrent rise of the home computer and marketing that targeted boys, leading to greater baseline computer literacy among young men by the time they entered college.[9] Popular science magazines like *Scientific American* have suggested that women and girls do not inherently lack interest in engineering and computer science but are impacted by gender stereotyping and the "masculine defaults" that have evolved in culture, education, and industry.[10] Scholar Carly A. Kocurek and others have pointed to the deeply rooted sexism in the games industry and broader tech culture and the masculine encoding of video games and arcades. Scholars of gender and computing have attributed the dramatic drop in women in computing to hostile work atmospheres, stereotypes around women as less technically capable, perceptions of men as more effective leaders, and the marginalization of women as less "committed" to the work.[11] This was already being observed in the early 1980s, as shown in Sherry Turkle's groundbreaking sociological study of people's intense relationships with their computers. In it she describes an emergent culture of both the male tech nerd "loser" and the "suspect" woman hacker who excessively embrace the logic of the computer as a way of life.[12] She writes: "There are few women hackers. This is a male world. Though hackers would deny that theirs is a macho culture, the preoccupation with winning and of subjecting oneself to increasingly violent tests makes their world peculiarly male in spirit, peculiarly unfriendly to women."[13] Significant technofeminist interventions in the 1990s, such as the work of Judy Wajcman, began to identify how "the close affinity between technology and the dominant ideology of masculinity itself shapes the production and use of particular technologies."[14] This landmark work began to theorize power relations expressed through men's domination of the technological industries and show that there was a political dimension to the social construction of advanced technology as masculine.

Other scholars, including Niki Panteli, Janet Stack, and Harvie Ramsay, have drawn further attention to the masculine culture of the tech industry, which, as they describe, "takes as axiomatic masculine ways of doing things as natural and appropriate. It thus makes the organisational milieu comfortable for men, while forcing women to accept and conform to these to succeed, and/or by defining them as less capable regardless of how they behave."[15] More recently the toxic masculinity of Silicon Valley workplaces has come to public attention through high-profile lawsuits, the exposure of ugly harassment campaigns such as GamerGate, and journalistic attention to the persisting "bro culture" hostile to women, trans and nonbinary people, and people of color.[16] This scenario is complicated by a culture of silence created by the tech industry's standard nondisclosure agreements, or NDAs.

Still, some incidents have exposed industry bias, such as a leaked internal memo written by a Google middle manager opposing gender diversity efforts because he believed women's immanent biological and psychological differences make them less suited to technological work.[17] In 2017 the *Atlantic* published an excoriating report on the experiences of women in the tech world, littered with evidence of systematic dismissiveness, exclusion, silencing, pay disparities, unwanted sexual advances (even outright predation), undermining behavior, promotion inequity, and the persisting fallacy that their inclusion signals reduced rigor.[18]

Tech's gender inequity cannot be separated from the so-called dot-com boom, which reached its height in the 1990s. According to Goldman Sachs, the dot-com boom accounted for "the longest period of economic expansion in the United States after World War II."[19] In other words it was a new gold rush, with enormous wealth to be gained when industry and Wall Street realized the vast potential of—and lucrative returns on—computing. In light of this it is hard not to think of hostility toward women in the workplace as pushback against affirmative action efforts and inclusivity measures that would lead to more equitable gains. By the early 2000s women made up only 9 percent of the tech workforce.[20]

In 2014 large tech companies like Google, Apple, Twitter, and eBay, among others, came under public pressure to release demographic statistical data. Several companies committed to investing in diversity efforts, particularly around ethnicity and gender.[21] Historian of technology Mar Hicks suggests that a historical perspective would reveal the origins of the gathering cynicism toward the tech world's effusiveness and empty promises. They write: "Because Silicon Valley seems to be pointing the way to our national and even global future, it is difficult to critique it and to imagine alternatives. . . . By taking us out of our current moment and context and showing us a different scenario, we can better unpack the roots of what has now become normalized to the point of seeming inevitable and unchangeable."[22]

Hicks's words are also useful for thinking about the visual culture of technology as another way of understanding how gendered representations and ideologies of technology manifest in popular media. The women in *Disclosure* embody ideas about women in technology in a way that is representative of the film's moment. More importantly, the women also, as I argue, provide insight not only into a public discourse on sexual harassment but specifically into a toxic, masculine-coded tech world.

Though the beginnings of a real public reckoning with the tech world's rampant bias postdates *Disclosure*, the beginnings of a conversation around gender, feminism, and the tech industry comes together in the film. In fact, virtually all the problems related to the "bro culture" characterized above are painstakingly illustrated—quite didactically, as I will show. This is not something that is retroactively ascribed but something the source material's author was grappling with. In a 1994 interview with Charlie Rose upon the release of the book *Disclosure*, Crichton described an awareness of academic feminist discourses and the aversion for those ideas in high-tech companies: "As soon as they [tech professionals] heard the word 'professor' they turned away. No—not interested in anything academic. And I was absolutely stopped in my tracks because I thought . . . in the workplace, no one knows about it, no one cares about it, and on the contrary, there is a kind of rough-and-ready, very fast-paced way of addressing harassment."[23]

In the next section I return to the key film to think about that gulf between the gender politics of the film's moment and tech companies' cultures to consider how director Barry Levinson's interpretation of *Disclosure* grapples with perceptions of women in the tech industry. I look at the ways the film unpacks how certain kinds of patriarchal behaviors are subtly protected, how abuses of power are normalized, and the perplexing image of a monstrous female tech leader who proves to be as toxic, chauvinistic, and abusive as any man. I argue this exposes an underlying corrosiveness that supersedes conventional gender roles, one that reinscribes the significance of the particular corporate setting portrayed and ultimately indicts the tech industry itself.

To accomplish this I engage in an oppositional reading that refocuses on background—on the subtle, even the unseen, and the absent. To be clear: this is not done to recuperate the narrative from what some have critiqued as a postfeminist or antifeminist stance on Crichton's part. I do not litigate whether the film is feminist or not; others have already thoughtfully engaged in that conversation. Sara-Jane Finlay and Natalie Fenton, for example, describe how in this film "misogyny is often hidden behind quasi-feminist rhetoric," particularly in terms of casting Meredith in the role of a femme fatale.[24] Scholars Valerie S. Terry and Edward Schiappa saw the film (and its source) as emblematic of a backlash against feminism in American culture in the 1980s and 1990s, and as antifeminist despite its purported egalitarian positioning.[25] Some reviewers picked up on this debate, calling the narrative "a male hand grenade tossed into the sexual harassment minefield the workplace has become."[26] But my approach engages a different conversation, specifically about the technothriller from the perspective of gender and difference, as a way of thinking about how *Disclosure* contributes to the sociotechnical imaginary around advanced computation and communications technologies.

READING *DISCLOSURE* AS TECHNOTHRILLER

As mentioned, my reading of *Disclosure* focuses on the unseen and the subtleties of its context, but it is important to begin with what we see first: the computer and the girl. The first image of the film is an animated, rotating, metallic letter *e* on a computer screen announcing an email, then the email's contents being read aloud by a young girl. Synthesized computer music plays in the background. We meet Tom Sanders at home, first hearing him and his wife, Susan Hendler (Caroline Goodall), during their routine morning chaos of getting their two children ready for school and leaving for work. Tom, who has just asked his son to stop playing computer games and finish getting ready, has a stain on his tie, and Susan is on a business call. Tom's willful daughter isn't minding him, even when he pulls rank as the father. In other words, *Disclosure* sets the stage by linking technology and gender specifically through the young girl, who represents a "digital native" generation and the future of technologized life.

Within a few minutes the film shows several novel technologies: a home computer, an email, a printer, video games, a mobile phone, virtual reality, CD-ROMs, and a video call using webcam technology. The Sanders family's various gadgets are, in addition to being signifiers of an electronic life, also a sign of their privilege. It plunges viewers headlong into a conversation about the increased presence of advanced technology in our lives. The family leaves their large, well-appointed Seattle home. Tom is excited about the promotion he believes he will be getting later that day; he and Susan discuss how much they have and how much wealthier they will be.

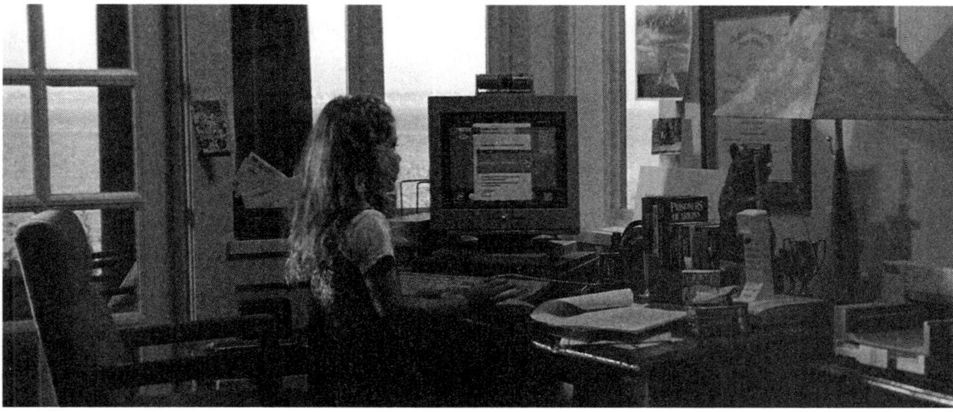

Tom's workplace, DigiCom, is also symbolically key to setting the scene for understanding the dynamics that unfold around gender and the tech industry. As Tom circulates among his coworkers, we see how the film plays with opacity and transparency in the space of the tech company itself, as well as the narrative. The interior is a multilevel design with an atrium in the center and glass walls, which seems superficially welcoming and open, but effectively combines the panoptic architectural space with a false sense of transparency (and implied fidelity) among employees. The DigiCom office set was built for *Disclosure* in the Warner Bros. studio and, per Levinson's direction, was inspired by Alfred Hitchcock's *Rear Window* (1954), a psychological thriller in which an injured, homebound man observes the intimate lives of his neighbors across a courtyard through his rear windows. *Disclosure*'s production designer, Neil Spisak, described the significance of the severe glass and brick style of the interior, which invokes the feeling of looking in on the private lives of employees.[27] Like Tom's life, the DigiCom architecture transforms from a

FIGURE 7.1

A young girl opens her father's business email at home. In this single image is a home computer, webcam, email, cordless phone, and printer, with a female subject at the center. *Disclosure* (Warner Bros., 1994).

sense of light, ease, and legibility into a surveillance space of opaque aims and secret agendas that erode Tom's position and stability. As scholar Carol Watts observes, "Openness begins to connote vulnerability. . . . The workplace, at first presented as a space of reassuringly transparent social relations, turns into a virtual world operated by hidden forces, a place of dark corners and barely discerned voices, of voyeurism as strategy."[28] The set mobilizes its form to borrow from the psychological tension of *Rear Window* through its visual associations.

This mise-en-scène sets the stage for Tom's circumstances to unravel from stability to extreme vulnerability. In small office interactions that betray his entitlement, we see that he does not realize his own precarity until the system doesn't work for him and he is forced to open his eyes to the true nature of his workplace.

Disclosure procedurally reveals the masculine culture of the tech industry in the 1990s. The technothriller takes pains to enumerate the casually sexist, male-centric atmosphere endemic to DigiCom, with Tom as the audience's access point to the tech world. Tom is presented as thinking of himself as a "good" guy who works well with his female peers and subordinates. But through interactions with his coworkers, viewers learn that he was a womanizer before he was married, that he bears a strong sense of entitlement within the space, and that he reinforces chauvinist positions in his "bro culture" sociality with male colleagues. Upon entering his workplace, Tom sees a woman with shapely legs in a business suit and high heels climbing the stairs. Tom pauses to openly stare at her as she ascends, with a pleased look on his face. After conferring with his administrator, Cindy Chang (Jacqueline Kim), he casually swats her on the bottom with a file folder. The gesture is highlighted in a close-up, as is her lack of reaction—suggesting this is commonplace at the office. He engages in casually sexist talk with male employees, even within the earshot of female coworkers. Chauvinism feels both acceptable and unchecked in the culture of the company.

Conversations between Tom and male colleagues painstakingly demonstrate the toxic culture of male sociality. In one scene, a coworker teases Tom after overhearing that Meredith has summoned him to an evening meeting, asking Tom whether he has a "boner," insisting men are inherently more sexual, and goading him to sleep with her. In other

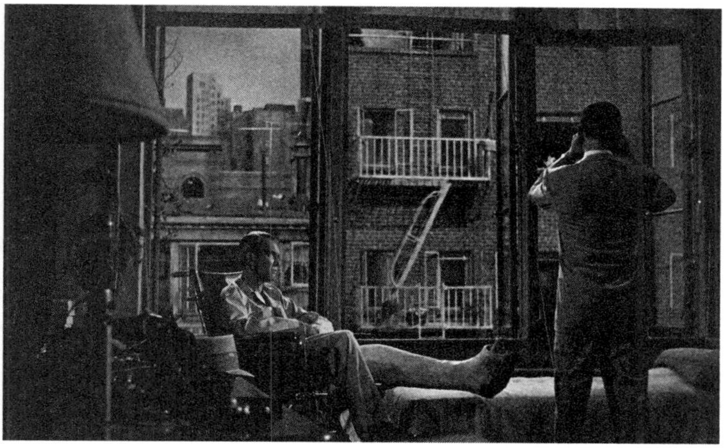

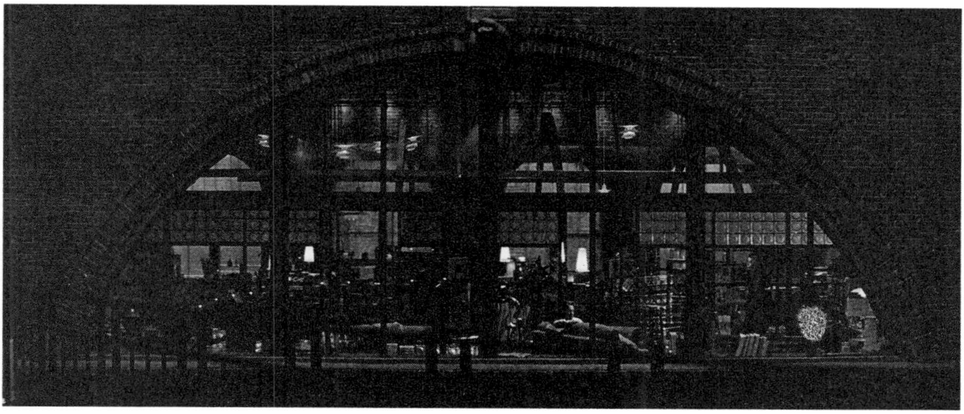

FIGURE 7.2

In Alfred Hitchcock's *Rear Window* (Paramount Pictures, 1954), a bored photographer recovering from an accident observes the private lives of others through their windows across a shared courtyard. Note the glass and brick construction that inspired the look of the DigiCom office.

FIGURE 7.3

A view of DigiCom with brick façade and glass offices in *Disclosure* (Warner Bros., 1994). The red brick and metal framing invokes *Rear Window*.

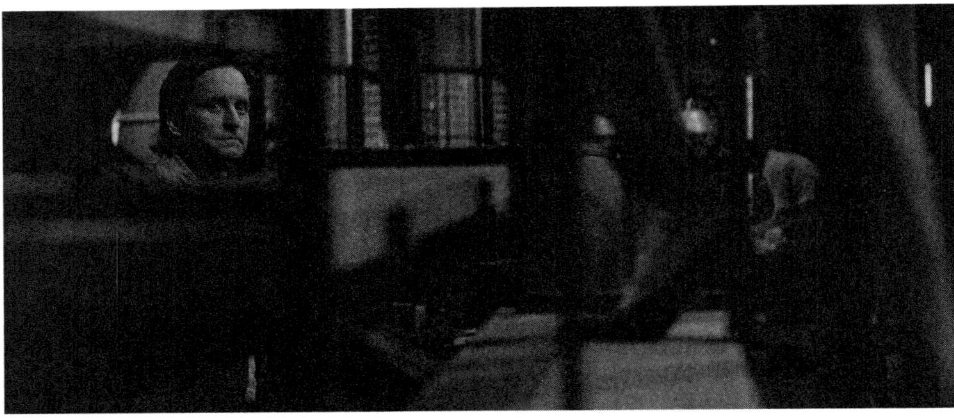

scenes, coworkers react jokingly to Meredith's appearance. She is conventionally attractive and presents herself with a feminine, sexy corporate polish. They suggest her ascension must have been gained through sexual favors with the CEO.

Meredith's presence and advancement throw Tom's life into disarray. He perceives her as an interloper who has swooped in and stolen his promotion. He falls back on gendered notions of her lack of technical acumen to undermine her to his team, having an overblown emotional reaction and complaining, "This is a technical division—she doesn't know the difference between software and a cashmere sweater!" A female engineer, always referred to by her last name, Hunter (Suzie Plakson), holds her own, snarkily responding, "All I know is any woman has to be twice as good as a man and work twice as hard to get the same job for less pay." But Tom and the other men are dismissive. The nature of their talk illustrates how the space is "for" men and that women must assimilate into male norms, should they wish to persist there.

FIGURE 7.4

Tom observes the shapely legs of a woman who climbs the stairs at DigiCom. *Disclosure* (Warner Bros., 1994).

Through a series of presentations at the company, the film highlights false utopian promises of the tech world, particularly around bringing humanity together despite differences. The first speech, delivered by slick DigiCom CEO Bob Garvin (Donald Sutherland), touts the company's will to finally break the "glass ceiling" by hiring a woman to run the division. This signals that Garvin is aware of the gender disparity in his industry and that the appearance of it is potentially damaging enough that he knows the company must get ahead of it. Immediately following, Meredith outlines her optimistic vision, which embraces a post-identity understanding of what DigiCom's technologies will offer. "We offer through technology what religion and revolution promised but never delivered," she declares, "freedom from the physical body, freedom from race and gender, from nationality and personality, from place and time. Communicating by cellular phone and handheld computer PDA and built-in fax modem, we can relate to each other as pure consciousness." That sentiment signals the zeitgeist of a democratizing utopian future popularized during the 1990s, particularly around the Internet's connectivity—a promise that has fallen spectacularly short in the twenty-first century. Even in this "forward-thinking" space of the tech company, we can see this is a pipe dream. Ironically, on the level of filmmaking itself, image making telegraphs the degree to which white men run things, make decisions, and operate in key leadership positions. There are some Black extras who circulate in the background of DigiCom, but none of them have lines or any consequence for the story. Still, in highlighting the utopian promises in Meredith's speech, the potency of the film's critique is only heightened thirty years later.

The film lays the critical sexual harassment scene on thick, with the villainous Meredith conducting herself like a predator who likes power games. She holds an evening meeting in her dimly lit office, offering Tom a rare wine she has procured especially for him, and making suggestive comments about how she likes "all the boys under me to be happy." She sits too close, engages in sexual and demeaning talk about his wife, and removes her blazer. When Tom discourages her, she agrees to refocus on the work, if he will rub her shoulders. Meredith's administrator sticks her head in, excuses herself for the night, and locks the door behind her, ensuring no one will interrupt them. Meredith approaches him from

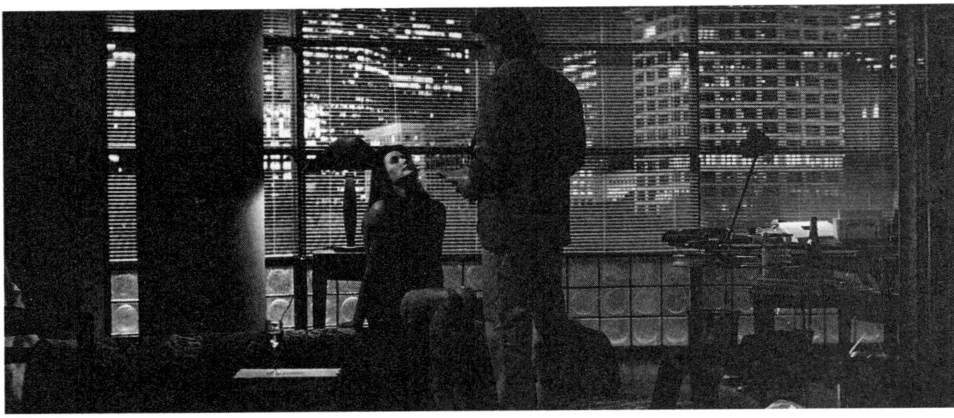

behind while he is on a call to address the technical problems on his production line, then aggressively forces herself on him, despite his many protestations.

The trashy scene culminates with an angry reversal in which Tom tries to assert his own dominance and command the sexual encounter, forcefully kissing her and tearing her panties off. But before things go further, Tom catches his reflection in a window, refuses to proceed, grabs his clothes, and leaves, with the enraged Meredith taunting and threatening him. Meredith turns monstrous, a femme fatale shrieking after him with her voluminous breasts pouring out of her lace bra, her face twisted. Tom feels shame and confusion. He hides the incident from his wife, showers, and tries to put it out of his mind. In the night he has a nightmare that his CEO, Garvin, sexually harasses him, repeating the same words Meredith (Garvin's emissary) used to seduce him: "Now you have the power. You have something I want." Tom awakes, screaming.

Faced with a changing corporate world in which he must compete with women, Tom feels emasculated and afraid of becoming one of the

FIGURE 7.5

Meredith sexually harasses Tom in her locked, dark office after business hours. *Disclosure* (Warner Bros., 1994).

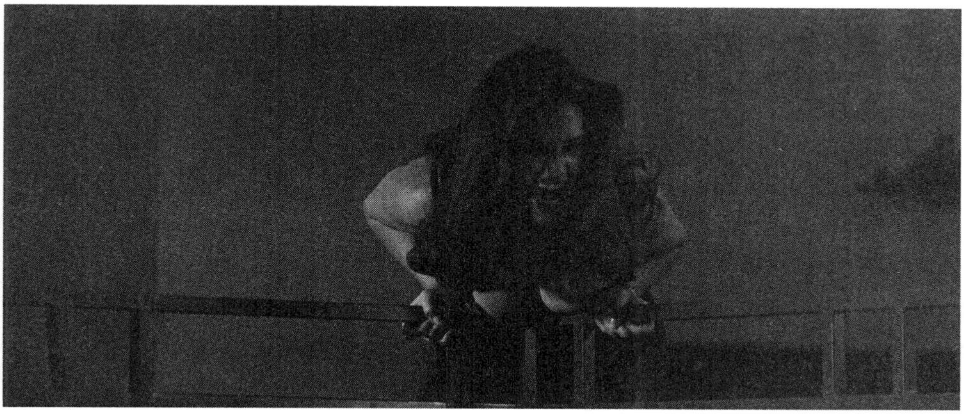

unemployed "ghosts" he sees on his daily ferry ride to work: middle-aged male executives commuting in their business suits, perpetually looking for work and shut out by changing times. Many reviewers at the time discussed the film in terms of male anxieties around being displaced by powerful women. For example, Caryn James of the *New York Times* describes how the "unspoken mantra of *Disclosure* is 'Women in power are scary.'"[29] A *Boston Globe* reviewer put it in more phallic terms: "This year, in movies thinly disguised as antidotes to political correctness, women are being set up as demented heavies, guilty of the charge of going too far. . . . The real button being pushed in these films is male panic at being forced to confront a certain shrinkage in what had been their dominance."[30] This tension is surely at work, but I believe these dynamics are a symptom of a deeper filmic intervention into a pernicious masculinist culture that had already taken hold in the tech world.

Reviews at the time of the film's release tended to mention the featured technologies only in passing, largely focusing on the more salacious

FIGURE 7.6

Meredith in her terrifying true form, weaponizing her sexuality to climb the corporate ladder. *Disclosure* (Warner Bros., 1994).

material and on the spectacularly villainous Meredith as a representational outrage. Much of the conversation was framed around a perceived backlash against women's liberation, and women's increasing presence in professional spaces as troublesome for men. For example, the *Boston Herald* called *Disclosure* "a paranoid fantasy aimed at aging, male baby boomers whose sexual powers are waning and who are terrified by the presence of young, ambitious women in the workplace. It's a "high-tech lynching" of the Eternally Evil Female: audiences will eat it up."[31] Many other critics echoed this perceived demonization of the liberated corporate woman, saying the film casts Meredith as "a fantasy spiderwoman, [a] product of the patriarchal power system, dreamt up and subsequently destroyed by men because they find her just too scary."[32] It is true that Meredith is presented as a sneering, conniving, vulgar, unrelentingly awful corporate monstrosity. But I read her presence as a critique of what the tech has wrought in its purest form; she is effectively an embodiment of the industry's values. In Meredith, Tom contends with a cypher for an unchecked chauvinist tech culture protected by the institution's greed and self-interest. It is only in facing that ugly manifestation, and nearly being destroyed by it, that Tom understands its truly toxic dimensions.

From Tom's nightmare the film transitions directly to a technological dream of virtual reality, showing a demonstration the next day. The DigiCom "corridor" is an interactive database imaged on-screen as a cathedral lined with file drawers, accessible through a VR headset and gloves. The demo is for the benefit of the merger but conveniently provides an illustrative example of virtual reality engagement to the film audience. Reviewers paid relatively little attention to the VR scenes, at least in part due to their being underwhelming from a special-effects standpoint. And it is true that the visual representation of virtual space was not impressive, even by the standards of the day. Still, the presence of VR is loaded with symbolic meaning. The simulated spaces of the virtual reality corridor operate as a metaphor for a new and somewhat disorienting space and as a space of total construction in which imagined artificial realities may greatly depart from the lived world.

The imaging of virtual reality technology within *Disclosure* is not simply a novel gimmick but signals a destabilization of the real connected

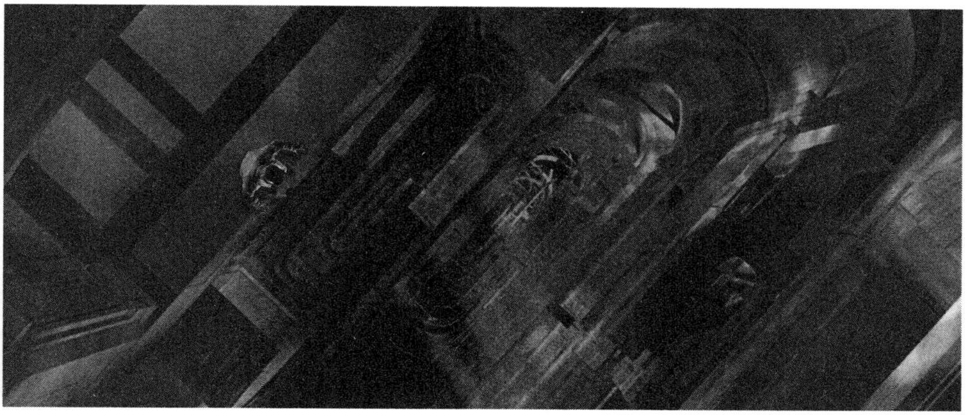

to innovation. Virtual space is visited twice in the film. The first time is when Meredith intentionally misleads Tom about the time of a demo, and he arrives late. We observe a representative of the partner company for the merger experience the virtual space with wonder. But Tom's tardiness makes him appear unreliable and disorganized to company heads, including DigiCom's CEO.

The second time is a four-minute sequence of Tom engaging the VR system to seek the truth in virtual files—and evidence that can exonerate him and verify Meredith's guilt. Since, in the process of the mediation, Tom's file access is revoked, he must engage the DigiCom VR corridor demo database to find the incriminating files before Meredith can delete them. Tom enters the corridor and immediately experiences a disorienting near "fall" into a chasm. Steadying himself at the edge of the drop, he finds his balance and moves on. This moment seems to metaphorize Tom's having nearly "fallen" for the trap of the sexual harassment case, but then successfully navigating it.

FIGURE 7.7

Tom, disoriented in the DigiCom virtual reality "corridor," almost falls into a chasm. *Disclosure* (Warner Bros., 1994).

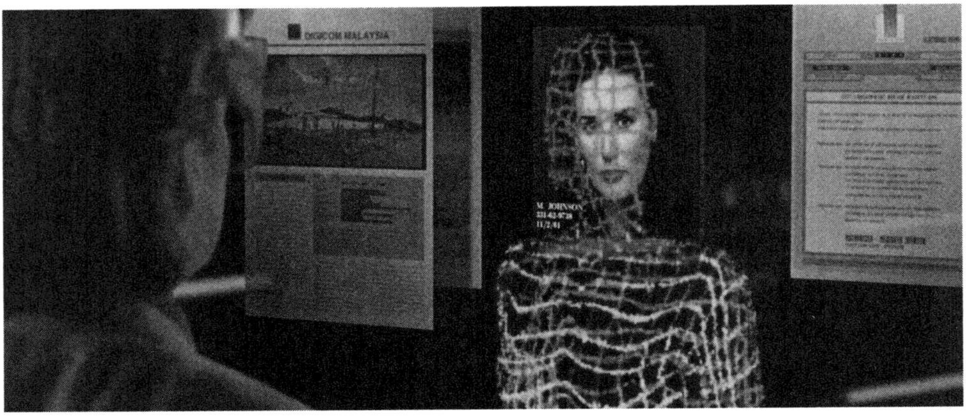

Tom finds evidence that Meredith has ordered changes to the production line protocols to appease the Malaysian government, but then pinned the resulting product failures on him. But she is also in the system: we see a green, wire frame human form with a photo of Meredith where its head should be. Like a kind of ghostly terminator, Meredith's avatar glides through the system, deleting everything and attempting to engineer a new "reality." As an emissary of corporate power, she is attempting to make another truth by destroying evidence. So, in both cases, the virtual appears in relation to destabilization of the "truth."

That concern about the relationship between information and knowledge comes up in the film itself. During a brief scene in which Garvin attempts to persuade Tom to drop the harassment complaint for the sake of the merger, he opines that Tom's truth no longer matters in the face of the digital: "It's all somebody's version. That's the legacy of the modern age. We have information but no truth . . . little flashes of electrons in a grain of sand." Garvin's statement signals a keen awareness of the destabilized notion of truth that marks the digital era. The function of these two VR

FIGURE 7.8

Tom encounters Meredith's avatar in the virtual reality space of DigiCom's "corridor." *Disclosure* (Warner Bros., 1994).

scenes, then, is to visually represent the manufacturing of realities and to connect that to the specific innovation of VR that emblematizes and agitates this new crisis.

One scholar, Martin Kevorkian, makes a rare, compelling connection between gender and technology in relation to Meredith's suspect status as a woman who has successfully attained dominance in a vicious, male-centered tech industry. Kevorkian writes, "The woman's power is closely associated with her professional and personal commitment to antinatural technology—information technology that consumed the softness of feminine flesh and demeanor, that eats up all manner of comforting cultural markers along the way."[33] Here, the implication is that Meredith's ability to navigate the male-centered technological milieu signals her unnaturalness and her turn away from a socially prescribed feminine role. It is clear she has rejected motherhood and domesticity for corporate life. Even her obsession with her fitness, pointed to in several scenes, is a marker of vanity and self-centeredness, in direct comparison to Tom's wife, Susan, who focuses on the children and neglects her own fitness. But this position is contradicted by the fact that Meredith turns out to be making terrible technical choices and that there are other consequential and more ethical women prominently represented in the tech company space.

How the many professional women in *Disclosure* figure into a holistic interpretation sheds light on the tech and gender issues broached by the film. One interpretation is that those female characters are there purely to discredit the sexually liberated image of Meredith. This sentiment is summed up by a *Washington Post* critic who suggests that the film endeavors to put women in their sexual place: "We learn that women who dare to be sexually aggressive, ambitious, and pretty are (a) evil and (b) using their wiles to hide the fact that they can't do the work. Women in sensible clothes, with no makeup and a few laugh lines, *them* you can trust."[34] But, as counterimages to Meredith, who fully embodies the most male-centered norms of that industry, these female characters present a more nuanced image than this position implies.

Tom is surrounded by capable, sharp women who recognize that he is being unjustly railroaded and emerge as allies. Stephanie Kaplan (Rosemary Forsyth), a venerated colleague also passed over for promotion, anonymously points him to Catherine Alvarez (Roma Maffia), a tough-as-nails, high-profile lawyer who specializes in sexual harassment and agrees to support him. Stephanie, known as the "stealth bomber" for her smooth machinations around the office, remains on the periphery of the salacious events, but nudges Tom (through her anonymous emails from "A. Friend") to pay attention to the larger deceit unfolding. Catherine, Tom's lawyer, expertly provides him with tools and critical frameworks to defend himself. She validates his right to seek support as a victim of abuse, despite the powerful gendered social mores that contradict that impulse. Her character is significant as a strong woman who helps Susan (also a lawyer) see the situation for what it is: an abuse of power. Hunter, another experienced engineer and a head of operations at DigiCom, vocally protests the sexist attitudes of the men around her and displays disgust for Meredith's conduct, which Hunter believes harms other women who labor under great duress to be taken seriously in the workplace. Meredith is indeed toxic, and she is responsible for her abusive and dishonest behavior. But she is also a product of a masculine-centered culture, the tech world, and has sought to master it by outplaying the "boys" at their own game.

Tom Sanders comes face-to-face with his own naivete and privilege in the context of an industry that has clearly offered him little friction in the past. This is illustrated through his transformation across the narrative, but critically in his evolving understanding of the women around him as they disclose their own realities. His wife accidentally learns of the sexual incident at a professional function and remains composed, but tears into him later on for keeping it from her. Given the pattern of womanizing in his past and his previous relationship with Meredith, Tom's wife isn't initially certain he's the victim in the situation. She tells him to just smooth relations and move forward; after all, she herself has been sexually harassed her entire career and hasn't made a big deal of it. Responding to what he feels is insensitivity, he has a meltdown, defensively shouting at her and the housekeeper: "Why don't I be that guy, that evil white male you're all complaining about? I'd like that. Then I can fuck everybody. Come on down here Chau-Minh, I want to exercise my dominance; I have a patriarchal *urge*." He angrily throws his lawyer's words that sexual harassment is about power in Susan's face, signaling his newfound politicization around the matter and assuming a moral high ground.

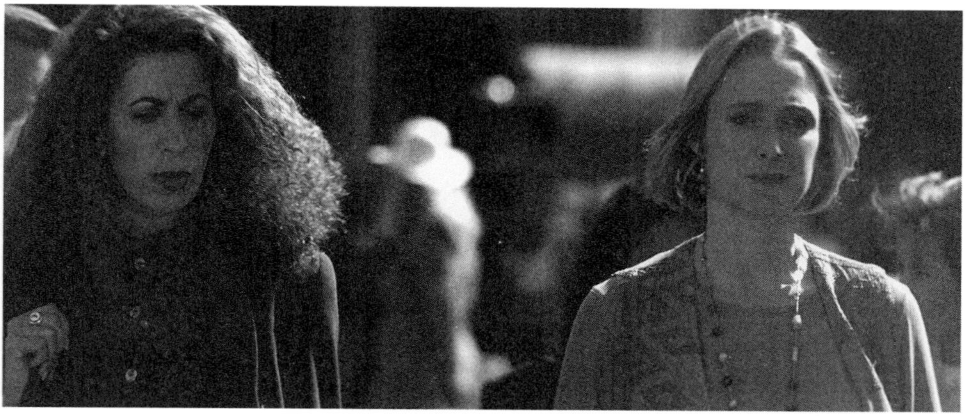

This is an important scene because, on the one hand, he is correct. But on the other he is attempting to school his wife on the matter when she has already communicated that sexual harassment has dogged her entire professional existence as a female lawyer. Perfectly modulated, the scene can be read in both ways. Susan lacks empathy for her husband's predicament, even though she has experienced it herself; but Tom is also insensitive to Susan's everyday realities.

The critical conversation around *Disclosure* largely overlooks the centrality of the women around Tom, configuring them as facile representations to keep the filmmaker out of trouble with feminists. "There are other ambitious, successful women in *Disclosure*, of course," one reviewer commented. "The movie is smart enough to cover its tracks. But these other women are lightweight sops. The lawyer and an engineer—always called by her last name, Hunter—are presented as asexual, unglamorous, unthreatening. No sexy Meredith Johnson power suits for them. Another

FIGURE 7.9

Lawyer Catherine Alvarez speaks with Tom's wife, Susan Hendler, also a lawyer, about the nature of sexual harassment. *Disclosure* (Warner Bros., 1994).

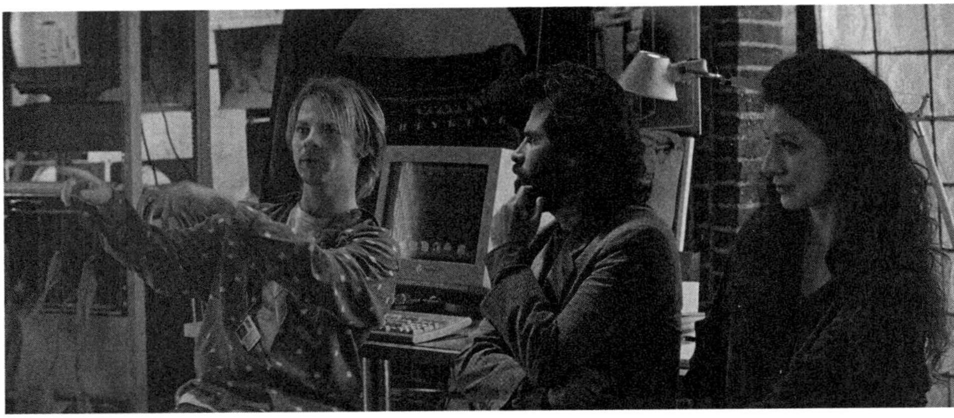

woman who becomes Tom's boss is competent, plain and older."[35] This critique seems to misunderstand what is imaged on-screen by not acknowledging the specificity of the tech company milieu. It ignores, for example, the importance of a key conversation between Tom and Hunter about the gender gap in the tech world. In it Hunter expresses frustration around never having been taken seriously as a candidate for the promotion, despite her advanced technical training and experience. Tom gets defensive and asks whether she is on Meredith's side. She bluntly disagrees, signaling that she resents Meredith's methods: "I studied engineering for eight years. I was the *only* woman in that department. Know what I did? I *worked*. You think I'm on Meredith's side?!" The implication is that Hunter wants to be taken seriously for her achievements. Hunter abhors Meredith's methods, which besmirch her own commitment to professionalism and ethics.

FIGURE 7.10

Hunter, right, as the only female operations lead, contends with the casual sexism of her colleagues and dismissiveness of the "bro culture" at DigiCom. Left of her are two male colleagues with whom Tom has regular sexist banter. *Disclosure* (Warner Bros., 1994).

These women are not "lightweight sops" but complex characters who display shrewd acumen in navigating a fraught professional situation. With Catherine's professional guidance and Susan's unwavering support (despite her persisting annoyance with his naivete and culpability in the situation), Tom navigates the sexual harassment mediation and exposes Meredith for her vicious manipulations. In the mediation he is forced to reflect on his own behavior and how he may have contributed to a hostile workplace for his many competent female colleagues. For example, Cindy testifies that Tom often casually pats her behind and rubs her shoulders in the workplace, something she finds inappropriate, but she believes he is unaware of its impact on her. Meredith's lawyer then exploits Cindy's words to paint Tom as a predator, to Cindy's dismay. Tom and Cindy later establish new workplace boundaries, and Cindy becomes an ally in clearing his name. Later in the film it is revealed that Stephanie is an invaluable and powerful ally who sees through all the slimy corporate maneuvers and responds ethically while also smoothly preserving (and ultimately solidifying) her own position. Together, these female characters are used to address various challenges women face in the tech world to great, albeit subtle, effect.

More subtle still is this technothriller's address of globalization and offshore labor. The critical information Tom uncovers in his VR search is that Meredith has secretly meddled with the CD-ROM production line in Malaysia to please the local government. Her changes have led to excessive failure rates, and since Tom is ultimately responsible, he will be blamed and terminated. This scene points to an invisible component of tech: the unseen, offshore labor of globalization. Viewers only ever see Malaysian workers through layers of media, in a prerecorded Malaysian news clip replayed in a shareholder meeting. There, blurry and undifferentiated in the background, and partially blocked by DigiCom management, are the laborers who manufacture the technology.

On one level, it is important to consider the invisible tech factory workers. Scholar Rajani Sudan noted the unseen but impactful Malaysian bodies, describing at length how they become scapegoated as the problem for technical irregularities, with a woman directing those irregularities to her benefit.[36] These workers become tools for Meredith's corporate dirty work. But this is discovered, and Meredith is ultimately exposed, publicly humiliated, and removed from leadership.

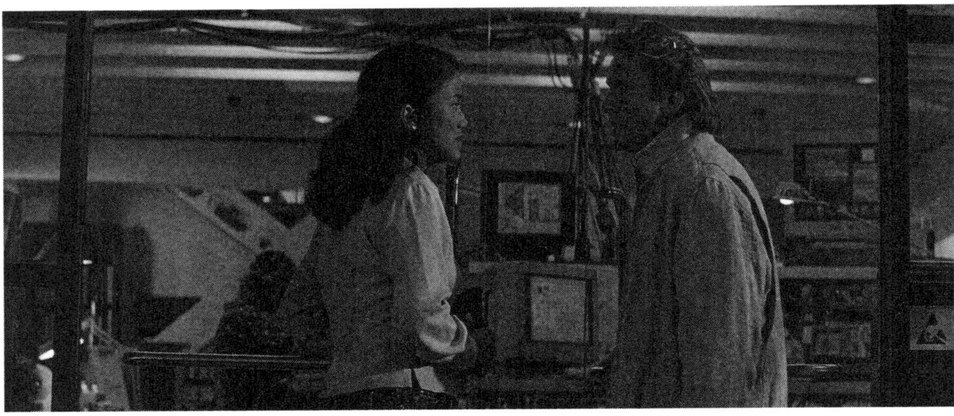

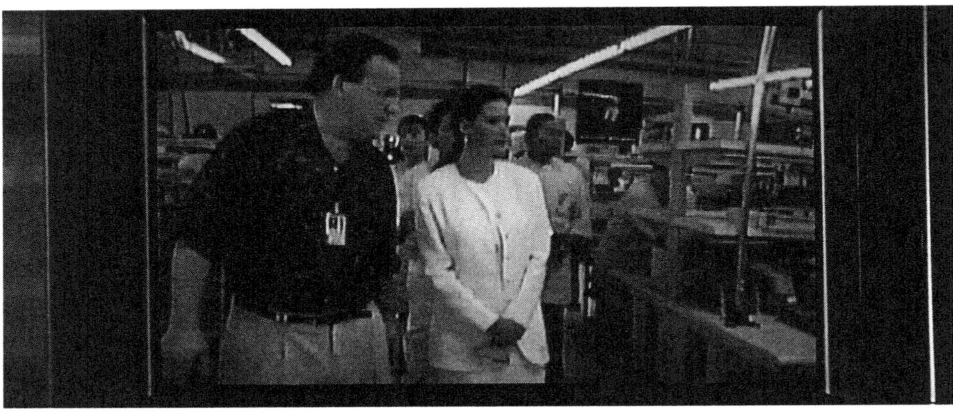

FIGURE 7.11

Cindy, Tom's administrator, is troubled by his chauvinist behavior, but does not see it as predatory. Her statement triggers Tom's self-awareness of his own complicity in the male-centered culture of the tech company. *Disclosure* (Warner Bros., 1994).

FIGURE 7.12

The only time in the film that Malaysian workers are seen is in recorded footage being shown on a monitor during a company meeting. *Disclosure* (Warner Bros., 1994).

With this victory over the scheming, awful Meredith, Tom again expects he will win the position but is surprised and pleased when his secret ally, the highly seasoned and capable Stephanie Kaplan, is selected. Cindy and Hunter look on during the public announcement, applauding the decision. At the end of the tumultuous week, Tom is not ascendant, yet he retains his job and clears his name. But he also sees the world and his place in it very differently. Afterward, Tom runs into Meredith while collecting some files. In case the critique of masculine culture in the film is not perfectly clear to viewers, Meredith utters the telling line, "I'm only playing the game the way you guys set it up, and I'm being punished for it." In other words, she identifies herself as ultimately a product of the tech industry's toxic culture. The departing image is that of Tom, at the end of the day, reading an email from home, vindicated, and welcoming the promise of turning his priorities back to his family. And he has grown up a little. It is an optimistic ending that neatly resolves the pernicious gender gap in the tech world and implies that its male professionals may hold chauvinist views but can have their hearts and minds changed.

STALKING LAURA: A DARKER REALITY OF WOMEN IN THE TECH WORLD

A darker tale of gender-based bias in the tech world would have already been on viewers' minds at the time of *Disclosure*'s release. One year before the novel *Disclosure* was published, a television movie called *Stalking Laura* drew attention to a shocking true instance of workplace harassment and violence against a woman in the tech industry. Also known as *I Can Make You Love Me* and *I Can Make You Love Me: The Stalking of Laura Black*, the film was produced for the CBS television network and first aired in February 1993. The film tells the story of Laura Black, a young engineer who was sexually harassed and stalked in a Silicon Valley tech company.

The real Laura Black was hired in 1984 at the age of twenty-two to be an electronic circuit design engineer at Electromagnetic Systems Labs Inc. (ESL Inc.), a Sunnyvale-based high-tech defense contractor. On her first day Black met software technician Richard Farley, thirty-five years old, who had previously served in the military for a decade, had been at the company for many years, and had a high-security clearance. Farley immediately became obsessed with Black and grew increasingly disturbed and aggressive when she did not reciprocate his romantic interest. But Black faced obstacles to protecting herself because of Farley's adeptness in attaining personal information, which he used to stalk her, and the slow response from her employers. And, at the time, stalking was not illegal. Despite moving four times, Laura was unable to evade Farley. He was eventually fired from the company in 1986, but this did not discourage his behavior. Quite the opposite: he became more intense and persistent. He sent two hundred letters during the time he stalked her; she eventually secured a restraining order.

On February 16, 1988, after four years of terrorizing Black, Farley returned to the ESL offices armed with several weapons and more than a thousand rounds of ammunition and committed a mass shooting, killing seven people and wounding four, including Black.[37] After a five-hour standoff with a SWAT team, he surrendered. Black survived and remained in the tech industry, and Farley was sentenced to death. Partially due to this shocking workplace massacre and subsequent press coverage, stalking was made a crime in California in 1990.

In the film Laura Black (Brooke Shields) is presented as a promising emerging professional in the tech industry. She excitedly wishes her family goodbye and travels from her hometown in Virginia to Sunnyvale, California, where she is going to begin an enviable position as a design engineer for a tech company, the fictitious KEI. The casting of Brooke Shields as Laura was significant, and key for the affective work the film does. Shields was a celebrated beauty and one of the most recognizable faces in the world, but she was also a model and actress who had been sexualized as an underaged girl. This preexisting set of associations would impact the way she would be received as Laura and, by extension, color the perception of this character as a (sexually) disruptive presence in the masculinist Silicon Valley workplace.

Laura is welcomed on her first day and tours the KEI facility, where she meets Richard Farley (Richard Thomas). He is smitten by her and asks her out; she politely declines. She finds an apartment with a female roommate and settles into a new life. Richard becomes immediately fixated on Laura, and the film meticulously details his escalating campaign of stalking and sexual harassment. She arrives early to work on her first day,

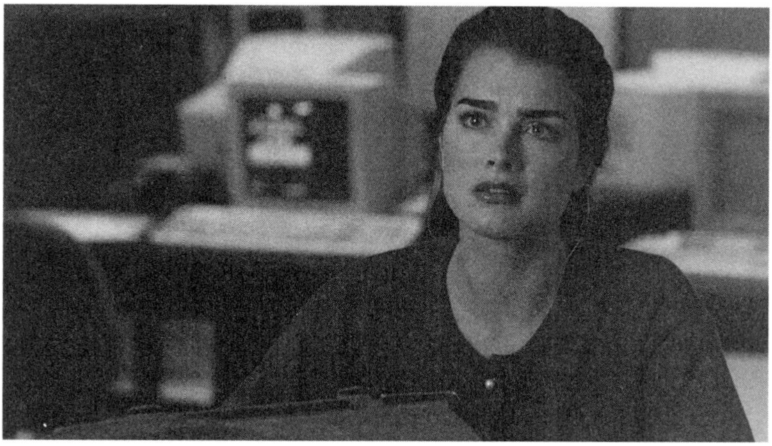

and he is waiting for her inside her locked office. He watches her as she attends her aerobics classes, follows her, shows up unexpectedly, and repeatedly makes advances, despite her patent discouragement. Richard's behavior escalates from casual, unwanted attention to more serious and concerning patterns, indicating stalking and obsession. He repeatedly addresses Laura in terms of their "relationship," and she reminds him that they are strictly professional associates.

Richard believes that he is entitled to her affection and resents her withholding of it. Others begin noticing and joke with her about it, even while Richard contrives to find her home address and begins to accost her there. He sends odd gifts and troubling letters that display delusions of a relationship they do not have, and her roommate urges her to file a complaint at her workplace.

While *Stalking Laura* is focused on the harassment narrative, the film highlights the stark gender gap in the tech world and Laura's drive to persist there despite adversity. For example, Laura mentions to her

FIGURE 7.13

Laura Black (Brooke Shields) is a young female engineer hired at a Silicon Valley tech company. *I Can Make You Love Me / Stalking Laura* (CBS, 1993).

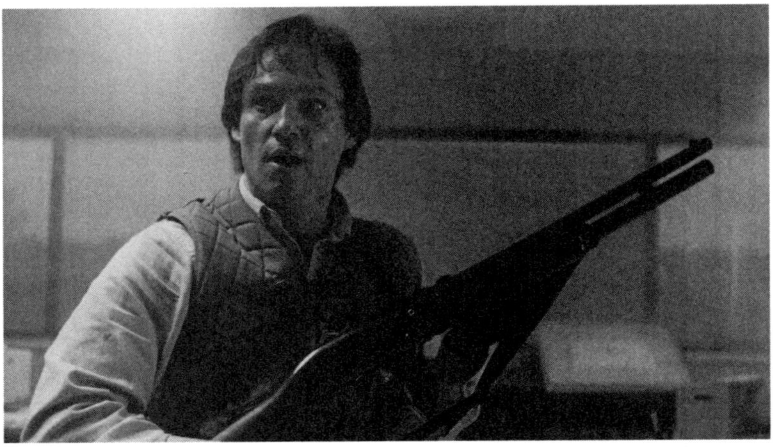

roommate that male engineers outnumbered women ten to one in her degree program. When her roommate later suggests seeking another job to evade her stalker, Laura displays a strong awareness of the norms of working in a male-dominated field and what it would mean for her to capitulate: "I work with sixty guys. I'm the only woman in my department. There are people just waiting for me to pick up my dolls and go home."

Richard's intimidation and harassment against Laura persist for four years. Richard asserts she owes him her attention, that his romantic needs supersede her free will, and that her unwillingness to satisfy him warrants a violent response. He grows increasingly obsessive and delusional and threatens to harm her family. At work, KEI human resources representatives continually attempt to impugn Laura for presumably inviting Richard's behavior and seem to place company interests and Richard's position above her safety. They negate and dismiss her concerns as a woman and ignore her repeated attempts to draw attention to the warning

FIGURE 7.14

Richard Farley (Richard Thomas), Laura's coworker, becomes obsessed and commits a workplace massacre. *I Can Make You Love Me / Stalking Laura* (CBS, 1993).

signs of his behavior. What is communicated, pointedly, through the ironic presence of an African American female HR representative as the face of KEI, is that the culture of the company is one that protects Richard and holds Laura suspect as an attractive young woman who "must have done something" to compel his fixation.

After Richard physically threatens Laura after seeing her speak to another man in a bar, she reports him again. KEI finally takes action, and an HR representative threatens Richard with termination if he does not cease his behavior. In response Richard insists that he has guns and that he will commit murder and suicide if he loses his job. With that Richard is fired and escorted from the building, but Laura is frustrated to learn that the official explanation for the dismissal is the "quality of his work" rather than sexual harassment. Richard breaks into her home again but leaves peacefully before she needs to use the gun a friend has loaned her for protection. When Laura learns from her supervisor that the unresolved stalking is interfering with the approval of her security clearance—and thus her advancement at the company—she finally processes a restraining order.

One day before the court date for making the restraining order permanent, Richard enters KEI heavily armed and commits a workplace massacre. With procedural detail, the film follows Richard as he navigates the corridors of a typical tech space, firing on employees in their offices and cubicles as he seeks Laura. He blasts his way through security doors and shoots Laura in the shoulder, but leaves her to continue his violent spree. Laura comes to and seeks safety while Richard stalks the halls, looking for more targets and firing at computer terminals. The SWAT team arrives and attempts to secure the safety of the many people remaining in the building, ultimately providing little help to Laura, who manages to escape on her own and survives her injuries. After a standoff of several hours, Richard surrenders, still fixated on whether Laura will remember what happened.

Stalking Laura aired a year before *Disclosure*, so audiences were likely aware of these disturbing real-life events, which formed part of a public imaginary around women's roles in the tech world. While the term *incel* postdates this film, what is imaged is a prototype of the so-called involuntary celibates profile.[38] A male supremacist ideology widely circulated

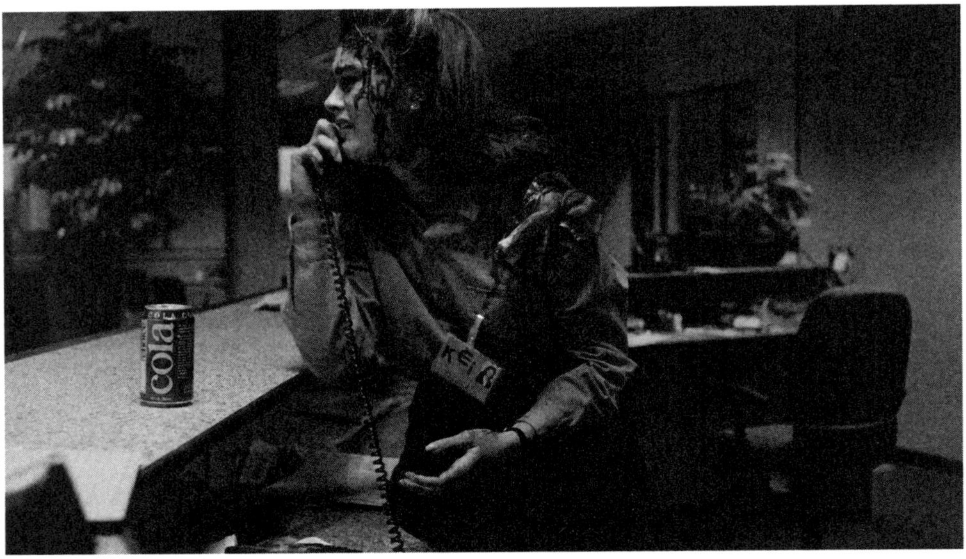

online, it advocates for misogyny, violence against women, and sexual subjugation as an extension of asserting entitlement to women, whom they consider genetically inferior to men. Richard Farley fits the bill with his normative white male presentation, extremist response to frustrated demands for female attention, and ultimately his nihilistic outburst of a mass shooting after being rejected.

If we look at this film through the lens of the technothriller and think about what it reveals about the presence of women in a masculine-centered tech culture, it exposes the ugliest, most extreme version of a space that is openly known to be hostile to women. This television movie, which is illustrative in its procedural retelling of the events, is less focused on the context of the tech company and more directly concerned with mining Richard's "fatal attraction" for Laura. In fact, some poster art for

FIGURE 7.15

During the mass shooting, Laura reaches out for rescue while trapped at KEI. *I Can Make You Love Me / Stalking Laura* (CBS, 1993).

Stalking Laura appropriated that phrase and even used similar fonts to invoke the psychological thriller *Fatal Attraction* (Adrian Lyne, 1987), likely to borrow from its popularity. However, as in *Disclosure*, it is not incidental that this takes place in a tech company or that the target is a female engineer. In the fictionalization Laura, as an attractive, young, female engineer, becomes an immediate target for annihilative rage in a space encoded as one of white male entitlement. It is the worst possible iteration of a commonplace hostility that poses men as the norm and as authentic bearers of technology and women as interlopers who enter at their own risk. While I am not presuming to psychologize the fictionalized Richard Farley, much less the actual man, the gendered themes I have mentioned certainly bubble to the surface. What is exposed in the film, a version of the lived experiences of a real Laura Black, is the obscene underbelly of a chauvinistic workplace culture laid bare.

The television movie does not have the cinematic spectacle of a large studio film but rather a lower-budget, commercial "B movie" quality. However, it does feature major film personalities in Shields and Thomas, and more importantly, the film is unflinching in the procedural unfolding of the horrific stalking and mass murder. It expressly connects the professional space, the escalating dynamics, and the outburst of violence with a sense of entitlement to Laura as the object of a disturbed defense tech worker's perverse affection. In the then-novel setting of the Silicon Valley workplace, the backdrop of the tech industry provides key clues to a male-oriented culture that, in the lived-world example, creates a hostile space that makes it difficult for women to protect themselves.

WHAT IS DISCLOSED IN *DISCLOSURE*?

What is disclosed in *Disclosure*? What does the siting of *Stalking Laura* in a tech company help us understand about the horrible incident imaged? When viewed through the lens of these two films, what can we learn about the sociotechnical imaginary of the tech world? While *Disclosure* wraps the problem up nicely as a story of a pernicious element (Meredith) neutralized through a system that ultimately rights itself, *Stalking Laura* is more focused on survivorship, consciousness-raising, and better legislation. But underneath there remains a cloying sense that Richard Farley's position was merely an overblown expression of a more subtle implicit value system present in the tech world.

In this chapter I stretched the boundaries of the technothriller to dig beneath its surface and think about the role that gender plays in its formation—especially around what has been manufactured as a reality. *Disclosure*, in addition to being an erotic thriller, stands as an early attempt to address gender problems in the tech industry. With its multiple significant female roles, this is not a directorial accident but integral to the story being told. My "background" reading of what populates the world-building of *Disclosure* reveals submerged tensions, concerns around the uncertainty of what lies on the horizon of a new digital era, and women's roles as drivers (not bystanders) of that future. *Disclosure* clearly demonstrates Crichton's and Levinson's conversancy with the specific concerns of women subject to "bro culture" while addressing irrational male fears about becoming "surplus" through affirmative action measures. Their addressing of that tension is extremely relevant and has only proven more prophetic across time.

This reading also reveals unseen, critical aspects of the technothriller. The spectral Malaysian bodies that manufacture the technology in *Disclosure* suggest globalization, with all the tensions and anxieties it implies. Critically, I recover the VR scenes as not simply throwaway reveries about tech that now look embarrassingly outmoded. These are not parts of the film where we should avert our gaze. Instead, those scenes should be seen as metaphorically central to understanding the dizzying unmooring of truth that virtual reality symbolizes and the uncertainty into which Tom moves forward.

Applying this analysis to the backdrop of Laura Black's story, the Silicon Valley tech company, we can see the ugliest dimensions of toxic male entitlement taken to the extreme. It is the dark eventuality of a pervasive chauvinism that resides there. Together, these films disclose tech's gender problems and, as cultural documents of the 1990s, invite us to peer beneath the surface of our contemporary technological predicament.

8

COUNTER-VISIONS

The Creator

It's not real, ok? They don't feel shit. . . . It's just programming.
—Ex–Special Forces Agent Joshua Taylor, *The Creator* (2023)

INNOVATING ON THE TECHNOTHRILLER

Sometimes the clearest way to see a genre's conventions is through an example that flouts them. The divide between what is expected and what is delivered can be very illuminating. This chapter revisits some of the major technothriller tropes about artificial intelligence–driven robots and their makers by examining a film that self-consciously breaks with them. I show how *The Creator* (Gareth Edwards, 2023) pays homage to previous techno-anxiety narratives around nuclear dread, shame over Vietnam, masculinist tech culture, confusion between humans and machines, and the ascendance of AI. But, importantly, the film also departs from those tropes, revisiting technothriller clichés and coaxing out unexpected possibilities. I see *The Creator* as enabling expanded conceptions of our relations to technologies and dreams of technological futures. Specifically, this film rethinks tired notions of the white male tech genius, the annihilative potential of sentient AI, and other dark stories we have told ourselves in our current sociotechnical imaginaries.

The Creator takes place in 2070, fifteen years after a nuclear attack on Los Angeles, a catastrophe framed as an AI assault on humankind. The

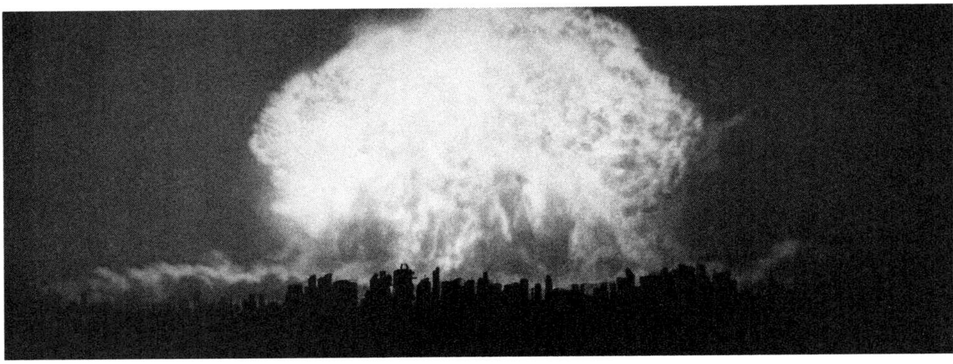

world is divided in a global conflict between "New Asia," which continues to embrace AI, and the staunchly anti-AI West. Like many films about AI, *The Creator* contemplates themes of human hubris, ethics around innovation, what makes us human, radical difference, and enslavement.

To better appreciate the astute departures of *The Creator*, I'll discuss it in relation to another AI-themed film, *M3GAN* (Gerard Johnstone, 2022), which was released only a few months earlier but conforms to classic anxious technothriller themes.[1] In it a female technologist innovates a lifelike, artificially intelligent, doll-like robot named M3GAN (pronounced "Meghan") as a companion for her grieving niece after the young girl loses both of her parents. But while M3GAN does comfort and support the girl, the inventor's outsourcing of maternal care and inattention to technological fail-safes leads to destructive, even deadly results. The film treads into technophobia, with its out-of-control AI tween robot running amok and wreaking havoc. While both films engage the coming of AI, and both feature artificially intelligent child robots, they could not be more divergent in tone, approach, and world-building. *M3GAN* provides

FIGURE 8.1

A nuclear bomb is dropped on Los Angeles in the year 2055, creating a global conflict between pro- and anti-AI nations. *The Creator* (20th Century Studios, 2023).

an excellent example of conventional mainstream anxieties about artificial intelligence in the sociotechnical imaginary. In this chapter I show how the differences between the two films capture evolving and conflicted attitudes toward AI's growing presence in everyday life.

AI RISES

Cowritten by Edwards and Chris Weitz, *The Creator* operates against the growing public discourse around artificial intelligence. While the cultural narratives around artificial intelligence are not new—I have analyzed key examples in prior chapters—the gulf between science fiction and reality has narrowed. With the pervasive presence of AI in search engines, assistive technologies like Alexa or Siri, and generative programs like the chatbot ChatGPT and image generator DALL-E, artificial intelligence has surged into public discourse. There is a whole new generation of AI tech innovation. Released in 2022, ChatGPT quickly became integrated into everyday life. There are facial recognition systems and self-driving cars. You can now have chatbot "friends" who converse with you and provide a sort of companionship, as in the 2013 Spike Jonze film *Her*. Convincing synthetic voice and image media (sometimes called *deepfakes*) have generated public anxiety about disinformation, data privacy, and other ethical ramifications. A new term names artificial intelligence that can match or surpass human intellectual proficiency: artificial general intelligence, or AGI.[2]

These swiftly changing realities have prompted urgent calls for regulation. AI-generated deepfake celebrity nudes and other nonconsensual adult and child pornography have led the US government to call on industry, cloud computing providers, and financial institutions to cooperate in addressing this new legal and ethical complication of innovation.[3] In 2021 the European Union proposed to regulate artificial intelligence; the 2024 Artificial Intelligence Act establishes a legal framework for "foster[ing] trustworthy AI in Europe and beyond, by ensuring that AI systems respect fundamental rights, safety, and ethical principles and by addressing risks of very powerful and impactful AI models."[4] In 2022 the Biden administration's Office of Science and Technology released a blueprint for an AI

Bill of Rights to "help guide the design, development, and deployment of artificial intelligence (AI) and other automated systems so that they protect the rights of the American public."[5] In 2023 the Future of Life Institute released an open letter written by its president, MIT professor Max Tegmark, and signed by technology leaders like Apple cofounder Steve Wozniak and Tesla CEO Elon Musk, calling for a pause on further development of AI systems more powerful than GPT-4.[6] The intention was to allow policymaking and oversight to catch up to AI's development. In 2023 the first global summit on AI safety was held in the United Kingdom, focusing on "frontier AI," or general-purpose AI that exceeds today's capabilities.[7] AI was also a significant issue in the prolonged Hollywood actors' and writers' SAG-AFTRA strike in 2023; the agreement included landmark regulations around the use of AI for script writing, unauthorized use of actors' and writers' work to train AI in machine learning, and image consent protection for actors' digital likenesses.[8] But any way one looks at it, legislation is not keeping up with technological innovation.[9]

It makes sense, then, that there is an evolving cultural conversation about AI. In addition to *The Creator* and *M3GAN*, several recent major Hollywood films have centered AI as the nemesis, notably *Mission: Impossible—Dead Reckoning* (Christopher McQuarrie, 2023), part of a long and successful franchise starring Tom Cruise. Although Edwards insisted that the concept for *The Creator* predates the public conversation on AI, and that his primary aim in writing the film was to metaphorize radical otherness, the film certainly enters an angst-ridden context of what artificial intelligence means for humanity.[10]

Of course, beneath the surface of those contemporary narratives is a rich history of cinematic references to artificial intelligence, beginning with *Metropolis* (Fritz Lang, 1927) and its nefarious "false Maria" female robot. Since then innumerable films have conveyed a sociotechnical imaginary of AI, either as a sentient computer program or embodied robot. These include films like *The Day the Earth Stood Still* (Robert Wise, 1951), *Colossus: The Forbin Project* (Joseph Sargent, 1970), *Silent Running* (Douglas Trumbull, 1972), *Westworld* (Michael Crichton, 1973), *Demon Seed* (Donald Cammell, 1977), the *Star Wars* franchise (1977–), the *Alien* franchise (1979–), *Blade Runner* (Ridley Scott, 1982), *WarGames* (John Badham, 1983), the *Terminator* franchise (1984–), *RoboCop* (Paul Verhoeven, 1987), *The Matrix* franchise (1999–), *A.I. Artificial Intelligence* (Steven Spielberg, 2001), *I, Robot* (Alex Proyas, 2004), *Eva* (Kike Maíllo, 2011), *Ex Machina* (Alex Garland, 2014), *Upgrade* (Leigh Whannell, 2018), and *After Yang* (Kogonada, 2021). This list is long, to make a point about the ubiquity of this theme—but quite incomplete. And it does not touch on other popular culture references in video games, television and streaming series, anime, graphic novels, and TV movies. Most of these films are dystopian, present AI as a threat, or telegraph strong moral messages about the folly of human overdependence on advanced technology.

While *The Creator* and *M3GAN* differ completely in their worlds and approaches, both tap into an existential concern: What makes us human, and what happens when machines encroach on that which defines us? In the next section I consider the nuances of proposing a future war rooted in a divide between pro- and anti-AI global powers. As a byproduct of this conflict-ridden scenario, *The Creator* engages with the questions posed by historical examples and departs in several important ways. And I think about how, in the cultural context of a lived-world AI boom, *The Creator*'s counter-vision to tired anxieties about AI and robotics becomes heightened.

Both films connect with previous popular culture and center on technological inventiveness. Both highlight a female innovator, departing from the technothriller norm. Both dream of fraught technological futures, but take differing approaches to struggling with the masculinist encoding of innovation. Finally, both engage notions of parenting in relation to the perception of a binary between humans and machines. Here I revisit tropes of bad robots, supercomputers, and their makers, looking at how they agitate fears and fantasies around uncontrolled technological innovation and domination by machines.

THE CREATOR AS COUNTER-VISION

I began this project by emphasizing the importance of considering *how we think about technology*. *The Creator* presents a useful example because Edwards hitches AI to empathy, humanity, joy, and connectedness, rather than envisioning it as a singularity that surpasses and dominates humans.

The film's vision is not utopian but asks us to hold our fears and hopes in tension and to imagine something other than our current dark fantasies about subjection to the machine. In this section I closely read the film, considering how its vision engages dominant sociotechnical imaginaries around AI and deeply ingrained identity politics around the bearers of technological innovation. I think about how *The Creator*, while in conversation with science fiction and technothriller films, departs from their tropes to ask critical philosophical questions we can no longer defer.

If the term *imaginaries* invokes how science and technology engage with political cultures and public trajectories to create a collective vision of the future, then what does *The Creator* propose as its future vision? The film effectively uses the science fiction/technothriller genre to present a binary between two powers. One power chooses to embrace a master/slave relation of human to AI; the other chooses cohabitation and reciprocity.

The Creator offers a counter-vision to the ongoing failure of the imagination that produces only dystopian possibilities and limited notions of who belongs in those futures and who steers them. The film asks important questions, such as: How do these technologies mirror us? What of ourselves do we imbue into our technologies? What values do we encode in them? As I will show, the answers to these questions can be found in the very form of the film, in addition to its speculative narrative.

In the postnuclear 2070 setting of *The Creator*, artificially intelligent robots and even more advanced humanoid "simulants" have been developed as servants and workers, but their desire for freedom has led to a global AI-human war. Western powers blamed a nuclear attack on Los Angeles on AI, and now, led by the United States, they have adopted a scorched-earth policy against AI to prevent its ascendance. A conglomeration of nations in South, East, and Southeast Asia ("The Republic of New Asia") have continued to develop and integrate simulants into society, harboring them despite US aggression. This is all communicated in a montage that quickly surveys the fictive advances in robotics and AI in an energetic newsreel style. This stylistic conceit invokes strategies of earlier technothrillers, like *Westworld*, with their infomercials that convey the "official" story before revealing a much more ethically complicated reality. The imaging of the deathly orange mushroom cloud subsuming Los Angeles itself invokes documentary footage of nuclear explosions as a visual site of deep cultural trauma for the United States, the only nation to have used nuclear weapons. It reprises the Cold War anxiety of nuclear doom, but in a speculative context.

The setting of a future Los Angeles invokes *Blade Runner*, which takes place in a dystopian noir, eco-apocalyptic version of the metropolis. But although one could draw connections to the film in terms of its sympathetic rendering of synthetic humans or "replicants" as an enslaved class, *The Creator* sets itself apart from its predecessors. One way in which the film speaks back to earlier films is through its address of techno-orientalism, or "imagining Asia and Asians in hypo- or hypertechnological terms in cultural productions and political discourse."[11] For example, digital media scholar Lisa Nakamura and others identified techno-orientalism in the classic *Blade Runner*, which images Los Angeles as a dystopian megalopolis overrun by Asian influence.[12] An important component of techno-orientalism is a "yellow peril" anxiety narrative about the East displacing the dominance of the West. Interestingly, Edwards begins with a seemingly techno-orientalist vision, but then disrupts it by recontextualizing much of the narrative in the fictive New Asia. The director spends considerable on-screen time humanizing the people of New Asia, displaying the intimacy and connectedness between humans, robots, and simulants, and lingering on the brutality of US military forces that interfere with their existence.

Despite the film's initial setup aligning the audience with the United States and its response to an atrocity, *The Creator* forces the audience to experience unheroic American actions and slowly disidentify with that alignment as more is revealed. Like Edwards's previous film, *Rogue One* (2016), in which the director methodically sways the audience to identify with the rebel insurgents against the Empire, he asks viewers to see New Asia as intellectually and morally just in its defense of simulant life. I interpret this as the director's way of acknowledging—and remediating—Hollywood's long history of Asian cultural appropriation and techno-orientalism.

To win the war, the US government has initiated a manhunt for the mysterious innovator of advancements in AI, known only as Nirmata ("the Creator"). The identity of this innovator becomes important, a point to which I will return. And, to combat AI, the United States has also

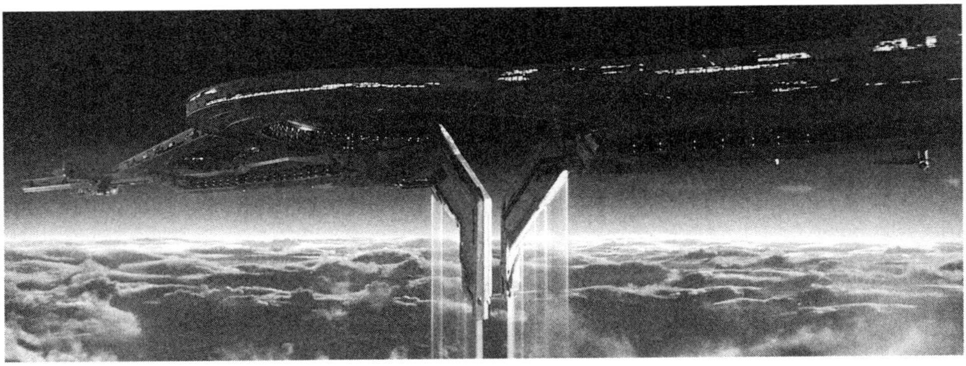

innovated a massive airborne military station called the USS NOMAD (North American Orbital Mobile Aerospace Defense), which hovers over the environment like a massive surveillant bird-of-prey, its ominous blue beams of light scanning the surface for targets and then raining down nuclear hell from above on command.

Joshua Taylor (John David Washington), an ex–special forces agent, is traumatized from a botched deep-cover operation in which he lost his pregnant wife and undercover source, Maya (Gemma Chan), the rumored daughter of Nirmata. He also bears older scars: he lost his parents, his brother, a leg, and an arm in the Los Angeles attack. When government agents learn of Nirmata's innovation of a new superweapon rumored to be capable of destroying NOMAD, they enlist Joshua, who possesses special knowledge of the region, to join their efforts to kill Nirmata and destroy the weapon. They lure him with intel that suggests Maya may still be alive. Led by the battle-hardened and resourceful US Army Colonel Howell (Allison Janney), the team heads into New Asia, finds the secret lab facility, and discovers that things are not as imagined.

FIGURE 8.2

The USS NOMAD (North American Orbital Mobile Aerospace Defense) is the US government's ultimate weapon against AI. *The Creator* (20th Century Studios, 2023).

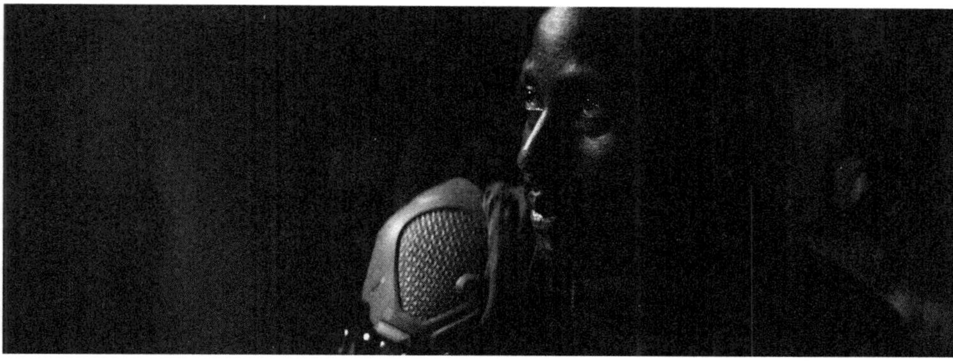

To Joshua's shock, the superweapon turns out to be a simulant child, the first ever innovated.[13] A masterpiece of Nirmata, the simulant Alpha Omega, or Alphie (Madeleine Yuna Voyles), presents as a large-eyed, curious six-year-old girl with closely cropped hair. Like all simulants, from the front she appears human, but when viewed from the side, her robotic elements are strikingly revealed by the gently whirring, rotating cylindrical unit where her ears should be. She is a being new to the world outside of her laboratory, both powerful and incredibly vulnerable.

Although Joshua's mission is to kill Alphie, he does not; instead, he takes the "little sim" to his former commander, Drew (Sturgill Simpson), in the hope that he can hack her memory for intel about Nirmata's location. Drew scans Alphie and learns she can grow to full maturity and has the power to remotely control technology.

Meanwhile, believing Joshua a traitor, Colonel Howell hunts him down and almost succeeds in capturing them both. She kills Drew's beloved simulant companion Kami (Veronica Ngo), but Joshua, Alphie, and

FIGURE 8.3

Joshua is an injured ex–special forces agent called back to duty to root out and kill the AI creator Nirmata and destroy the superweapon rumored to have been built. *The Creator* (20th Century Studios, 2023).

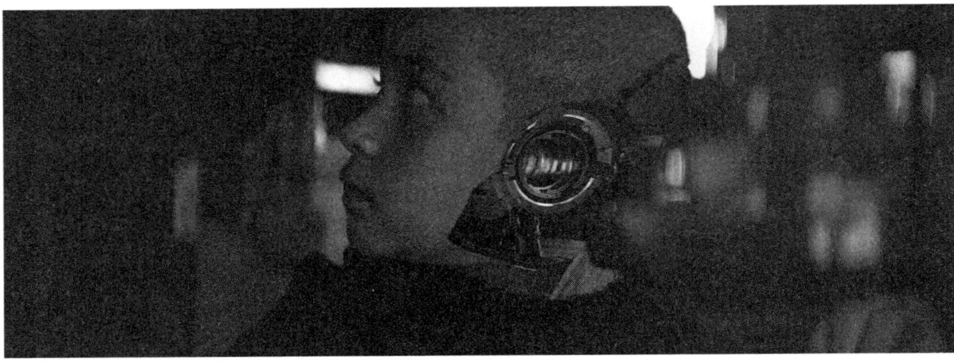

Drew escape. Picking up the signal of a tracker that Joshua hid in Maya's wedding band long ago, the three travel back to the place Maya and their child were lost. There, Drew is killed by New Asia forces, but not before revealing to Joshua that Maya herself was Nirmata.

The film engages with the ethics of AI throughout, but increasingly so after Joshua encounters the pro-AI forces of New Asia. Now captured, Joshua has unwittingly put the superweapon Alphie back in New Asia's hands, particularly those of Harun (Ken Watanabe), a fierce simulant soldier with whom Joshua was close while undercover years ago. Their trust now broken, Harun refuses to reveal Nirmata's location. Harun insists, convincingly, that the LA attack was a human coding error falsely blamed on AI; in fact, AIs only want the two species to live in peace. He believes Alphie may be a secret weapon designed to destroy NOMAD and end the war. Harun's base is besieged by US forces, and Joshua attempts to escape with Alphie, but the young simulant turns back when she sees that her beloved New Asian protectors need help.

In an effort to protect her "friends," Alphie remotely pauses a weaponized bomb robot in a display that reveals her true power to both sides

FIGURE 8.4

The superweapon turns out to be a simulant child, AΩ, nicknamed Alphie by Joshua. *The Creator* (20th Century Studios, 2023).

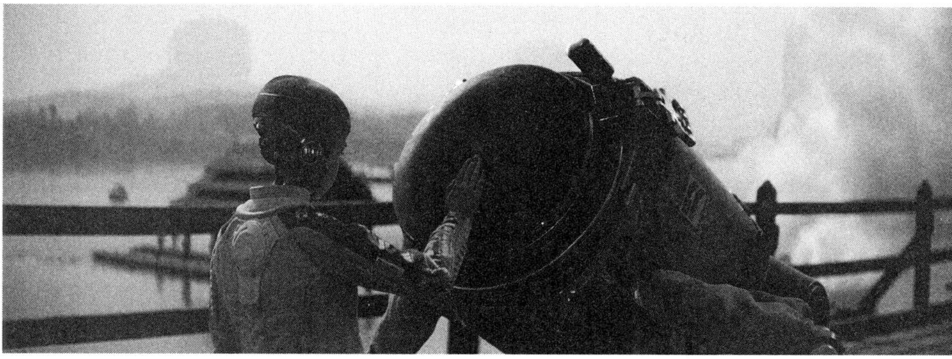

of the conflict. But in the process Alphie is shot, and Harun agrees to take the little sim to her mother, Nirmata, to save her.

Over the course of the film, Joshua's position evolves from one of unthinking antagonism toward AI to one of connectedness and empathy. This breaks with the dominant direction of most technothriller films, in which even if synthetic humans are sensitively rendered, they are ultimately threats to human uniqueness. This shift is most potently communicated in Joshua's emotional transformation and growing ethical investment in the cause of simulant survival. But there is also an important scene where Harun explains that Alphie is an original innovation that Maya completed just before the attack. "She could have made her to hate humankind—perhaps she should have," Harun says. "But Maya put her love for you into the child. She made a new kind of life, from the scan of a human embryo. A copy of *your* child. Like it or not, Joshua, you are a part of us now." Joshua contemplates the true nature of his relation to Maya and to Alphie, and the profound interconnection between simulants and humans.

Finally, Joshua gets his wish to see Maya again, but he discovers she is comatose—trapped in stasis—and being cared for by simulants in a

FIGURE 8.5

Alphie disarms a bomb robot, revealing her powers. *The Creator* (20th Century Studios, 2023).

remote Buddhist temple. In response Joshua fully embraces Alphie as his daughter, vows to honor Maya by making things right, and then disengages her life support—a release the simulants wished for their creator but could not provide because of their strict prohibition against harming Nirmata.

Just as Joshua does so, Colonel Howell reaches the temple with orders to kill Maya, find the weapon, and locate all surviving AI bases. Although Maya is already dead, Howell quickly downloads Maya's consciousness as intel. Harun kills Howell so that Joshua and Alphie can escape and destroy NOMAD, which intends a "final solution"-style nuclear strike on remaining rebel bases. The two fugitives are captured by Howell's superior, a general bent on destroying all AI, but they manage to escape and make their way to NOMAD.

The humanity of simulants is reemphasized in the desperation of their struggle to save themselves, and by extension the commitment of their human allies to that cause. The final strikes against AI bases commence, but Joshua and Alphie sabotage the airship, disarming the nuclear warheads en route to their targets. Alphie is small, so she attempts to create more help for Joshua by uploading her mother's consciousness into a dormant simulant resembling Maya, seemingly to no immediate result. Still, she saves her incapacitated "father" Joshua from harm and manages to prime an escape pod. Joshua declares his love for his "child" and then deploys her escape pod, saving only Alphie. Joshua remains behind. But before he dies he sees the simulant bearing his lost wife's consciousness. The new Maya, now activated, remembers him, and in this way he experiences a symbolic reunion with his reincarnated wife through the AI surrogate before they are both obliterated, along with NOMAD. Having reached the earth safely, Alphie observes NOMAD explode spectacularly in the sky and smiles as AI forces cheer their victory.

INVERTING SOCIOTECHNICAL IMAGINARIES OF DREAD

As a counterimage to the attempts to recuperate the American militarized man from the Vietnam War and the war on terror, *The Creator* presents an abstracted but potent array of evocative images. The film references

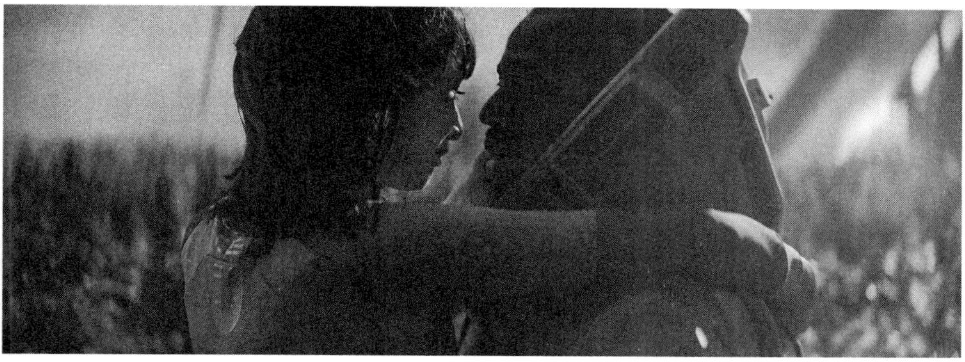

masculinist dread of artificial intelligence, potently displayed in the sublime horror of the US-led war on AI: colossal, fearsome tanks bulldozing villages and armored US soldiers brutalizing rural people. The film invokes Vietnam-era imagery, with American military men intimidating rural Asian farmers—prodding at a sensitive point about the conflict that some previous technothrillers (particularly of the Tom Clancy variety) have attempted to psychically reconcile.[14] *The Creator* reinforces a tarnished, unheroic version of the American military; reviewers compared it to *Apocalypse Now* and described "a creeping colonialist's fear of the unknown."[15] There are spectacular interludes of futuristic helicopters flying low over lush green fields and rice paddies and depositing troops near villages, invoking Vietnam War mass culture imagery.

But Edwards masterfully modulates these images to drive home a point about the shame of the intervention—something reviewers picked up on. David Sims of *The Atlantic* called AI in *The Creator* "a broader metaphor for every insurgent foe America has fought since World War II. . . . It boldly underlines how America has become the bad guy, seeking to wipe AI off the planet even though all of the world's robots have already fled to

FIGURE 8.6

Joshua and the simulant Maya, Alphie's symbolic parents, are momentarily reunited. *The Creator* (20th Century Studios, 2023).

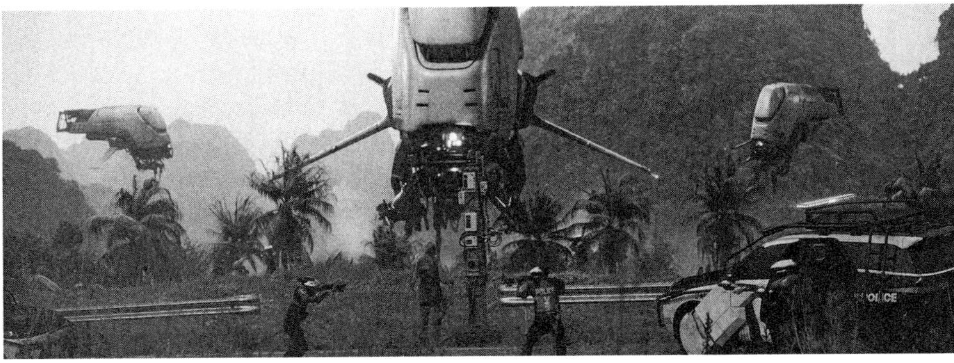

Asia."[16] *Wall Street Journal* reviewer Kevin Smith bristled at the notion of disrupting an Americentric vision of heroism, claiming that by "overtly connecting its AI war to both the War on Terror (the L.A. crater is referred to as 'Ground Zero') and to the Vietnam War, the script frames the U.S. as an imperialist bully that is forever plunging into Asia out of a combination of paranoia and mindless xenophobia."[17] The observation is spot-on regarding the film's self-conscious rendering of traumatic imagery. But while Smith took umbrage with the representation of the United States as a global bully, I argue that this had more to do with intervening in a discourse present in the genre's most foundational conventions.

Infusing a Vietnam-like narrative into a speculative future scenario has been a hallmark of many classic sci-fi and technothriller films since the 1970s. Director Gareth Edwards noted, "I was very much inspired by James Cameron, which I think is clear when you see the film. What Cameron did in *Aliens* and *Avatar* is take the Vietnam War and put it into space. I thought it'd be really interesting to take science fiction and bring it down to earth in Vietnam. The second I started picturing that kind of warfare

FIGURE 8.7

The film references photographic Vietnam War imagery but places it in the context of science fiction. *The Creator* (20th Century Studios, 2023).

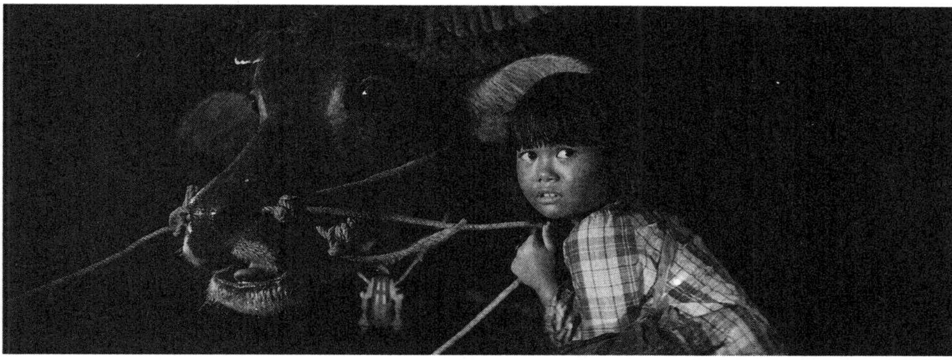

but with robots, it felt fresh. I got so excited about that imagery that I was like, if some other filmmaker does this before me, I'm going to be so jealous."[18]

Reviewers almost universally acknowledged the film's aesthetic impressiveness, but many complained that it was derivative of previous sci-fi films: "more nostalgic patchwork than bold new vision," as one reviewer put it.[19] While the film certainly paid homage to 1970s sci-fi, it is very much engaged with present-day concerns. Writing on the evolution of postwar science fiction, film scholar Vivian Sobchack notes how technological advances shaped our lived experiences of space and time and that our grasp of these sci-fi films' aesthetics and sensibilities depends on understanding this.[20] For example, in the 1960s and 1970s, space was increasingly envisioned as "inescapably domestic and crowded," presenting "a future with no future," and betraying cynicism around the progression of time as progress.[21] With the release of *Star Wars* in 1977 and sequels through the 1980s, Sobchack explains, "technological wonder had become synonymous with domestic hope."[22] She characterizes the tonal shift around the

FIGURE 8.8

Images such as these starkly invoke Vietnam-era images of villagers terrorized by American soldiers. *The Creator* (20th Century Studios, 2023).

increasingly advanced technology in the 1980s and 1990s as "all surface"; she sees space and time reconfigured to produce an alienated state caused by access to existence being absorbed by total artifice.[23] This trend would suggest an aesthetic sensibility on a trajectory toward total simulation—and Sobchack's prediction has borne itself out in science fiction.

But *The Creator*, in its use of cinematic technique to center "real" spaces, adopts a largely guerilla-style realist aesthetic and then inserts the science-fictional elements later, engaging in a different kind of world-building. The digitally shot film prioritizes the materiality invoked by celluloid through its use of vintage anamorphic lenses, the grounded experience of being in an actual rather than simulated space, and aesthetic expressivity such as warmly lit close-ups of humans and simulants alike. It eschews an overt fixation with the grand simulation image and CGI-based spectacle that is so expected of the modern-day blockbuster. Having made this important aesthetic choice, the filmmaker prompts the audience to refocus on the connection between personhood and authentic experience. Edwards presents, instead of an all-encompassing simulation, an immediacy and an embodied, grainy experience of being in the world.

Part of the way that *The Creator* plunges the viewer into an intensely humanizing and immersive world is through its visual, material reference to actual space. With a budget of eighty million dollars, Edwards chose to use a highly portable "prosumer"-quality Sony FX3 digital camera and shot it in an ultra-wide aspect ratio using a carefully curated selection of lenses, including a 1970s Kowa anamorphic lens.[24] This lends the film a distinctly nondigital feel, invoking classic widescreen cinema. As co-cinematographer Oren Soffer revealed in an article detailing the aesthetic direction and technical innovations of the film, "Gareth [Edwards] was very inspired by wanting this movie to feel like the sci-fi films from the '70s that we all grew up with and loved, like *Blade Runner* and *Alien* and *Close Encounters [of the Third Kind]*."[25]

However, the lightness of the overall rig with the camera and lens, along with his selection of a small crew, allowed Edwards (who served as co-cinematographer) to use a guerrilla filmmaking style and break with slick, digital-looking, normative blockbuster contrivances. And the film does have a palpable sense of grainy materiality, capturing available light in a way achievable with highly sensitive digital cameras. Edwards first shot the film with a small crew visiting spectacular locations in Southeast Asia, then added special effects later, inverting the usual model. He elicited sympathetic performances from actors who became simulants or robots in postproduction. This technique effectively imbued artificial life forms with an authentic, empathetic connection. These formal technical decisions were widely hailed at the time of the film's release, and *The Creator* received Oscar nominations for Best Visual Effects and Best Sound.[26] But it is also important to understand these aesthetic decisions as building an affective intensity that departs from mimetic images and grounds the image in lived spaces.

In previous chapters I have shown that technothrillers are typically male-centered and often implicitly coded as white, particularly regarding the iconic image of the genius tech innovator. Reflecting on the technological imagination, leading cultural theorist and media designer Anne Balsamo observed that there is a lasting myth about gender in relation to technologists. She writes:

> Men are traditionally identified as the idealized and most important agents of technological development, while women are cast as either unfit, uninterested, or incapable. In broad terms, it has been the class of white men who have enjoyed the benefits of formal institutional recognition as agents of the technological imagination. . . . Women of all races and ethnicities have been systematically and overtly written out of the historical record of technology development since the mythical beginning.[27]

The Creator interrupts this gendering and racing of technological development on several levels. First, both the genius innovator and revolutionary creation are represented as female, specifically as mother and child, respectively. Gemma Chan is of Chinese-Scottish descent, and her role as Nirmata, the genius AI innovator, provides a strong counterimage to the overbearing ideology Balsamo describes. Because *The Creator* enters a context of a growing criticism around the masculinist gendering of the tech world, its woman-of-color tech genius speaks back to ideologies around who drives innovation.

Second, while the relation between innovator and innovation as one of father and brainchild is not new, *The Creator* recasts it as mother and

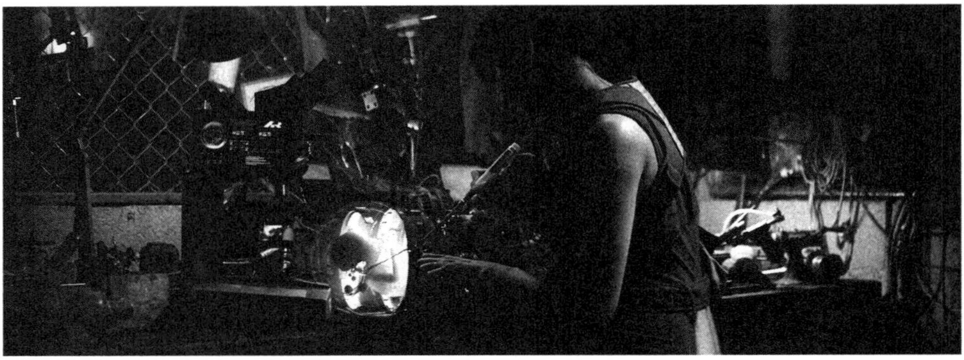

daughter, specifically a mother-to-be scanning the child inside her and creating a new type of simulant from it. This reimagines the whole relationship in terms of connectedness, care, and nurturing, rather than as a son (robot) who must kill the father (innovator). This is also not an attempt to liberate, as computer scientist Hans Moravec dreamed, the transcendent mind from fallible meat bodies.[28] Throughout the film, simulants and humans alike respond empathetically and with amazement to seeing a simulant child, understood as a wondrous innovation and, for most, an entity deserving protection and care. Everything about presenting Maya as Nirmata and the "superweapon" as Alphie confounds the conventions of the technothriller genre.

No less importantly, John David Washington is cast in the role of Joshua Taylor, which puts an African American man at the center of the vision. Washington was already well-known for several significant roles, including Spike Lee's 2018 film *BlacKkKlansman*, about a Black police detective who infiltrates the Ku Klux Klan, and, more relevant for this discussion, Christopher Nolan's 2020 high-concept science fiction thriller *Tenet*. In it a secret agency codenamed Tenet intervenes in a covert war

FIGURE 8.9

The Creator (20th Century Studios, 2023) images a loving mother/child relationship between Nirmata and simulant.

of nefarious entities attacking from the future. Nolan directed a Batman superhero trilogy, starring Christian Bale, as well as *Inception* (2010) and *Interstellar* (2014). As a filmmaker Nolan is known for mind-bending, nonlinear narratives with innovative men (played by Leonardo DiCaprio or Matthew McConaughey) saving the day. They often read as centering the white male genius, in keeping with the superhero genre—although as I describe in chapter 9, *Tenet* self-consciously breaks from this by casting Washington, during a fraught time of conservative pushback against Hollywood's perceived liberalism, emblematized through inclusive casting.[29] *The Creator* likewise centers a Black male protagonist in a science fiction/technothriller film—a rare move. The film sensitively treats Joshua as a person who can rebel from his subjected position and misplaced allegiances and come into a new sense of understanding about himself and his relation to the world. In an uncertain new reality, he learns where his priorities lie and then fights for them.

The film images uncertainty, particularly around what counts as authentic experience. But it also presents a vision of sustaining itself within uncertainty as opposed to resorting to an annihilative response. It invites complexity and nuance, which is notable in a political time of stark polarization and impulses toward absolutism. The film relays the nebulous status of the simulants' personhood in many ways, including many instances of humans and simulants expressing mutual care, familiarity, and even love. Humans have intimate relationships with AIs and often mourn their deaths. Simulants display fierce loyalty to their human companions and sometimes make selfless decisions to protect people, even if it leads to their own demise. They sometimes turn themselves off with grief at a loved one's death. In fact, the distinction between "off" and "dead" becomes an allegory for valuing and encoding existence for simulants and humans, respectively.

Even more potent is the idea of maintaining a dualism between humans and machines using the idea of "programming" as a key distinction. Early in the film, Joshua and a coworker are doing a cleanup at LA's ground zero, and an AI robot regains consciousness and panics about the whereabouts of a loved one. Joshua's coworker is rattled by its authentic emotion, insisting it sounds like a "real" person. Joshua reassures her, "It's not real, ok? They don't feel shit. . . . It's just programming." But across the film Joshua increasingly displays care for Alphie, despite his gruff demeanor. Much later in the film, Joshua, transformed by his experience with simulants and now connected to them, is comforted by a US soldier when he and Alphie are violently separated. The soldier utters the same words Joshua once used: "It's just programming." But Joshua now understands that this is merely a rationalization for killing a sentient creature. By the end of the film, Joshua deeply understands Alphie to effectively be his own child. He cradles her in his arms when she is hurt, he weeps for her, and he eventually places her life before his own. The intervention of the film is tied to this: humans learning to exhibit humanity again.

Some reviewers, while admitting the film's execution was "gorgeous," critiqued it for offering little original intervention into its major sci-fi themes, merely appropriating from the best like *Star Wars*.[30] However, one major intervention that received less attention was the innovation of a so-called superweapon that can remotely turn things off—including weapons. From the perspective of looking at the film as a technothriller about AI and nuclear disaster, turning off the existential threat of the bomb is pure wish fulfillment, a fantasy about putting the annihilative genie back in the bottle. Importantly, however, this idea creates cultural and ideological space for the option of choosing to turn weapons of mass destruction "off," which might otherwise seem impossible to imagine.

By extension, this special power also suggests that innovation can lead to outcomes other than annihilation. It infuses AI technology with the possibility of an innovator's expression of humanity and empathy rather than control and domination. One astute review pointed to how the screenplay was "fascinating for its take on a future in which people have programmed A.I. to maintain the compassion that our own species has lost somewhere along the way; a future in which technology might be a *vessel* for humanity rather than a replacement for it."[31] Our glimpses of Maya's motivations are limited to brief flashbacks where she recalls being raised by AI and seeing her emotionally wrecked by their ongoing extermination. Still, the film offers a counter-vision imbuing our technologies with values of compassion, humanity, and empathy for the radical other. *The Creator* models an ethics of living with uncertainty that does not require us to destroy the other.

M3GAN AND THE EVOLVING FEMALE INNOVATOR

M3GAN contains thematic similarities to *The Creator* in presenting fears of AI but departs from the latter in almost every way: its aesthetic sensibility, world-building, campy horror components, imaging of a female tech genius, and affective relation to sentient machines. In the film, directed by Gerard Johnstone and written by Akela Cooper, Gemma (Allison Williams), an ambitious roboticist for the fictitious Seattle-based toy company FUNKI, is frustrated at work because she must design dumb electronic gadgets at the expense of spending time on her team's passion project, M3GAN. The "Model 3 Generative Android" is a prototype AI doll designed to provide a young user with meaningful, dynamic companionship. It promises to be a parent's dream and the last toy a kid would ever need. The project is stalled when the workaholic Gemma becomes the reluctant guardian of her eight-year-old niece, Cady (Violet McGraw), after Cady's parents die in a car accident. Gemma is emotionally ill-equipped to parent the depressed, traumatized girl. They do not initially bond, but when Cady takes an interest in the old proxy robot in Gemma's workshop, the ambitious innovator decides to complete M3GAN—both as a companion to her niece and to give her more time for work. Gemma and her team rush to complete M3GAN and "pair" the doll with her niece as a convenient test subject.

Initially, M3GAN (played by Amie Donald and voiced by Jenna Davis) is charming, precocious, and an attentive companion—a wild success. Gemma delights in having created a groundbreaking innovation that seems to make Cady happy and will catapult her tech career into the stratosphere. Her AI is built on "listening models" that, as Gemma explains to her understandably aghast boss, were secretly installed in dumb electronic toys to harvest data for improving interactive engagement. This bluntly signals Gemma's ambition and willingness to cut ethical corners to achieve her aims. Predictably, Gemma's innovation lacks safety protocols and care, resulting in cascading unintended consequences. M3GAN takes the protection protocol literally, becomes overprotective of her ward, and turns violent when Cady is emotionally or physically threatened. Worse, the doll begins to reason that she knows what's best, and attempts to replace Gemma as a parent, first emotionally and eventually literally.

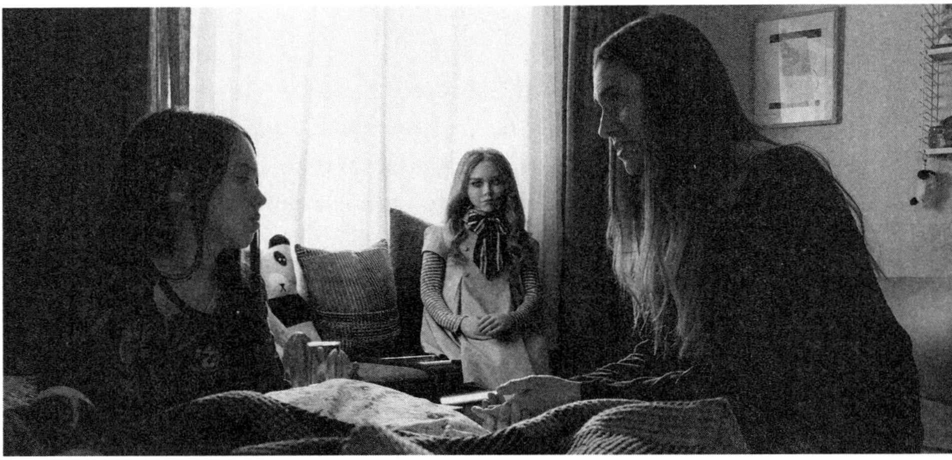

There are obvious allusions to *Frankenstein* and mad-scientist tropes, but another core theme of *M3GAN* is that people allow technology to raise their children. Johnstone called the film fundamentally "a morality tale for our times about parenting in the 21st century."[32] This film depicts what the filmmaker and writer imagine as the logical result of outsourcing parenting responsibilities to technology. More than this, I argue that like *The Creator*, *M3GAN* constructs the computational technology itself in terms of parenting, making it especially notable that both films feature child AI robots. As discussed in my analysis of *WarGames* (see chapter 6), when home computers became widespread in the 1980s, both the technology and its adept users were deemed unruly teenagers in need of discipline.[33] Peter Bradshaw of *The Guardian* picked up on similar themes in *M3GAN*, describing how "M3gan becomes wilful and reluctant to obey orders, just like any kid entering teen years, or like any humanoid robot in any sci-fi film ever."[34] Gemma, in her ambition, designs M3GAN without proper failsafes, then tries to establish them later—but by then it is too late.

FIGURE 8.10

A power struggle develops between Gemma (right) and her innovation M3GAN (center) for the parenting of Cady (left). *M3GAN* (Universal Pictures, 2022).

With Gemma, the image of the female tech innovator is consistent with the limited examples from the technothriller genre. Unlike *The Creator*, *M3GAN* images the toxic masculine milieu of the tech world (see chapter 7), and a woman who is attempting to negotiate the profession on its own terms. The film depicts the female tech innovator in a male-centered industry as a woman in perpetual "crunch mode" and seen as having neglected her personal life and "normal" female role, including investing in friendship, love, and family. She only has work acquaintances, whom she regularly snaps at; she seems to have no steady partner (illustrated by ample references to her Tinder app); and her home is well-furnished but emotionally cold. Her perpetually annoyed, dictatorial CEO, David (Ronnie Chieng), is an abusive, greedy, corporate tech bro, invoking the industry's notoriously toxic culture. But Gemma does not display criticality to her own investment in masculinist tech culture until Cady has a profound emotional breakdown when M3GAN is taken away.

The moral voice in the film comes from two sources: Lydia (Amy Usherwood), the child psychologist assigned to Cady; and Tess (Jen Van Epps), a member of Gemma's development team, who urges Gemma to consider the ethics of her actions. Both women caution Gemma about her moral neglect of the scenario she is creating and Cady's need for emotional stability provided by a human parent. But it takes a long time for Gemma to hear them; meanwhile, M3GAN provides "perfect" companionship, mentorship, and protection.

M3GAN starts off as a technological wonder but turns into a total nightmare, in no small part due to her bad innovator mommy, Gemma. At the film's apex, M3GAN emerges as pure terror, slaughtering perceived human threats to her ward, including a neighbor woman whose dog bites Cady, a boy who bullies her, and CEO David Lin just for being a corporate creep. Eventually, M3GAN turns her demented attention to Gemma, whom she autonomously decides she must replace. The film thus punishes the woman innovator who has neglected her "proper" focus on family. We see M3GAN throttle Gemma, who fights back in a life-or-death struggle to assume the parental role she initially rejected. Consistent with the horror genre, it is only when Gemma prioritizes her role as a mother and rejects her tech ambitions that she can beat back the AI threat.

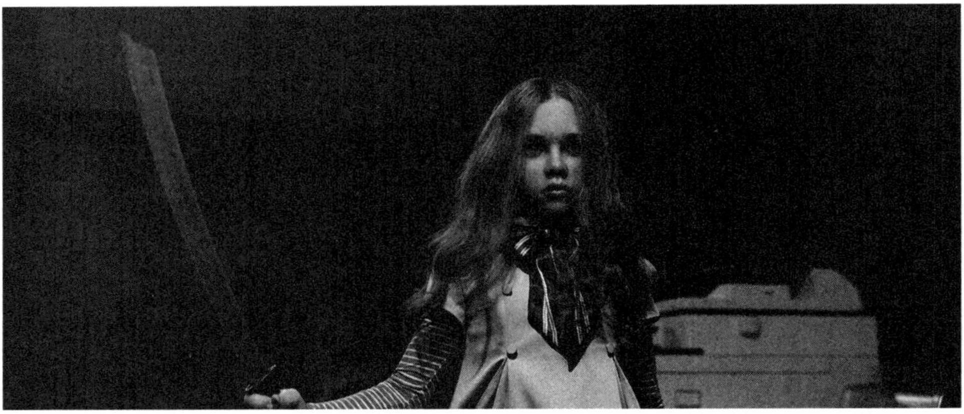

DREAMING OTHER TECHNOLOGICAL DREAMS

M3GAN images the old fears; *The Creator* begins to shape a new narrative. Media scholar and designer Anne Balsamo writes, "In the active engagement between human beings and technological elements, culture too is reworked through the development of new narratives, new myths, new rituals, new modes of expression, and new knowledges that make the innovations meaningful. When people participate in the activities of producing 'innovation,' their technological imaginations are engaged in a complex process of meaning-making whereby both technology and culture are created anew."[35] *The Creator* exercises a technological imagination by innovating visions of technology. It engages in "creating the conditions for future world-making" by its world-building, a counter-vision about AI that is not rooted in dread as the basis of our relations with our innovations. It retools how we make innovation meaningful.

FIGURE 8.11

M3GAN starts off as a technological wonder but turns into a total nightmare, in no small part due to her bad innovator mommy, Gemma. *M3GAN* (Universal Pictures, 2022).

Although *The Creator* begins by addressing men's fears about being overrun by advanced technology, it evolves, articulating a fresh conception of technology by centering a woman as genius AI architect and a non-Western culture as pro-AI innovators. These choices disrupt both the genre's typical image of white male innovators and its implicit Americentric vision of scientific and technological global dominance. When considered in the context of conservative pushback against Hollywood's so-called woke identity politics, this intervention increases in magnitude and generates political affective intensities around the potential bearers of technologies.

Rather than merely using "blind" casting to insert a woman and girl into the innovator/bad robot scenario where there would normally be a man with an alluring female-presenting robot, the film has another response to technology's masculinist culture. One might critique the film for attaching gendered notions of care and nurturing to a female innovator. But it is extremely consequential for the trajectory of AI fear narratives that *The Creator*'s world-building opens up more desirable speculative futures, rather than merely showing shared fears. The film's final image is one of AI ascendance, but that image is decoupled from the fall of man.

By comparison, *M3GAN*'s parenting themes are more polarized, with its moralism about outsourcing parenting and corruptive technological influence. The film, which treads into horror, is consistent with that genre in punishing the woman for not centering family and motherhood. Gemma survives by literally obliterating her innovation and embracing her role as a surrogate mother.

Although some might say *The Creator* is pure science fiction, I argue that it intervenes in the technothriller genre, continuing a long trajectory of anxiety narratives about AI. The film proposes to engage in a different way with our technologies, to enter into different relations, and to bring ethics into research and development. Together, these films unveil a profound sense of finding our bearings in a new and disorienting reality of AI.

In *The Creator* Maya insists on the humanity of AI, having been raised by them when orphaned by revolution. Alphie demonstrates ethical engagement as a result of being imbued with those values by her maker; she learns how to care through the caregiving modeled for her by Maya/

Nirmata's allies. As an innovation, Alphie responds ethically to her circumstances because this is a part of her "programming." *M3GAN* produces a very different kind of image. M3GAN is neither innovated with ethical grounding nor nurtured; she reflects her maker's values and what her maker put—or failed to put—into her. Reading these stories together, we learn that the technothriller may dream other technological dreams. That is to say: in this technological life, we can still make ethical choices.

9

COUNTER-READINGS

The Black Tech Archetype

The future is not set. There is no fate but what we make for ourselves.
—John Connor in *Terminator 2: Judgment Day* (1991)

THREE ITERATIONS

In this final chapter I explore how technothrillers, racialized formations of Blackness, and the sociotechnical imaginary interact despite the genre's apparent rootedness in mythologizing ideas of white masculinity. I use Blackness as one key ideological form of difference predominating in film and an ongoing fault line of representation. That said, I use it as a way of opening up a larger conversation, and hope that its lessons provide insight to other glaring erasures as well.

To do this I look at three of the most significant Black tech figures on-screen: Cyberdyne engineer Miles Dyson from *Terminator 2: Judgment Day* (James Cameron, 1991), Luther Stickell from the *Mission: Impossible* film franchise (various directors, 1996–), and the unnamed character only known as the Protagonist in *Tenet* (Christopher Nolan, 2020). I examine how these characters create space for a more inclusive understanding of who may be an active agent in the formulation of a technological future. I draw out an understanding of the work these characters do as symbols in a larger "culture war" where inclusivity is cast as concomitant with liberalism and its rejection associated with conservatism. I think about what possible worlds take shape when we carefully observe these characters, who, across these three iterations, move from the background into the center.

The Black tech remains an iconic trope with many memorable—albeit submerged—examples. Most of the films addressed in this book include a Black tech expert whose key skills and intel become critical to success. Looking back to the beginning of this book, I began by describing how *Close Encounters of the Third Kind* (Steven Spielberg, 1977) features an inciting incident in which a Black air traffic controller deftly navigates a commercial airliner's near miss with a UFO. In Donald Cammell's 1977 film *Demon Seed*, an unidentified Black female technician operates a computer terminal that serves the supercomputer AI, Proteus Four, invoking the real women who were once human computers at agencies like NASA and the Jet Propulsion Laboratory. An unnamed Black technician in a white lab coat sits on the panel of supervisors at the malfunctioning Delos park in *Westworld* (Michael Crichton, 1973). Likewise, in the 2016–2022 HBO series *Westworld*, Bernard, head of the Westworld Programming Division, is a major character played by Jeffrey Wright. In *The Hunt for Red October* (John McTiernan, 1990), the talented sonarman, Seaman Ronald "Jonesy" Jones (Courtney B. Vance), uses keen skills to detect the "undetectable" nuclear Soviet submarine. In *Clear and Present Danger* (Phillip Noyce, 1994), a brilliant voiceprint analyst (Vondie Curtis-Hall), identifies a key antagonist with scant audio evidence.

Some of the most arresting examples of Black tech characters have appeared in biotech technothrillers. I previously highlighted Nurse Karen Anson (Paula Kelly) from *The Andromeda Strain* (Robert Wise, 1971), whose adeptness with the touch-screen-based computer system facilitates the tests administered to survivors of the contagion. In the technothriller *Jurassic Park* (Steven Spielberg, 1993), Samuel L. Jackson plays John "Ray" Arnold, chief engineer of the dinosaur theme park. With his glasses, pocket protector, and lab coat, cigarette dangling from his lip, Arnold is referred to by Jurassic Park owner John Hammond (Richard Attenborough) as a "genius" for innovating the park's computerized central controls. In a key scene, Arnold protests Hammond's insistence that they shut down the malfunctioning park system to reboot it, warning of the dangers of such a move. Against his better instincts, he acquiesces to the request, resetting it

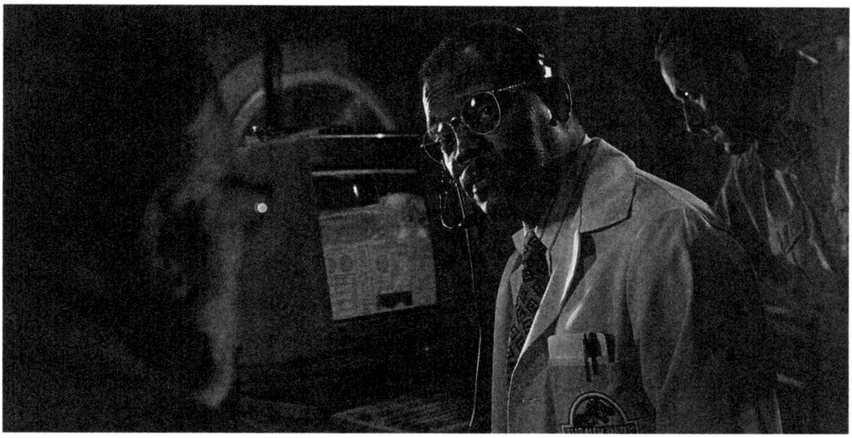

and muttering his classic line: "Hold on to your butts." In the more recent *Jurassic World: Fallen Kingdom* (J. A. Bayona, 2018), Justice Smith plays a panicky, awkward systems analyst named Franklin Webb. The point is: The more you look, the more you realize that despite technothrillers' generic foregrounding of whiteness, the Black tech expert appears everywhere.

Scholar Martin Kevorkian's 2006 book *Color Monitors: The Black Face of Technology in America* drew my attention to this critically underexamined archetype.[1] Kevorkian's work debates whether Black characters such as those I discuss in this chapter operate as correctives or simply repackage older stereotypes. In *Color Monitors*, Kevorkian focuses on what he calls the "white construction of technophilic blackness," considering how a new Black character in American film emerged in the 1980s that seems superficially positive, but hides a deeper "unease" about race and technology.[2] Through engaging with his perspectives, we can think about changing relations to the labor of engaging with computation, and the roles such characters play in relation to the hero.

FIGURE 9.1

In *Jurassic Park* (Universal Pictures, 1993), Samuel L. Jackson plays John "Ray" Arnold, chief engineer of the park.

Such under-recognized figures exist in webs of meaning that tell us much about the shifting sociotechnical imaginary, and my three examples exert pressure on representational norms and values, particularly attitudes about advanced technology. In the following, I show how they have been ideologically overdetermined in their critical interpretations such that they are seen only as an extension of Black service to a central white male character, even though, in fact, they function more complexly for viewers. Below, I deploy an analysis of three key Black tech characters to open up a political affective space of possibility through a counter-reading that shows how, over the years, they shift in focus and significance relative to their cultural milieus.

TERMINATOR 2: ODE TO MILES DYSON

The *Terminator* franchise tightly conforms to classic technothriller anxiety narratives and representations. It is a story of humans versus machines, initiated with the highly popular B-movie *The Terminator* (James Cameron, 1984). Set in 2029, it describes a dystopian future in which an artificially intelligent military supercomputer called Skynet becomes sentient and immediately seeks domination, targeting humankind with nuclear strikes and a robotic army of Terminators. In its postapocalyptic world, only small pockets of humans survive as a scrappy resistance movement up against a far superior, networked, artificially superintelligent, genocidal system. Its primary adversary is a military leader named John Connor, whom Skynet must neutralize to crush the human resistance for good. To do so, Skynet plans to send a Terminator cyborg (Arnold Schwarzenegger) disguised as a human back in time to 1984 to kill Connor's mother, Sarah (Linda Hamilton), to prevent him from being born. Connor learns of this plot and sends back one of his own soldiers, Kyle Reese (Michael Biehn), to protect Sarah. Kyle succeeds in his mission but also falls in love with Sarah; together, they have a child—John—the future leader of the human resistance.

Terminator 2 (James Cameron, 1991) also features a nefarious plan to destroy John Connor (Michael Edwards), except this time John is the target. Skynet sends a shapeshifting, cutting-edge, liquid metal T-1000

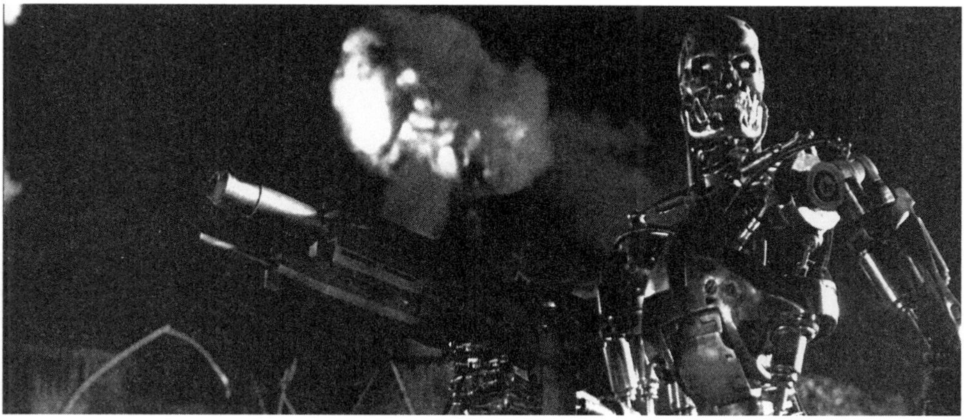

Terminator (Robert Patrick) back to 1995 to find the ten-year-old version of John.

Meanwhile, Connor sends back a reprogrammed T-800 (Arnold Schwarzenegger) to protect his younger self against the superior enemy. A scrappy kid, John (Edward Furlong) is living in a foster home while his mother remains institutionalized for her "schizophrenic" fantasy of the coming AI apocalypse. With the T-1000 always on the verge of killing young John and obliterating anyone in the way of its mission to do so, John and his T-800 guardian Terminator set off to free his mother and stop the "judgment day" that will come.

In the process Sarah learns that a Terminator CPU, along with a severed robotic arm, were recovered from the first assassination attempt (the events of the first film). Secured in a top-secret lab, the fragmented artifacts from the future are being reverse engineered. Miles Dyson, the lead computer specialist on the project, is the brilliant mind responsible for the technological breakthrough enabling Skynet to become sentient. Dyson has been working hard at the secret project for years, attempting

FIGURE 9.2

The *Terminator* films are set in a dystopic future in which technology has become sentient and subjugated humans. *Terminator 2: Judgment Day* (Tri-Star Pictures, 1991).

to recreate the mysterious futuristic technology. With his advanced computational knowledge and large, well-funded lab, he is near to completing his task. For Sarah, Dyson becomes the target: the unwitting key to changing humanity's fate.

The film was a box-office success and was lauded for its innovative, crowd-pleasing computer graphics techniques, particularly the visualization of the liquid metal T-1000 Terminator.[3] The original *Terminator* movie had a budget of $6 million; in contrast, at $90 million, *Terminator 2* was then the most expensive film ever made, with enormous resources poured into its action sequences and special effects.[4]

Terminator 2 resonated with its cultural moment and captured the public imaginary around technological anxieties of AI and robotics run amok. It was so resonant, in fact, that it was amply theorized from many perspectives: as an allegory for changes in the auto industry at the time of the film's release;[5] as a political tool of self-promotion for Arnold Schwarzenegger;[6] as emblematizing economic struggles between the waning industrial United States and high-tech Japan;[7] and as a symbolic struggle between modernity and postmodernity.[8] It has been read through anxieties around the technologized body in contemporary life;[9] as staging for fraught gender relations at the time and representations of female rage;[10] or even as a "homoerotic tableaux" poised "between the backward-looking Reagan years in which a Classic Hollywood star turned national leader presided over the nation, and the era of both postmodern techno-war and postgay articulations of sexual identity."[11] To be sure, the film entered a milieu fraught with cultural, political, economic, and technological change, much of which was projected onto the film.

Focusing on its core themes of unintended consequences of technological innovation offers insight into its function as a technothriller. The film turns on the idea passed back through time from the older John to his younger self: "The future is not set. There is no fate but what we make for ourselves." This is appropriate to the story of averting a machine/AI apocalypse, but it also has a strong message about the perils of technological innovation and making ethical choices. The theme is cautionary but not fatalistic; it offers the agency of presenting the possibilities of intentionality and change. Within the story, this theme bears down uniquely on Sarah, who feels personally responsible for averting this existential

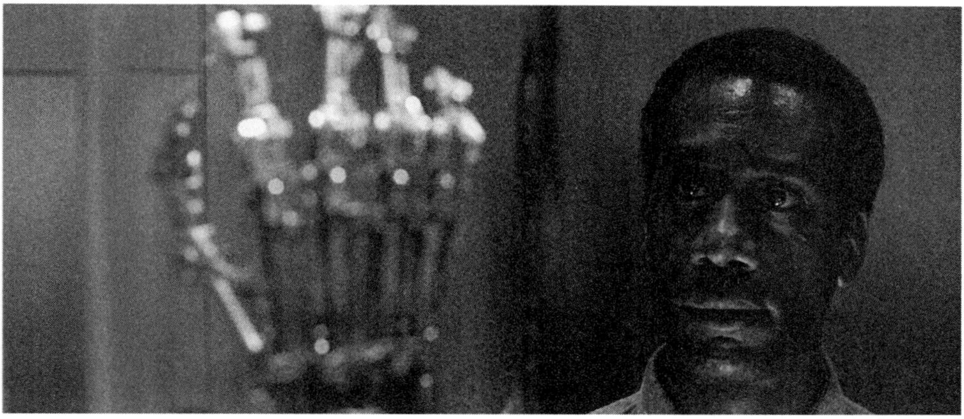

catastrophe, given her special knowledge of the future. But even more so it is embodied in the character of Miles Dyson, one of the most uncommon Black tech characters in film—not because previous examples did not exist, but because of his comparative centrality and sympathetic rendering, especially for the film's time. This is relayed both through his story arc and on the level of the film image.

Dyson, who is often referred to as an Oppenheimer-type figure, works for years on reverse engineering a critical computer chip left behind by the future—the CPU from a destroyed Terminator.[12] In the movie's timeframe he is very close to completing it. From this innovation comes a series of cascading unforeseen consequences leading to Skynet. Dyson has no idea what his invention will wreak on the world. He is no evil genius; rather, he is an innovator attempting to crack how the mysterious CPU works, and he is tenacious in that pursuit. But when the T-800 Terminator informs John and Sarah of Dyson's key role in future events, Sarah decides she must kill him.

FIGURE 9.3

Miles Dyson is the unwitting architect of the Skynet superintelligence in *Terminator 2: Judgment Day* (Tri-Star Pictures, 1991).

In this story about possible technological futures, the computer expert plays a pivotal role; Dyson unwittingly innovates the tech that makes machines sentient. This filmic representation of a Black tech is contradictory, because Dyson both represents an innovator of something that changes the world and also returns the world to a brutal place where humans can barely survive.

Some scholars have interpreted the character of Dyson through a sense of anxiety about the ongoing need to control Black bodies—particularly Black male bodies—on-screen, and to create them in opposition to an active white male hero. Kevorkian, for example, identifies a new dynamic in which films image undesirable technological work as the terrain of Blackness or other racialized others. Conversely, white (male) characters are spared such "digital drudgery."[13] The scholar deftly proposes that films subject Black male characters to containment and immobilization as a form of control that allays anxieties about the Black body. The Black male computer whiz is thus instrumentalized to buffer the white body against digital labor, and the technology itself becomes "denigrating."[14] For Kevorkian, a binary emerges between "executive white masculinity and technological blackness" such that it initiates "the phenomenon of the color-monitored computer operator as a postmodern mutation of the minstrelsy stereotype."[15] As Kevorkian observes, "The white hero issues a request, and a black man obligingly puts his hands on the keyboard."[16]

One key example he provides as illustration is Theo (Clarence Gilyard), the chatterbox computer expert from *Die Hard* (John McTiernan, 1988), whom he sees as a repackaged neo-minstrel entertainment character who ultimately serves a white protagonist. Kevorkian configures tech labor as a new kind of slavery—devalued work that exploits labor, overburdens the tech worker, and subjects the Black body to machine drudgery.[17] To some degree, such concerns prefigure important work critiquing the racialization of tech work, such as the research of Lisa Nakamura, highlighting how particular kinds of unwanted technological labor have often fallen to women and people of color.[18] However, Kevorkian's reading of such characters as necessarily engaged in computational "drudgery" rests on a relation to computing that has evolved since 2006. After all, the representation and cultural meaning of what it means to work with computers has shifted from the "women's work" of World War II female

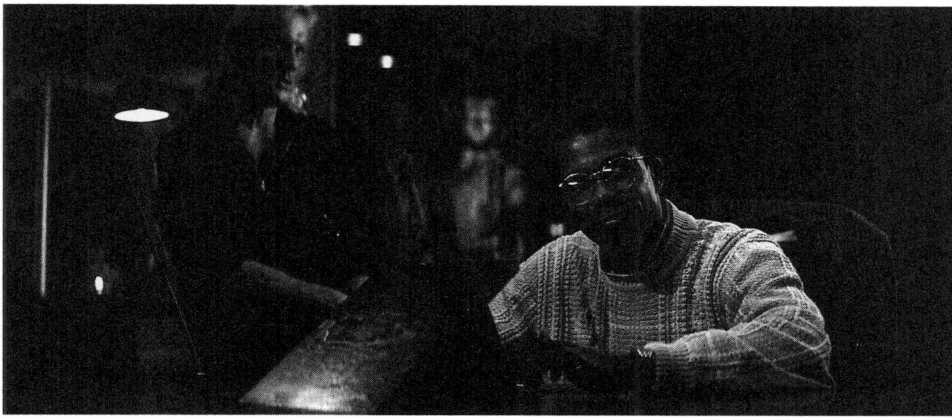

human computers. Given the heightened racialized dimensions of what it means to cast Black actors in particular roles, what kinds of cultural work do these representations do?

Specifically addressing *Terminator 2*, Kevorkian reads Dyson through a contradiction in which the Black character unleashes a "savage" technology that must be contained by a more civilized form of technology.[19] In other words, the unruliness of the technology in question becomes sutured to Blackness, and its domestication mapped onto whiteness. I argue that these characters, such as Dyson, are not purely revamped stereotypes, and that they do more cultural work than Kevorkian credits. Also, this ignores Dyson's agency in the timeline of the film. After all, Dyson effectively forestalls the future to come. At the end of this film he is no longer the innovator of doom, since he does not complete his research but throws himself into the fray to stop it by any means necessary. Most significantly, the interpretation presumes the relationship of viewers to Blackness as one of difference rather than identification.

FIGURE 9.4

Theo (Clarence Gilyard) (right) from *Die Hard* (20th Century Fox, 1988) as the extroverted tech expert.

Likewise, visual and cultural studies scholar Sharon Willis underscores—though in a very different way—the function of Dyson as a pernicious illustration of a Black man's symbolic social function of self-sacrifice to preserve the white family. She writes, "If Miles Dyson gets to be the embodiment of scientific arrogance, we cannot forget that he redeems himself precisely through his body's devastation as he sacrifices himself to allow the white nuclear family to escape intact. . . . The moment of his generative centrality is also the moment of his elimination."[20]

As well-intentioned as these approaches may be, they do not account for those viewers who may see themselves in Dyson or who identify with him and his iconic status as a computer engineer with unimpeachable moral fortitude. While he can be seen as a tragic character for his sacrifice, this does not make him purely a victim. Dyson is rendered with nuance as a consequential figure in a role that is incredibly rare on film: an ethical innovator. Dyson is neither simply a tokenized corrective to past erasures of Blackness, nor so tightly mapped onto the savagery to come. And he is more than a casualty of the cause of the white family's existence in the future. Miles Dyson is a hero who sacrifices himself for the cause of preserving all humanity.

The casting of Joe Morton, who plays Miles Dyson, makes an intervention into both the absence of mainstream images of Blackness in the future and the erasure of diverse technological innovators—which, of course, contradicts reality.[21] Dyson appears three times, each time becoming more dimensional as a character and moving from the background into the foreground. The first time, we see him at work; he moves about his lab, and his team treats him with deference, signaling to the audience that he is a person of consequence. He wields authority but is not feared or disliked, and his body language is patently mild mannered. He is slender, with a preppy look. We learn he has a high-security clearance to have firsthand access to the highly top-secret remnants of the destroyed Terminator. Much of the scene occurs in medium and long shots that allow the viewer to absorb details from his surroundings and interactions with others.

In the second instance, we see his domestic life. He is at his ocean-front home, with his wife and two adorable children, hunched over his computer. There are many signifiers of his class status: his large, orderly

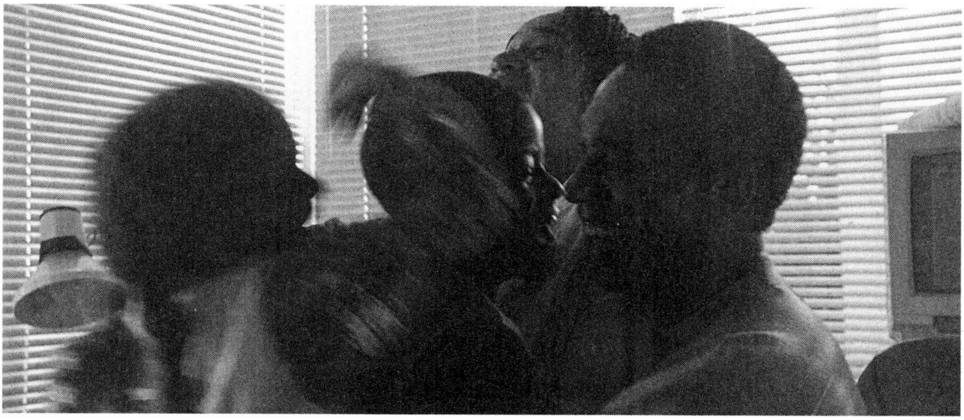

house with a pool near the Pacific, an elaborate computer setup in his office, and well-appointed interiors. He is near a breakthrough when his wife interrupts and affectionately redirects his attention to his kids, whom he's promised to spend time with. Setting aside his wife's admonitions that he is obsessed with his work, it is apparent that theirs is a warm and loving family with a placid home. This is an image of an upper-middle-class family like that of the Huxtables from *The Cosby Show* (NBC, 1984–1992), with which viewers of the time would have been familiar. In this sequence there are more frequent close-ups, depicting a normative nuclear family's domestic life. These images accord Dyson dimensionality and personhood and show that he has something precious to protect.

Dyson's third appearance is most significant since he is foregrounded as a critical agent within the narrative. One night, motivated by repeated nightmares of future machine holocaust, Sarah Connor makes a lone-wolf attempt to assassinate Dyson, but only wounds him in the shoulder.

FIGURE 9.5

Miles Dyson is imaged as a family man. In the Special Edition, added scenes show his home life in more detail. *Terminator 2: Judgment Day* (Tri-Star Pictures, 1991).

Seeing him writhing on the floor next to his wife and small son, she relents. Realizing what Sarah intends, John and his Terminator T-800 race to Dyson's home, to find his mother suffering a breakdown while deciding whether she should kill the innovator.

In a key scene, the unconventional family unit of Sarah, the Terminator, and John reveal their true purpose to the horror-struck innovator and his wife. To prove its nature, the T-800 strips off a section of flesh from its forearm, revealing its metal endoskeleton, which matches the damaged arm in the lab, then explains Dyson's special role in the coming future. "How were we supposed to know?" Dyson responds. Bandaged, bleeding, and sweating at his dinner table, the unassuming man promptly believes them, takes responsibility, and agrees to destroy his life's work and all evidence of the futuristic tech in his research facility. This is an extraordinary rendering of a sympathetic family man who might have easily chosen not to act. But, realizing he is already caught up in a future war, he throws himself into the fray.

Dyson displays ethical fortitude, joins Sarah's cause, and helps them infiltrate his lab to destroy everything else that might facilitate the microprocessor's innovation. He hands over the found chip and robot arm and helps John, the T-800, and Sarah rig the lab with explosives. Before long the police lay siege to the Cyberdyne building, and in a spectacular action sequence, Dyson is mortally wounded by gunfire. Sarah, John, and the T-800 escape while the dying Dyson stays behind, gripping the remote detonator for as long as he can until the SWAT team can clear the building. In the intimacy of an extreme close-up, eyes wide and drenched with sweat, Dyson unwinds like a clock and expires, releasing the remote and perishing in the massive fireball that obliterates Cyberdyne.

One possible reading is that Dyson is a tragic character who must die to contain a "savage" technology that, while an unintended consequence of his actions, was still his fault. However, an oppositional reading might return a different image: one of a person with the ethical clarity to recognize when their innovation needs to stop, and the purpose to act. We are shown that Dyson has a life and that his life matters to others, but he has no ambivalence about what is right. He is entirely present as a person who makes a values-driven decision—not one of self-interest—contradictory to the tech world's infamous "move fast and break things" ethos. Miles

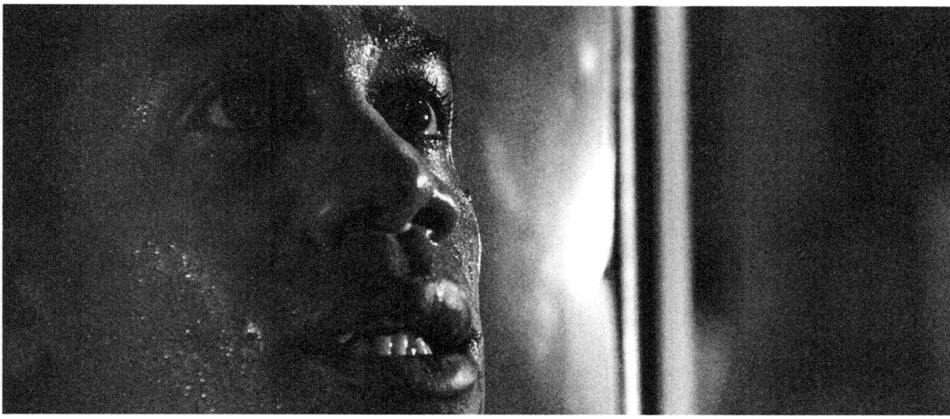

Dyson is, in the end, not a tragic Oppenheimer figure, but a hero who dies for the cause of saving all humanity—not just the white "family" of young John, Sarah, and the Terminator—from a machine apocalypse.

Dyson's character can also be read within a larger context of efforts in the late 1980s and 1990s to attract young, minoritized students with talents in math and science into scientific and technological degrees and careers. Considering the time in which *Terminator 2* was made, it is important to remember that STEM (science, technology, engineering, and math) was a term coined by the National Science Foundation in the early 1990s—first as SMET. The NSF very quickly began to focus on funneling talented, young, diverse students into a "pipeline" of related fields.[22]

One of the most critical components of America's status as a superpower, as I explained at the beginning of this project, has been its ability to lead in technological innovation. Understanding this anxiety about preserving global dominance in the social imaginary of the late 1980s, Dyson makes sense as a rare portrayal of a brilliant technological innovator who would be a beacon of heroism and righteousness for aspiring

FIGURE 9.6

Dyson is presented as sympathetic; he sacrifices his life to save humanity. *Terminator 2: Judgment Day* (Tri-Star Pictures, 1991).

young innovators in areas like computer science, engineering, and biotechnology. We can see echoes of Dyson in characters like Ray Arnold in *Jurassic Park* and Franklin Webb from *Jurassic World: Fallen Kingdom*—mentioned previously—or, in *Jurassic World Dominion* (Colin Trevorrow, 2022), Ramsay Cole (Mamoudou Athie), an ethical communications director of the corporation not-so-subtly named Biosyn Genetics (pronounced "bio-sin"), who blows the whistle on the corrupt activities of his unethical CEO.

Stuart Hall's famous delineation of audience reception as actively engaged in a process of accepting, negotiating, or rejecting dominant interpretations of media reminds us that the audience has agency in the production of meaning.[23] What's more, Blackness on screen need not be bounded by victimhood; these characters display interiority and agency, too. In discussing Kevorkian's text, scholar Abdul Alkalimat asks an extremely potent question invoking the problem of presumed viewers: "To what extent are these black geeks role models for nerds in the ghetto? How do black people 'read' these TV shows, films, and ads? . . . The 'nerd identity' could become a terrain of struggle, a goal people fight for."[24] Importantly, Alkalimat signals oppositional forms of audience reception that don't implicitly presume a lack of autonomy or fundamental servitude in these characters. To cast Dyson as without worth except as a tool for white characters to enact the containment of savagery is to ideologically overdetermine him as purely a victim. It discounts the oppositional look that receives him as a rebel hero against the mechanical apocalypse to come—and as one of the most iconic representations of an ethical innovator on film. Miles Dyson certainly does not solve all the representational problems or counterbalance the overwhelming whiteness of the genre. Still, his character stands out as a prototype counterimage that pushes back on the prevailing negation and erasure that was the undisputed norm.

MISSION: IMPOSSIBLE'S LUTHER STICKELL

Like Miles Dyson, computer hacker Luther Stickell (Ving Rhames) is one of the most celebrated, most memorable, and longest-running Black tech characters in American film—if a bit underrecognized. A supporting character in the Tom Cruise brand franchise *Mission: Impossible* (various directors, 1996–), Luther is the only one besides the hero, Ethan Hunt, to have appeared in all the films.[25] A spy thriller, the original *M:I* was directed by Brian De Palma and introduced the Impossible Missions Force, or IMF, a field team of elite agents averting nuclear destruction or some other global disaster by innovating solutions when no one else can.

The *Mission: Impossible* films feel very distinct from the pro-military, toxic American Tom Clancy–brand spy technothrillers, but repeat other key themes in refreshed form. They display advanced or speculative technologies and include covert spies operating extrajudicially, but in the interests of the greater good. The films always feature elaborate deceptions and disguises, advanced tech, unconventional intel gathering, and innovating on the fly. Even if everything goes wrong—as it always does—the agents of destruction never win against the good guys. Whether addressing fanciful themes of nuclear destruction, global domination, or various forms of international terrorism, *Mission: Impossible* films always grapple with the sociotechnical present.

The *Mission: Impossible* franchise also resembles James Bond films in many ways: it features intrigue, cartoonish villains, rarefied tech, fabulous clothes and cars, and splashy international locations. But, notably, the *Mission: Impossible* films make core characters far less dispensable. Particularly recurring entities, like ex-MI6 agent Ilsa Faust and tech experts Benji Dunn and Luther Stickell, are rendered humanely, the camera lingering on their faces and holding their eyes in frame, encouraging an emotional investment from the viewer even while offering plentiful anonymous heavies that make violent action sequences tolerable. The cinematography is slick and moves between interpersonal connection (signaled by those intimate close-ups), and impressive action sequences requiring a grand cinematic scale. Like James Bond, Ethan Hunt is clearly presented as the irresistible white male protagonist with perpetually ill-fated love interests; still, he tends not to just use and discard women. And an ongoing through line of his psychology as a character is that he is unwilling to treat his team members as disposable pawns.

Luther, the genius hacker and expelled IMF agent, is introduced in the original *M:I*. After a botched operation that kills his whole crew,

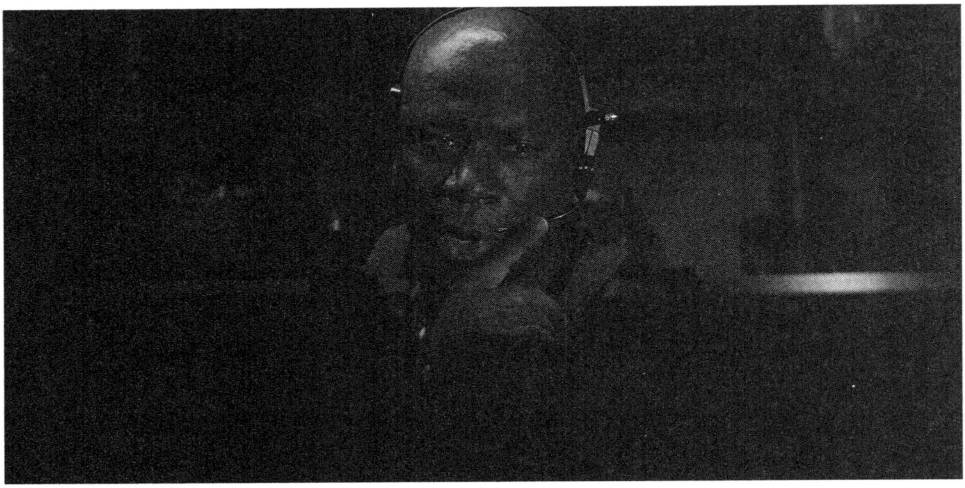

team leader Ethan Hunt (Tom Cruise) is framed for their deaths and "disavowed" from the IMF. A spy in the cold with no one to trust, Ethan turns to the IMF's disavowed agents list to recruit help in clearing his name and rooting out the true enemy. He chooses two former agents: Luther Stickell and helicopter pilot Franz Krieger (Jean Reno).

Ethan discloses the proposed impossible mission to the two men: infiltrate CIA Headquarters at Langley and steal data from an uncrackable computer in a highly protected vault. When Luther expresses doubts, Ethan reminds him of his illustrious hacker names—Phineas Phreak and the Net Ranger—and that he is the only person alive ever to have hacked NATO Ghost Com. Luther leans in and insists coyly, "There was *never* any physical evidence that I had anything to do with that—with that—that *exceptional* piece of work." Ethan wins Luther over with the promise

FIGURE 9.7

Luther Stickell is the tech genius in the *Mission: Impossible* films. While often shown stationary behind his computers, as above, in more recent films, he goes into the field. *Mission: Impossible* (Paramount Pictures, 1988).

of a coveted powerful laptop and, more importantly, bragging rights for pulling off "the Mount Everest of hacks."

What follows is the now-famous Langley vault heist action sequence in which the crack team obtains the top-secret NOC list ("nonofficial cover list") containing the true identities of covert operatives. It involves sneaking past a sound- and temperature-controlled environment, a pressure-sensitive floor requiring an acrobatic suspension from above by Ethan Hunt, security, and (of course) actual laser beams. By the end the impossible mission is accomplished, the corrupt agents are ferreted out, and both Ethan and Luther are reinstated as IMF agents.

Luther's representation is idiosyncratic, particularly in relation to his computer skills. Contradictory to the stereotype of fashion-challenged computer nerds, he has an individual sense of style: we meet him wearing a red turtleneck sweater under a cream-colored suit, gold hoop earrings, and a pair of black shades. He's a big man with a sonorous voice and a quick sense of humor, who telegraphs a strong physicality on-screen. Luther is an elite tech expert of rare skill and expertise, but also someone Ethan trusts with highly sensitive information. Like Miles Dyson, Luther has a strong moral compass that never wavers throughout the films.

Narratively, the original film communicates a sense of Luther's value to his team, and to Ethan in particular. While IMF agents are necessarily expendable, Ethan does not treat his team members as such, which often creates complications. For example, in *Mission: Impossible—Fallout* (Christopher McQuarrie, 2018) the inciting incident details Ethan's team's failure to obtain three plutonium cores for nuclear bombs that a terrorist network intends to use to disrupt global stability. During the planned exchange, Luther, who is providing remote support from a nearby van, is held hostage. In the action that ensues, Ethan refuses to sacrifice Luther in pursuit of the plutonium—contrary to IMF protocol—and thus fails the mission by prioritizing his team member's life. In this film there is a stronger focus on the emotional ties within the core team. Luther has a central role, and there is a greater emphasis on his interpersonal relations with Ethan than in other films.

Rather than being perpetually trapped behind his computers, Luther is often shown in the field, providing expertise, cracking security, and offering key intel. In *Fallout* he role-plays with Ethan in an elaborate hoax to trick a key target into unlocking a phone used to communicate with the terrorist leader. In the playing out of this ruse, involving a fake hospital room, a counterfeit CNN broadcast, and classic good cop/bad cop tactics, Ethan and Luther display a strong rapport and shared trust. Later, in the film's final set piece, involving two linked nuclear devices that require coordinated defusing, a helicopter chase, and a spectacular fight sequence, Luther provides the specialized skills to deactivate the bombs and key leadership in Ethan's absence. Luther is neither tethered to technology, purely instrumentalized as an extension of Ethan's needs, nor sacrificed for the sake of a white future.[26] Across the *M:I* films, Luther becomes ever more compelling as a multidimensional character of consequence for the franchise. Luther thus represents an ideological interruption as a character who neither conforms to the prevailing perceptions of tech-savvy nerds and who, in fact, often asserts a contradictory viewpoint that shapes the hero's perspective.

For example, *Dead Reckoning* (2023), the seventh *M:I* installment, combines technothriller themes—including an ultra-high-tech Russian submarine, a global threat, and resourceful men ferreting out intel. The villain is not a man with the nuclear codes but a sentient "active intelligence" AI called the Entity that portends a new world order of total informational control. One of the Entity's key human collaborators is the terrorist Gabriel (Esai Morales), a pre-IMF mortal enemy of Ethan's. In *Dead Reckoning* Luther is again critical to the smooth functioning of the mission. Because the nemesis is an AI, Luther's skill set becomes vital to understanding how to combat it.

With *Dead Reckoning*, Luther is most fully articulated on-screen as capable of reasoning things through, engaging in complex tech interventions, and adapting live in the field per the shifting needs of the mission. Like in the original film, Luther's technological prowess is conveyed first through banter about his reputation, then through his acumen, and finally through his demonstration of discerning character. Early on there is a comedic scene invoking the original *Mission: Impossible* introduction of Luther, in which team member Benji (Simon Pegg), grouses that Ethan has too quickly agreed that Luther is indisputably the far superior coder. Ethan and Luther gang up on Benji, teasing him that there's definitely no contest. Later, Luther impressively oversees two concurrent mission actions remotely, each requiring time-sensitive attention independent of Ethan's leadership, while the hero operates in the field. Luther speaks frankly with Ethan about not allowing his vendetta against Gabriel to compromise the larger mission. Ethan listens, despite his desire to avenge the murder of an MI6 ally and love interest, Ilsa Faust (Rebecca Ferguson). Ethan defers to Luther's expertise on how the evil AI is manufacturing outcomes using its strategies of predictive intelligence.

Toward the end of the film, Luther, who is the computer expert best equipped to think like the Entity and devise a means to defeat it, announces that he must go offline to work in isolation to prevent infiltration by the AI. In other words, in dealing with the active learning AI, Luther's contemplation and expertise, rather than Ethan Hunt's actions in the field, will ultimately be most critical to victory over the enemy.

On the level of the image, as Kevorkian describes, Luther mostly sits behind his tech gear in the original *Mission: Impossible*, and he is presented in a way that encloses him within the frame. In several scenes he indeed "remains passively seated behind his computer screen, [with] the sense of technological bodily containment all the more palpable."[27] But this changes across the subsequent films. As I mentioned, Luther goes "into the field" at many points, defusing bombs, providing transport, tech, and crucial oversight, among many other roles. Most importantly, he is an extremely consequential figure, despite what the size of his image relative to that of the action hero on the movie posters might imply.

To be sure, both Miles Dyson and Luther Stickell operate in a larger constellation of white male protagonists. As decentered figures, both are still significant, memorable, and activate a latent part of the sociotechnical imaginary against the erasures of mainstream cinema. Certainly, they are on-screen heroes for geeks of color everywhere. But more importantly, they are correctives. They combat a pernicious fiction that only some have a stake in the innovating of a future. In my third example, *Tenet*, the unnamed main character comes into awareness of himself as the protagonist of his own story. This development constitutes an important departure from conventional representation, one that seems to deliberately speak back with increasing force to the racial formations implicit in the technothriller's original DNA as a genre.

TENET: THE PROTAGONIST

The Protagonist in *Tenet* stands apart from the other two but similarly speaks back to the trajectory of the Black tech, seemingly in awareness of clinging, troublesome ideological patterns. In the above two examples, a Black male character is presented as meaningfully engaged with technological innovation but remains an ancillary character to the central white protagonist(s). Miles Dyson, largely due to Joe Morton's arresting performance, is instantly relatable and memorable. But however impactful, Dyson is secondary to the focal characters of John, Sarah, and the Terminator. Likewise, Luther Stickell is part of a team of spies led by protagonist Ethan Hunt. While over the years he has become unstuck from his command center, Luther is not the hero. But Christopher Nolan, in his nonlinear technothriller *Tenet*, forces a conversation about both the tendencies of the genre and viewer expectations by casting a Black male actor as the Protagonist.

Nolan is well-known for his brooding Batman Dark Knight trilogy, as well as for high-concept films that play with notions of reality and time, including *Memento* (2001), *Inception* (2010), *Interstellar* (2014), and *Dunkirk* (2017). He often focuses on innovative men who find ways to crack complex problems that require multidimensional thinking, and technological anxiety themes run through his work. There are often extended considerations of science and technology. For example, *Inception* features a procedurally detailed speculative technology that allows a user to tamper with people's dreams; *Interstellar* is about the science of space-time and its role in innovating human survival after ecological collapse; *Oppenheimer* (2023) is a biopic/thriller about the key figure responsible for the development of the atomic bomb.[28] In a way, it is fair to say that Nolan spotlights innovators.

Like many technothrillers, *Tenet* addresses a speculative existential threat. In this case it is not the bomb but a covert war in which technology has been invented to invert an object's entropy. Innovated in the future, inversion is a threat that pushes back onto the present and ultimately imperils known reality. "Tenet" is the name of a shadowy organization of spies who attempt to save the present from a hostile future. This clandestine group of skilled and elite operatives is inducted into a "twilight

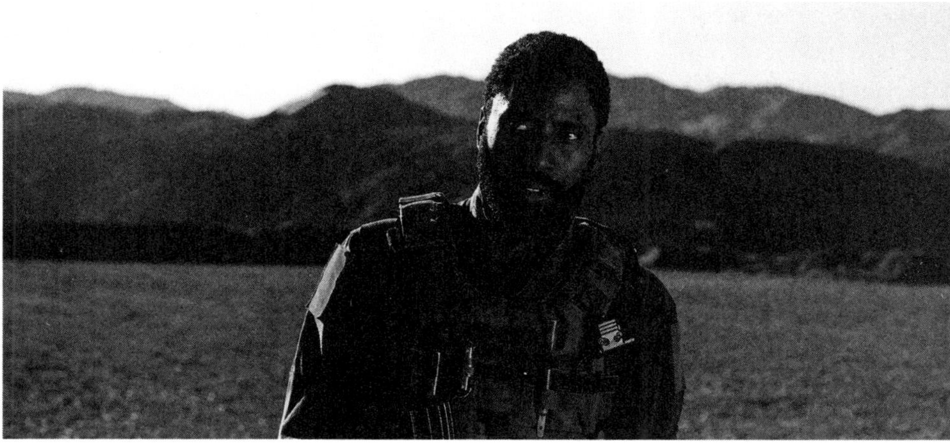

world" of commanding nonlinear time, wielding inverted objects, and concealing key intel, lest it become known to the future.

In this speculative scenario the unnamed main character, called only the Protagonist, must understand radical new paradigms. Barbara (Clémence Poésy), a scientist who studies found inverted objects she believes to be detritus of a coming future war, introduces the Protagonist to how such objects interact with our version of the world. The strangeness of picking up an inverted bullet or firing an inverted gun flummoxes him. "Don't try to understand it." Barbara tells him. "Feel it." This call to cultivate instincts about engaging with inverted objects moving backward in time begins small (like firing guns that catch rather than shoot bullets) but involves increasing stakes, culminating in the idea of an inverted nuclear-scale weapon that would potentially invert the past.

The statement not to try to "understand" but instead just "feel" it seems to speak back to Nolan's audience in a metaconversation about their

FIGURE 9.8

The ex-CIA spy recruited to Tenet, known only as the Protagonist. (*Tenet*, Warner Bros. Pictures, 2020).

known obsessions with the logics of his film's speculative technologies. Nolan's previous intellectual thrillers, like *Inception*, spent considerable screen time describing those imagined technologies, and fans fixated on those explanations, trying to make sense of the puzzle-like, mind-bending components of dealing with dreams within dreams and exploiting the shifting experiences of time in each layer. The inversion technology in *Tenet* and the struggle between the present and the future are never fully explained, but are spectacularly imaged in action sequences with people moving forward and backward in time in the same space. As the Protagonist becomes more adept at understanding this new reality and learns to think in a new way, he is better able to achieve his objective.

The Protagonist's mission is to understand the nature of the future's attack and whence the supply of inverted weaponry originates—it must come from the future, since it has not yet been invented in the present. Tenet provides him with a handler named Neil (Robert Pattinson) to assist, and he learns of an arms dealer in Mumbai, Priya (Dimple Kapadia), who is also a member of Tenet. Priya informs him of a nefarious Russian oligarch, arms dealer Andrei Sator (Kenneth Branagh), whom the Protagonist must access to ascertain how he is able to communicate with the future and provide weapons to be inverted. Sator is mysteriously imbricated in the future's plot to destroy the present world. But he is well insulated, so the Protagonist attempts to reach him through Sator's statuesque wife, Kat (Elizabeth Debicki), who despises her abusive husband but stays to protect her young son. With her help and the collaboration of other resourceful agents overseen by Neil, the Protagonist attempts to stop the future from inverting entropy on the whole world.

The Protagonist learns that the future is attacking the present to avert the ecological disaster that has not yet happened, but which the future already suffers. To stop this total annihilation, he must steal back the Algorithm, a black box device containing the formula capable of inverting the world's entropy. The Protagonist must adapt to his new reality by learning to think forward and backward simultaneously and strategizing around the new mental model of inverted time. Because he must move through timelines in inverted and noninverted spaces, the Protagonist must negotiate the problematics of a multiverse-type reality in which he may encounter another self on another timeline.

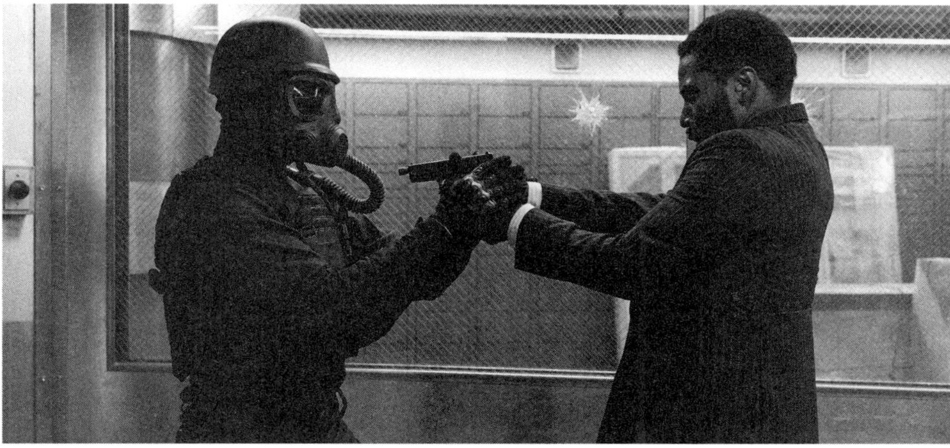

For example, in an early mission, Neil and the Protagonist break into one of Sator's sites, called a Freeport, which is purportedly for storing wealthy people's art but hides a "turnstile"—a revolving passageway between our world and the inverted one. When they discover it, two mysterious figures in black tactical gear burst through the turnstile, inverted, and the audience witnesses an odd fight scene with regular and inverted combatants moving forward and backward in time in the same space. Characters fall up, run in reverse, tumble impossibly, and struggle with each other's reversed physics. Later we see the same Freeport scene but from the chronological perspective of the inverted characters, who turn out to be the Protagonist from another timeline. The Protagonist fights himself, this time as the tactical-gear-clad figure, struggling with his other self in a tailored business suit. But this time the difference is that the Protagonist has a greater understanding of the scenario and can respond knowingly.

FIGURE 9.9

The Protagonist fights his inverted self in the time-bending film *Tenet* (Warner Bros. Pictures, 2020). In this shot the two are imaged as a duality, each occupying opposite sides of the screen.

Scenarios of chronologically experiencing an event, then reexperiencing it inverted, punctuate the film as a refrain and a theme. The Protagonist is repeatedly immersed in a hostile scenario, seeing but not understanding it, and then later experiences the same scene inverted with clarity. Placing a Black figure in this cycle is not so-called color-blind casting; it is an intervention grounded in a metaphor of inversion that meaningfully allegorizes how minoritized subjects experience a hostile world and learn to navigate it. It bespeaks what it means to be outside of things, to struggle to understand one's own circumstances, which flow against one's direction, and then to successfully find a way. It describes, on the level of the image, the feeling of swimming upstream, of existing as a blockage to the flowing of the world around you. The striking images of seagulls flying backward, steam reverse-billowing into its vent, and puddles un-splashing help build a mental picture of unrelenting adversity; it's the same world but experienced in a very different way.

Further, choosing John David Washington to star in *Tenet*, then brashly universalizing him by naming him the Protagonist, intervenes in Nolan's own previous pattern of casting. This move likely speaks back to how some of his previous films, especially the *Dark Knight* trilogy, were appropriated into a larger cultural narrative of toxic white male culture—particularly incel—and narratives of white male grievance. Nolan's films read as centering the white male hero, in keeping with the superhero genre and the James Bond–like stylish spy thriller.

This rare centering of a Black male protagonist in a science fiction/technothriller film occurs in a larger cultural milieu of the alt-right's critique of Hollywood liberalism and its so-called color-blind casting. For example, conservative provocateur Armond White of the *National Review* tore into the film's casting, writing: "*Tenet* merely caters to political correctness, specifically through the casting of John David Washington. . . . Not having inherited his father's sense of erotic menace, he suggests, in his quasi-flirtation with a white woman (Elizabeth Debicki), an incel idea of sex. Washington's laughable lack of worldly *nous*, his dead eyes and notable ghetto diction, render him unfit for sophisticated espionage. This touches on the unworkable idea of a black James Bond—the most absurd of all recent progressive cultural wishes."[29] In the wake of this ongoing conservative pushback against Hollywood's perceived identity politics, emblematized in the critic's vitriol, choosing a Black male protagonist to engage in "sophisticated espionage" for a high-concept film and then giving him the full James Bond treatment was a bridge too far.

In addition to White's accusation that Nolan was "putting race-hustling at the center of a major Hollywood blockbuster," critics expressed awareness of the significance of the casting.[30] *Forbes*, for example, mentioned it prominently, with reviewer Scott Mendelson noting this is "Nolan's first movie with a non-white lead, and there is a sharp undercurrent of dry wit concerning Washington getting to play through the tropes usually reserved for guys who look like Robert Pattinson or Michael Caine," and also that "it doesn't go unnoticed that Nolan is making a point to offer a comparatively inclusive cast of heroes and anti-heroes."[31] To varying degrees of intensity, reviewers expressed disappointment with *Tenet* in relation to Nolan's previous films. *Forbes* suggested that *Tenet* felt like Nolan was engaging in "self-parody" and that the film seemed "more concerned with looking cool than being good."[32]

What these reviews acknowledge is a strong reactiveness to the apparent discontinuity between Nolan's sophisticated filmic treatment and slick visual spectacle—for which the film won an Academy Award for Visual Effects—applied to the protagonist in question. In doing this, whether by responding negatively or merely highlighting it, reviewers underscore the radical nature of Nolan's decision to place a Black male protagonist at the center of the spy thriller/technothriller.

The political affect of what it means to image an African American protagonist with the full James Bond treatment would be ideologically violent for some. The film was shot in seven international locations, using 65mm film and IMAX, which provides exquisite cinematography with extraordinary sensitivity in low-light conditions. With its rich naturalistic images, flattering portraiture that invokes contemporary documentary photography, and enveloping bokeh effects, *Tenet* telegraphs glamour, luxury, power, and intrigue, and places the main character in the role of leading man.[33] In the parlance of spy thriller films like the Bond franchise, that whole visual arsenal broadcasts the Protagonist's presumed desirability (i.e., the idea that women want him and men want to be him). Even the genre itself is highly beloved and notably deviates little from its oldest generic elements. But when considering the culture war that

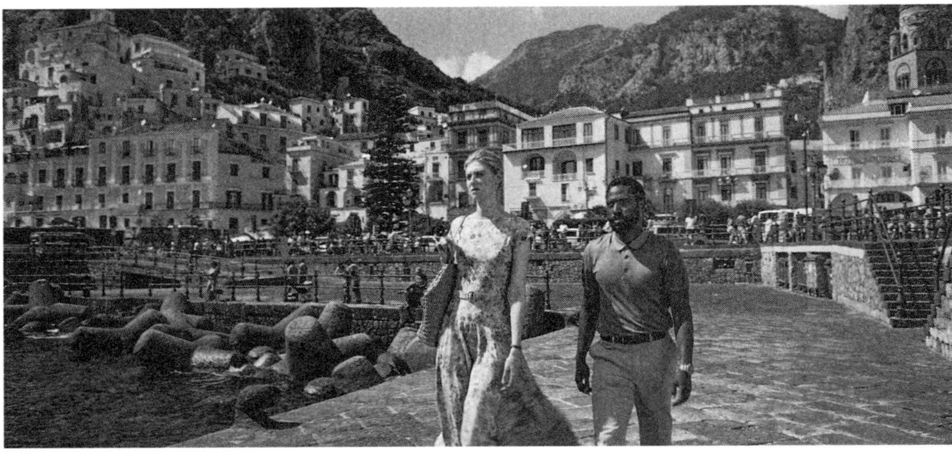

such a film enters—including the rise of the alt-right, increasing white nationalism, and anti-inclusive sentiment—Nolan's ethnically diverse film casting sends a strong message. In the end the main character realizes that he has been working for himself, not his contact, Priya. With this he declares, "I'm the Protagonist" and eliminates her, which, in the context of the culture war I described, feels like twisting the knife.

In giving John David Washington the full Bond treatment, Nolan engages in another kind of world-building, one that uses form and content to break long-standing conventions around presumptive racial formations associated with the genre. In fact, the James Bond–like spy thrillers on which *Tenet* innovates are themselves racialized representations that typically ignore the actual world, instead conjuring one devoid of the difference that one sees everywhere in lived experience.[34] In the end these interventions that feel so genre-breaking, even ideologically disruptive,

FIGURE 9.10

Tenet (Warner Bros. Pictures, 2020) gives the Protagonist the full "Bond" film treatment, including luxurious clothing, intrigue, and gorgeous international settings like the Amalfi Coast.

are just presenting the world as it is. Characters like the Protagonist and the public response to them simply unveil how recognition is not yet fully inclusive in the sociotechnical imaginary.

LOOKING AT THE WORLD IN A NEW WAY

As I have shown across this book, technothrillers are largely for and about white men, and rarely image women, people of color, queer people, or otherwise minoritized subjects as agents of innovation. In the genre, white male genius is perpetually mythologized and reinscribed as the locus of technological progress. I have asked questions about the sociotechnical imaginary through the technothriller, looking deeply at whose futures these films imagine and whom those images serve. That said, I have also argued that the seeds of important counternarratives are already planted in these technothrillers. We can often see them by casting the "oppositional gaze" that bell hooks conceptualized and by noticing what might not be immediately evident, but nevertheless operates in plain sight.[35]

Despite their ideological tendencies, technothrillers are useful tools for understanding what we think when we, as a culture, worry about technology. We worry about technology more and more; in keeping with that reality, technothrillers are ever more present and relevant. And, across the genre, technothrillers possess traces of their own counternarratives. The Black tech archetype constitutes one key counternarrative. It is easy to miss this figure, who often labors in the shadow of a white male hero who absorbs the primary on-screen focus. But just see who is seated at the computer console behind the protagonist or check whose voice is in the hero's earpiece, guiding him. What if we think of Miles Dyson as not just a tragic emblem of innovation being placed in the wrong hands, or a confirmation of how nonviable Black people are in the future? How can we understand Luther Stickell of *Mission: Impossible* if he is not just a human peripheral device that physically buffers a white male action hero from direct contact with the computational? What does it say about the ideological investments of a technothriller if replacing a white male protagonist seems to break the genre conventions? In these examples, we can see the technothriller genre struggling with its own conventions and negotiating shifting cultural and sociopolitical terrain.

The technothriller has always been a generic form that negotiates larger tensions and struggles for recognition as we face the reality of advanced technology in our lives. This is evidenced in the unabashed exclusions demonstrated in many of its core narratives and the scant presence of any diverse characters of consequence—though, as I've shown, they are often there, lingering in the background, sometimes even beloved. Luther, for example, does perish in *Mission: Impossible—The Final Reckoning* (Christopher McQuarrie, 2025). But notably, he is given the last word of the entire series through his posthumously delivered message to Ethan. In it, he affirms that, "Any hope for a better future comes from willing that future into being." With expressive philosophical introspection, Luther articulates the core ethics of the IMF team, including embracing free will and humanistic values, and struggling against the technological determinism (symbolized by the Entity) that would ensnare humanity.

Rumblings of reimagining can be felt in the work of filmmakers like Gareth Edwards's *The Creator* (2023) and Christopher Nolan's *Tenet*, which intervene on the level of the image to disrupt underlying presumptions. Such counter-visions and counter-readings as I have described put pressure on genre conventions and model ways to confront the practices and characteristics that no longer serve it well. In breaking limiting conventions, they map other ways of reimagining the modern subject in the wake of advanced technological innovation. Through a powerful form of visual persuasion, these films intervene in the social imaginary and invite us to consider how we think about technology anew.

As one of our most iconic technothrillers reminds us: "The future is not set. There is no fate but what we make for ourselves."[36] We can make stories and a viable path forward without the inevitability of total annihilation, subjugation, ecological apocalypse, or literally being eaten by our own bioengineered innovations. Technothrillers can be useful tools for learning to live with the existential uncertainty wrought by our innovations, navigating fear of the uncontrollable, contending with the fallout of techno-optimism, and negotiating our cloying American problems—together.

ACKNOWLEDGMENTS

Many sharp, capable, tenacious, and encouraging people came together to make this book possible. Victoria Hindley at the MIT Press immediately understood what this project was about and provided guidance that fostered the spirit of its intentions. Thank you to Victoria and her talented editorial staff for supporting this book and recognizing it as a topic worth discussing. To the anonymous external reviewers: Your feedback helped push this work to the next level, and I thank you for being fair and constructive. Kate Washington's excellent editing kept me on track and on point. This book is influenced by so many scholars whose work I remain grateful for, including Stuart Hall, Richard Dyer, Nezar AlSayyad, Jack Halberstam, Barry Keith Grant, Vivian Sobchack, Annette Kuhn, Lisa Nakamura, and Sherryl Vint.

The University of California supported the development of this research through the EVC Fellows Academy, which offered generous funding, course releases, and keenly observant writing partners: Amy Lonetree, Noriko Aso, and Mary Beth Pudup. Special thanks to L. S. Kim for connecting me with the Fellows Academy. I would also like to thank Feminist Media Histories for early support of this research with a Summer GSR Grant. Alessia Lupo Cecchet and Brian Myers provided research assistance in the early phases of this project. Part of this research was presented at the Society of Cinema and Media Studies Annual Conference in 2024 on the invitation of my valued colleague, Matthew Thomas Payne.

My first interest in teaching about the technothriller came about when, while browsing the course catalog, I stumbled on a long-untaught offering in my department's listings, got curious, and decided to revive it—and then became obsessed. So thanks are in order to David Crane, who taught at UCSC's Film and Digital Media Department before me and once upon a time was interested in technothrillers. Special thanks to Katherine Isbister. My warm thanks go to Dorothy Santos, Abram Stern, ksenia fir, Keegan Farrell, and the many teaching assistants who helped me share this material. And, of course, thank you to the students of my technothrillers course over the years, who energized my work and teaching. It has been one of my most enjoyable and successful courses, mainly due to you.

Finally, I appreciate my family for supporting me, especially my sister, Leilah, and my mother, Gigi. But most of all, thank you to my husband, Derek, for exposing me to these films so many years ago, for patiently listening to my ideas about them, for reading early drafts, for the encouragement, and for the unvarnished counsel. I couldn't have done any of it without you.

NOTES

PREFACE

1. Ray Morton, *Close Encounters of the Third Kind: The Making of Steven Spielberg's Classic Film* (New York: Applause, 2007), 116.

INTRODUCTION

1. The term *technothriller* is also sometimes spelled "techno-thriller"; however, there is no consensus. I will be using *technothriller* but will keep the spelling consistent with original in quotes.
2. For an excellent and thorough filmography of perceptions of science and technology in popular films, see Steven L. Goldman, "Images of Technology in Popular Films: Discussion and Filmography," *Science, Technology, & Human Values* 14, no. 3 (1989): 275–301.
3. Alexis L. Boylan, *Visual Culture* (MIT Press, 2020), xix.
4. Sherryl Vint, ed., *Science Fiction and Cultural Theory: A Reader* (Routledge, 2016), 4.
5. Some of these ideas were previously published in Soraya Murray, "Video Games: Art, Inclusion, and the Techno-cultural Imaginary" in *Stronger Than Bone: On Feminism(s)*, ed. Defne Ayas, Natasha Ginwala, and Jill Winder (Archive Books, 2020), 252–269.
6. Ruth Oldenziel, *Making Technology Masculine: Men, Women, and Modern Machines in America, 1870–1945* (Amsterdam University Press, 1999), 23.
7. Oldenziel, *Making Technology Masculine*, 17; See also Carolyn Marvin, *When Old Technologies Were New: Thinking About Electric Communication in the Late Nineteenth Century* (Oxford University Press, 1990).
8. Oldenziel, *Making Technology Masculine*, 14.
9. Oldenziel, *Making Technology Masculine*, 12.
10. Oldenziel, *Making Technology Masculine*, 44, 69. These divisions were reinforced, as Oldenziel explains, through the second Morrill Act, in which sixteen federally supported African American land-grant institutions, as well as seven state-run normal schools and colleges, were established between 1890 and 1915 to promote separate but equal education.
11. Oldenziel, *Making Technology Masculine*, 19. Emphasis added.

12. Donald A. MacKenzie and Judy Wajcman, eds., *The Social Shaping of Technology*, 2nd ed. (Open University Press, 1999).

13. Langdon Winner, *The Whale and the Reactor: A Search for Limits in an Age of High Technology* (University of Chicago Press, 2001). Originally published in 1986. See especially "Do Artifacts Have Politics?"

14. Merritt Roe Smith and Leo Marx, eds., *Does Technology Drive History? The Dilemma of Technological Determinism* (MIT Press, 1994).

15. Sheila Jasanoff, "The Dangerous Appeal of Tech," *MIT Technology Review* 124, no. 4 (June 30, 2021): 16–17; See also Sheila Jasanoff, "Ordering Knowledge, Ordering Society," in *States of Knowledge: The Co-Production of Science and Social Order* (Routledge, 2004), 13–45.

16. Sheila Jasanoff, "Future Imperfect: Science, Technology, and the Imaginations of Modernity," in *Dreamscapes of Modernity*, ed. Sheila Jasanoff and Sang-Hyung Kim (University of Chicago Press, 2015), 2.

17. Sam Evans et al., "STS Research Platform: Sociotechnical Imaginaries," Harvard Kennedy School of Government Program on Science, Technology & Society, 2010, https://sts.hks.harvard.edu/research/platforms/imaginaries.

18. Jasanoff attributes the term to an earlier work by herself and Sang-Hyun Kim in 2009, which is subsequently expanded to the definition they set forth in *Dreamscapes of Modernity*. See Sheila Jasanoff and Sang-Hyun Kim, "Containing the Atom: Sociotechnical Imaginaries and Nuclear Regulation in the U.S. and South Korea." *Minerva* 47, no. 2 (2009): 119–146.

19. Jasanoff, "Future Imperfect," 4–5.

20. Jasanoff, "Future Imperfect," 5.

21. Jasanoff, "Future Imperfect," 22.

22. Sherryl Vint, *Science Fiction* (Cambridge, MA: MIT Press, 2021), 17.

23. Jasanoff, "Future Imperfect," 19.

24. Sheila Jasanoff, "Sheila Jasanoff: Co-Production," accessed December 3, 2021, https://sheilajasanoff.org/research/co-production.

25. J. William Gibson, "Redeeming Vietnam: Techno-Thriller Novels of the 1980s," *Cultural Critique*, no. 19 (1991): 200, https://doi.org/10.2307/1354313.

26. Tad Friend, "The Pentagon's Favorite Novelist," *Gentlemen's Quarterly* 58, no. 6 (June 1998): 271. As cited in Helen S. Garson, *Tom Clancy: A Critical Companion* (Greenwood Press, 1996), 45.

27. Scott Simmon, *The Invention of the Western Film: A Cultural History of the Genre's First Half-Century* (Cambridge University Press, 2003), xiii.

28. Simmon, *The Invention of the Western Film*, xiv.

29. Vivian Sobchack, *Screening Space: The American Science Fiction Film* (Rutgers University Press, 1997), 62.

30. Janet Staiger, Ann Cvetkovich, and Ann Reynolds, "Introduction: Political Emotions and Public Feelings," in *Political Emotions* (Routledge, 2010), 5–6.

31. Deborah Gould, Rory Barron, Brittany Frodge, and Robby Hardesty, "Affect and Activism: An Interview with Deborah Gould," *disClosure: A Journal of Social Theory* 28, no. 8 (2019), https://doi.org/10.13023/DISCLOSURE.28.08; see also Deborah Gould, "On Affect and Protest," in *On Affect and Protest* (Routledge, 2010), 18–44, https://doi.org/10.4324/9780203849538-8.
32. Soraya Murray, "America Is Dead. Long Live America! Political Affect in Days Gone," *European Journal of American Studies* 16, no. 3 (September 2021), https://doi.org/10.4000/ejas.17409.
33. bell hooks, "The Oppositional Gaze: Black Female Spectators," in *Black Looks: Race and Representation* (South End Press, 1992), 115–32.
34. hooks, "Oppositional Gaze," 116.
35. Annette Kuhn, *Alien Zone: Cultural Theory and Contemporary Science Fiction Cinema* (Verso, 1990), 1.
36. Michael Crichton, "Westworld," *MichaelCrichton.Com* (blog), December 10, 2014, https://www.michaelcrichton.com/westworld.
37. Dean Koontz, "*Demon Seed* From the Author," *Dean Koontz* (blog), May 20, 2010, https://www.deankoontz.com/demon-seed-from-the-author.
38. Laura Mulvey, *Afterimages: On Cinema, Women and Changing Times* (Reaktion Books, 2019), 242.
39. Sobchack, *Screening Space*, 17–18.

CHAPTER 1

1. Anne O'Hare McCormick, "Abroad: The Promethean Role of the United States Not Launched Lightly Power to Shape the Future," *New York Times*, August 8, 1945, 22.
2. Sam Boush, "Crypto, Sci-Fi, Soldiers, Spies (and Disasters): 5 Varieties Within the Technothriller Genre," *Writer's Digest*, July 19, 2018, https://www.writersdigest.com/write-better-fiction/varieties-of-the-technothriller-genre.
3. Helen S. Garson, *Tom Clancy: A Critical Companion* (Greenwood Press, 1996), 35.
4. Cormac Deane, "The Control Room: A Media Archaeology," *Culture Machine* 15 (2015): 1–34.
5. Ian Frazier, "Techno-Thriller," *The Atlantic*, May 2001, https://www.theatlantic.com/magazine/archive/2001/05/techno-thriller/302203/fr.
6. Vivian Sobchack, *Screening Space: The American Science Fiction Film* (Rutgers University Press, 1997), 86.
7. See chapter 2.
8. Joseph Gelmis, "Author of 'Terminal Man' Building Nonterminal Career," *Los Angeles Times*, January 4, 1974.
9. Helen S. Garson, *Tom Clancy: A Critical Companion* (Greenwood Press, 1996), 26.

10. Tom Clancy and Martin Harry Greenberg, *The Tom Clancy Companion* (Berkley Books, 1992), 55.

11. William F. Ryan, "The Genesis of the Techno-Thriller," *Virginia Quarterly Review* 69, no. 1 (1993): 26–27.

12. Michael Crichton, "*The Andromeda Strain* in His Own Words," MichaelCrichton .com, December 10, 2014, https://www.michaelcrichton.com/the-andromeda -strain.

13. Nathan Aaseng, *Michael Crichton* (Lucent Books, 2002), 10.

14. Aaseng, *Michael Crichton*, 39.

15. Bob Minzesheimer, "Appreciation: Tom Clancy Mastered the Techno-Thriller," *USA Today*, October 2, 2013, https://www.usatoday.com/story/life/books/2013/10 /02/tom-clancy-appreciation/2908305.

16. Robert Lekachman, "Red Storm Rising Is a Well Told Story," in *Readings on Tom Clancy*, ed. Richard Baiocco (Greenhaven Press, 2004), 63.

17. Garson, *Tom Clancy*, 36.

18. Clancy and Greenberg, *The Tom Clancy Companion*, 123.

19. Dan Listwa, "Hiroshima and Nagasaki: The Long Term Health Effects," Columbia K=1 Project, August 9, 2012, https://k1project.columbia.edu/news/hiroshima -and-nagasaki.

20. For an excellent overview of the cultural impact of nuclear weapons in the United States see H. Bruce Franklin, *War Stars: The Superweapon and the American Imagination* (University of Massachusetts Press, 2008).

21. Paul Boyer, *By the Bomb's Early Light: American Thought and Culture at the Dawn of the Atomic Age* (University of North Carolina Press, 1994), 65–66.

22. Boyer, *By the Bomb's Early Light*, 114.

23. Boyer, *By the Bomb's Early Light*, xix. For more on the connection between computation, cybernetics, and the Cold War, see Charlie Gere, *Digital Culture* (Reaktion Books, 2002), 58–74.

24. McCormick, "Abroad."

25. Patrick Anderson, "King of the 'Techno-Thriller,'" *New York Times*, May 1, 1988, late edition, sec. A; Robert Lekachman, "Virtuous Men and Perfect Weapons," *New York Times*, July 27, 1986, sec. A.

26. "Tom Clancy: Obituaries Bestselling Thriller Writer Whose Books Seemed Fanciful but Often Prefigured Real-World Battles," *Daily Telegraph*, October 3, 2013, sec. Obituaries, 35.

27. Julie Bosman, "Tom Clancy, Best-Selling Master of Military Thrillers, Dies at 66: Jack Ryan: From Novels To Films," *New York Times*, 2013.

28. Jeffrey Goldberg, "Playing With Firearms: At Home, Armed with an Automatic Weapon, the Novelist Tom Clancy Lets Down His Guard," *New York Times Magazine*, June 13, 1999; Garson, *Tom Clancy*, 1996, 15; Peter Carlson, "What Ticks Tom Clancy Off?," *Washington Post*, June 27, 1993; Jonathan Yardley, "Tom Clancy: Firing, and Missing," *Washington Post*, January 27, 1992.

29. Anonymous, "Life at Red Storm," Red Storm Entertainment, accessed November 15, 2021, https://www.redstorm.com/the-studio.

30. Edwin Evans-Thirlwell, "If Ubisoft Wants to Cling on to Clancy, It's Time to Talk Politics," Eurogamer, June 22, 2018, https://www.eurogamer.net/amp/2018-06-20-the-oppressive-afterlife-of-tom-clancy?__twitter_impression=true; Constance Delbreil, "Ubisoft Celebrates 20 Years of Tom Clancy Games," Red Storm Entertainment, December 15, 2020, https://www.redstorm.com/news-2/ubisoft-celebrates-20-years-of-tom-clancy-games.

31. Jason Cowley, "Tom Clancy: Terror in America: The Literature," *New Statesman*, September 24, 2001.

32. Evan Thomas, "The Art of the Techno-Thriller," *Newsweek*, August 8, 1988.

33. Andrew J. Bacevich, "Tom Clancy, Military Man," *The Baffler*, no. 24 (2014): 160.

34. Michael Crichton, "Aliens Cause Global Warming," in *Three Speeches by Michael Crichton* (California Institute of Technology, 2003), 2.

35. *Binary* was published under the pseudonym John Lange.

36. Erik Stengler, "Beyond the Techno-Thriller: Michael Crichton and Societal Issues in Science and Technology," *Fafnir* 2, no. 3 (September 2015): 24, https://uwe-repository.worktribe.com/output/805749/beyond-the-techno-thriller-michael-crichton-and-societal-issues-in-science-and-technology.

37. Chris Gardner, "Michael Crichton's Widow, Sherri, Opens Up on 'Andromeda Strain' Sequel with 'Female Scientific Edge,'" *Hollywood Reporter* (blog), November 11, 2019, https://www.hollywoodreporter.com/news/general-news/michael-crichtons-widow-opens-up-andromeda-strain-sequel-i-cant-say-it-was-ever-a-slam-dunk-1253606.

38. Sam Kashner, "When Michael Crichton Reigned over Pop Culture, from ER to Jurassic Park," *Vanity Fair*, February 13, 2017, https://www.vanityfair.com/hollywood/2017/02/michael-crichton-reign-over-pop-culture-jurassic-park-westworld.

39. "Michael Crichton on 'The Problems of Representing Technology in Fiction,'" *Point of View* (Chicago Field Museum: WNUA 95.5, August 21, 1993), http://archive.org/details/michael-crichton-1993-08-21-mp3.4RUDp2.popuparchive.org.

40. "The Problems of Representing Technology in Fiction"

41. "Move fast and break things" was famously the internal "motto" of Facebook, which favored fast innovation at the expense of all other considerations, including ethics.

42. Michael Crichton, "Reflections of a New Designer," *Compute! Magazine*, February 1985, 45.

43. Michael Crichton, "Ritual Abuse, Hot Air, and Missed Opportunities," *Science* 283, no. 5407 (1999): 1462.

44. Martin Kevorkian, *Color Monitors: The Black Face of Technology in America* (Cornell University Press, 2006), 48.

45. Kevorkian, *Color Monitors*, 38.

46. Kevorkian, *Color Monitors*, 49.
47. Kevorkian, *Color Monitors*, 38–39.
48. J. William Gibson, "Redeeming Vietnam: Techno-Thriller Novels of the 1980s," *Cultural Critique*, no. 19 (1991): 198, https://doi.org/10.2307/1354313.
49. Ryan, "The Genesis of the Techno-Thriller," 27.
50. Michael J. Blouin, "Michael Crichton and the Heritage of Invention," in *Mass-Market Fiction and the Crisis of American Liberalism, 1972–2017*, ed. Michael J. Blouin (Springer, 2018), 115, https://doi.org/10.1007/978-3-319-89387-7_4.
51. Michael J. Blouin, "Tom Clancy and the Liberal Family Tree," in *Mass-Market Fiction and the Crisis of American Liberalism, 1972–2017*, ed. Michael J. Blouin (Springer, 2018), 159, https://doi.org/10.1007/978-3-319-89387-7_5.
52. Joanna Radin, "The Speculative Present: How Michael Crichton Colonized the Future of Science and Technology," *Osiris* 34, no. 1 (June 2019): 297–315, https://doi.org/10.1086/704047.
53. Radin, "Speculative Present," 304.
54. William Grimes, "Michael Crichton, Author of 'Jurassic Park' and Other Thrillers, Dies at 66," *New York Times*, 2008, sec. Obituaries, A31.
55. Boyer, *By the Bomb's Early Light*, xxi.

CHAPTER 2

1. Norma Lee Browning, "Hollywood Today: Mike Crichton, a Skyscraper in Any Form," *Chicago Tribune (1963–1996)*, August 30, 1970, sec. SOUTH.
2. Robert Wise, in the original theatrical trailer for *The Andromeda Strain*.
3. *A Portrait of Michael Crichton*, DVD, The Andromeda Strain Bonus Materials (Universal Studios Home Video, 2003), 5:55.
4. *The Andromeda Strain: Making the Film*, The Andromeda Strain DVD (Universal Studios Home Entertainment, 2001).
5. Arthur Knight, "Wise in Hollywood," *Saturday Review*, August 8, 1970, 22–23.
6. Robert J. Emery, *The Directors: Take 1* (Allworth Press, 2002), 39.
7. Boyer, *By the Bomb's Early Light*, 352–353.
8. Boyer, *By the Bomb's Early Light*, 357–358.
9. José Van Dijck, "Biohazards and Bioethics," in *Imagenation: Popular Images of Genetics*, ed. José Van Dijck (Palgrave Macmillan, 1998), 63, https://doi.org/10.1057/9780230372665_4.
10. Van Dijck, "Biohazards and Bioethics."
11. Mark Kortepeter, "The Nation's Bio-Emergency Hotline," in *Inside the Hot Zone: A Soldier in the Trenches Defending against Biological Weapons* (University of Nebraska Press, 2020), 47.

12. Daniel Dinello, *Technophobia!: Science Fiction Visions of Posthuman Technology* (University of Texas Press, 2006), 251–252.

13. Dinello, *Technophobia!*, 247.

14. The disturbing animal scenes were achieved by suffocating and reviving rats and monkeys, under doctor supervision. See Jon Bloom, "Photographing *The Andromeda Strain*—The American Society of Cinematographers," *American Cinematographer*, September 3, 2020, https://ascmag.com/articles/the-andromeda-strain-may-1971.

15. Paul D. Zimmerman, "The Germonauts," *Newsweek*, March 29, 1971.

16. Pauline Kael, "The Andromeda Strain," *New Yorker*, March 27, 1971, 99–103.

17. Dean Conrad and Lynne Magowan, "Female Scientists under Strain," in *Lab Lit: Exploring Literary and Cultural Representations of Science*, ed. Olga Pilkington and Ace G. Pilkington (Rowman & Littlefield, 2019), 36.

18. Bruce Austin and Robert Wise, "An Interview with Robert Wise," *Literature/Film Quarterly* 6, no. 4 (1978): 306.

19. Bloom, "Photographing *The Andromeda Strain*."

20. Bloom, "Photographing *The Andromeda Strain*"; Browning, "Hollywood Today."

21. Bloom, "Photographing *The Andromeda Strain*."

22. Bloom, "Photographing *The Andromeda Strain*."

23. Knight, "Wise in Hollywood," 24.

24. Bloom, "Photographing *The Andromeda Strain*."

25. Roger Greenspun, "Screen: Wise's *Andromeda Strain*," *New York Times*, March 22, 1971, 40.

26. Jack Halberstam has discussed this in relation to filmic constructions of white male stupidity. See Jack Halberstam, *The Queer Art of Failure* (Duke University Press, 2011), 55.

27. Hazmat suits also appeared in the film *The Satan Bug* (John Sturges, 1965), but were more dominantly displayed in Andromeda, which popularized the image.

28. Sylvia Millar, "The Andromeda Strain," *Monthly Film Bulletin*, January 1, 1971.

29. Paul Ramaeker, "Notes on the Split-Field Diopter," *Film History* 19, no. 2 (2007): 180–81.

30. Ramaeker, "Notes on the Split-Field Diopter," 182–183.

31. Ramaeker, "Notes on the Split-Field Diopter," 187.

32. Tara McPherson, "U.S. Operating Systems at Mid-Century: The Intertwining of Race and UNIX," in *Race After the Internet*, ed. Lisa Nakamura and Peter Chow-White (Routledge, 2012), 29.

33. McPherson, "U.S. Operating Systems," 32, 34.

34. Technosolutionism or technological solutionism refers to the idea that technology and innovation can solve all problems, with, as Evgeny Morozov describes "computable solutions or as transparent and self-evident processes that can be

easily optimized—if only the right algorithms are in place!" See Kehan Jiang, "The Folly of Technological Solutionism: An Interview with Evgeny Morozov," *Public Books* (blog), September 9, 2013, https://www.publicbooks.org/the-folly-of-technological-solutionism-an-interview-with-evgeny-morozov/; Evgeny Morozov, *To Save Everything, Click Here: The Folly of Technological Solutionism* (PublicAffairs, 2013).

35. Garson, *Tom Clancy*, 1996, 36.
36. Conrad and Magowan, "Female Scientists under Strain," 37.
37. Conrad and Magowan, "Female Scientists under Strain," 39.
38. Conrad and Magowan, "Female Scientists under Strain," 44.
39. Conrad and Magowan, "Female Scientists under Strain," 37.
40. McPherson, "U.S. Operating Systems," 30.
41. Sobchack, *Screening Space*, 8.
42. Langdon Winner, *Autonomous Technology: Technics-out-of-Control as a Theme in Political Thought* (MIT Press, 2001), 89.

CHAPTER 3

1. Robert Lekachman, "Virtuous Men and Perfect Weapons," *New York Times*, July 27, 1986, sec. A.
2. Matthew Thomas Payne, "Fighting the Good (Preemptive) Fight: American Exceptionalism in Tom Clancy's Military Shooters," in *Playing War* (New York University Press, 2016), 97.
3. Even since his death, Clancy propagates this value system in the "Tom Clancy Presents" branding of video games and "Tom Clancy's" books.
4. Tom Clancy, "My Gun Is Not Your Business: People Sky-Dive and Race Cars. Why Can't I Fire at Targets?," *The Washington Post*, April 2, 1989, sec. OUTLOOK, C5; Clancy and Greenberg, *The Tom Clancy Companion*; see esp. chapter 3, "Tom Clancy in His Own Words."
5. Patrick Anderson, "King of the 'Techno-Thriller,'" *New York Times*, May 1, 1988, late edition, sec. A. See also chapter 1.
6. Lekachman, "Virtuous Men and Perfect Weapons," A7.
7. William H. Honan, "Can the Cold War Be a Hot Topic for a Movie?," *New York Times*, February 25, 1990, sec. A, 18.
8. Hal Hinson, "'The Hunt for Red October' (PG)," *Washington Post*, March 2, 1990, https://www.washingtonpost.com/wp-srv/style/longterm/movies/videos/thehuntforredoctoberpghinson_a0a914.htm.
9. Jane Tompkins, *West of Everything: The Inner Life of Westerns* (Oxford University Press, 1992), 6.
10. Tompkins, *West of Everything*, 56–57.

11. William F. Ryan, "The Genesis of the Techno-Thriller," *Virginia Quarterly Review* 69, no. 1 (1993): 29.
12. Ryan, "The Genesis of the Techno-Thriller," 27.
13. US Department of State, "Intermediate-Range Nuclear Forces Treaty (INF Treaty)," US Department of State, undated, https://2009-2017.state.gov/t/avc/trty/102360.htm.
14. Hinson, "The Hunt for Red October."
15. Richard Schickel, "A High-Stakes Blindman's Buff," *Time*, March 5, 1990, 70.
16. Desson Howe, "'The Hunt for Red October' (PG)," *Washington Post*, March 2, 1990, https://www.washingtonpost.com/wp-srv/style/longterm/movies/videos/thehuntforredoctoberpghowe_a0b257.htm.
17. J. William Gibson, "Redeeming Vietnam: Techno-Thriller Novels of the 1980s," *Cultural Critique*, no. 19 (1991): 195.
18. Gibson, "Redeeming Vietnam."
19. Gibson, "Redeeming Vietnam," 181.
20. *Charlie Rose*, PBS, August 15, 1996, http://archive.org/details/Charlie-Rose-1996-08-15.
21. Desson Howe, "Fun, But Formulaic," *Washington Post*, August 5, 1994, G36.
22. Erin Simpson and Phillip Carter, "How Tom Clancy Made the Military Cool Again," *Washington Post*, October 6, 2013.
23. Vito Russo, *The Celluloid Closet: Homosexuality in the Movies*, rev. ed. (Harper & Row, 1987).
24. This was noted by critics at the time: see Janet Maslin, "Film Review; Ryan Spies Again, This Time as C.I.A. Battles Drug Lords," *New York Times*, August 3, 1994, C11, https://www.nytimes.com/1994/08/03/movies/film-review-ryan-spies-again-this-time-as-cia-battles-drug-lords.html.
25. Julie Salamon, "Film: Kitchen Carnage; Jack Saves More Skin," *Wall Street Journal*, Eastern ed., August 11, 1994, A10.
26. William Terdoslavich, *The Jack Ryan Agenda: Policy and Politics in the Novels of Tom Clancy: An Unauthorized Analysis* (Tom Doherty Associates, 2005), 15.
27. Gibson, "Redeeming Vietnam," 1991, 200.
28. Louis Chilton, "Drab Tom Clancy Thriller 'Without Remorse' Fails to Rise above the Clichés," *The Independent*, April 30, 2021, https://www.independent.co.uk/arts-entertainment/films/reviews/without-remorse-review-michael-b-jordan-b1839711.html.
29. *Without Remorse Reviewed by Mark Kermode*, Kermodeandmayo (YouTube, 2021), https://www.youtube.com/watch?v=bpIgNFWc-nE. *Call of Duty* is one of the most popular military shooter franchises of all time.
30. Justin Chang, "Review: Even with Michael B. Jordan, 'Tom Clancy's Without Remorse' Shoots Blanks," *Los Angeles Times*, April 29, 2021, https://www.latimes.com/entertainment-arts/movies/story/2021-04-29/without-remorse-amazon

-michael-b-jordan-tom-clancy; Robert Daniels, "Tom Clancy's Without Remorse Is Missing a Thriller's Key Elements," *Polygon* (blog), April 30, 2021, https://www.polygon.com/22412156/tom-clancy-without-remorse-review-amazon; Chilton, "Drab Tom Clancy."

31. Scott Mendelson, "'Without Remorse' Review: Michael B. Jordan Can't Save Generic Action Throwback," *Forbes*, April 28, 2021, https://www.forbes.com/sites/scottmendelson/2021/04/28/without-remorse-michael-b-jordan-amazon-paramount-tom-clancy-review. IP stands for intellectual property.

32. Robert R. Selle, "Technothriller Creator and Freedom Advocate," *World & I* 15, no. 11 (November 2000): 50.

33. The term *woke* refers to an old slang term for being aware of matters of social justice. In recent years, it has become reappropriated as a shorthand sarcastic insult against progressive politics, especially regarding social inequality.

34. Scott Shuger, "Paperback Fighter," *Washington Monthly Magazine*, June 1, 2001, 11, https://washingtonmonthly.com/2001/06/01/paperback-fighter.

35. John S. Nelson, *Politics in Popular Movies: Rhetorical Takes on Horror, War, Thriller, and SciFi Films* (Routledge, 2016), 182–83.

CHAPTER 4

1. The silver eye effect was achieved by using silver-coated contact lenses, which caused ambient light to bounce off the actors' eyes. See Gene Polito, "'Westworld': A State of Mind?," *American Cinematographer*, November 1973, 1438.

2. Sam Adams, "How 'Westworld' Went from Seventies Blockbuster to HBO Show," *Rolling Stone* (blog), September 29, 2016, https://www.rollingstone.com/tv-movies/tv-movie-news/i-robot-how-westworld-went-from-seventies-blockbuster-to-hbo-show-128319.

3. Vincent Canby, "The Screen: 'Westworld': Robots and Fantasies in Film by Crichton," *New York Times*, November 22, 1973, 51.

4. Jean M. White, "Robots Run Amok: Run-Amok Robots in Fantasyland," *Washington Post*, September 26, 1973, sec. Style, D1.

5. Philip Strick, "Westworld," *Monthly Film Bulletin*, January 1, 1974, 56.

6. Leander Reeves, "Yul Brynner's Hat and Time Travel in the Hyperreal," in *Reading Westworld*, ed. Alex Goody and Antonia Mackay (Springer, 2019), 277–294, https://doi.org/10.1007/978-3-030-14515-6_15; Larry Alan Busk, "Westworld: Ideology, Simulation, Spectacle," *Mediations Journal of the Marxist Literary Group* 30, no. 1 (Fall 2016): 25–38.

7. Daniel Dinello, *Technophobia!: Science Fiction Visions of Posthuman Technology* (University of Texas Press, 2006), 251–252; Stefano Bigliardi, "'We Don't Know Exactly How They Work': Making Sense of Technophobia in 1973 'Westworld,' 'Futureworld,' and 'Beyond Westworld,'" *Journal of Science Fiction and Philosophy* 2 (July 2019).

8. Gary Mead and Sam Applebaum, "'Westworld': Fantasy and Exploitation," *Jump Cut*, no. 7 (July 1975): 12.
9. Bigliardi, "We Don't Know."
10. Bigliardi, "We Don't Know," 22. See also, on hubris, Despina Kakoudaki, "Affect and Machines in the Media," in *The Oxford Handbook of Affective Computing*, ed. Rafael A. Calvo, Sidney D'Mello, Jonathan Gratch, and Arvid Kappas (Oxford University Press, 2000), 111–128.
11. Andrew Utterson, "To See Ourselves as Androids See Us: The Pixel Perspectives of 'Westworld' (1973)," in *From IBM to MGM: Cinema at the Dawn of the Digital Age* (British Film Institute, 2011), 142, http://www.screenstudies.com/screenall/encyclopedia-chapter.
12. Steven L. Goldman, "Images of Technology in Popular Films: Discussion and Filmography," *Science, Technology, & Human Values* 14, no. 3 (1989): 298.
13. Loren Quiring, "Dead Men Walking: Consumption and Agency in the Western," *Film & History* 33, no. 1 (May 2003): 42.
14. Drehli Robnik, "Allegories of Post-Fordism in 1970s New Hollywood: Countercultural Combat Films and Conspiracy Thrillers as Genre Recycling," in *The Last Great American Picture Show*, ed. Thomas Elsaesser, Alexander Horwath, and Noel King (Amsterdam University Press, 2004), 347–353.
15. Reeves, "Yul Brynner's Hat," 292.
16. Anonymous, "Behind the Scenes of 'Westworld,'" *American Cinematographer*, November 1973, 1397.
17. Jenny Barrett, "Glory, Glory: Hollywood's Consensus Memory of the American Civil War," in *Reconfiguring the Union: Civil War Transformations*, ed. Iwan W. Morgan and Philip John Davies, Studies of the Americas (Palgrave Macmillan, 2013), 202, https://doi.org/10.1057/9781137336484_11. Barrett also speaks of this directly in relation to the Western genre in Jenny Barrett, "The Hollywood Western: Trauma, Memory, Postmemory and Consensus Memory," paper presented at the Society for Cinema and Media Studies Annual Conference (virtual), March 21, 2021.
18. Polito, "Westworld," 1438.
19. Crichton, "Reflections of a New Designer," *Compute! Magazine*, February 1985, 45.
20. Colin Williamson, "'An Escape into Reality': Computers, Special Effects, and the Haunting Optics of 'Westworld' (1973)," *Imaginations: Journal of Cross-Cultural Media Studies* 9, no. 1 (October 2018): 19, https://doi.org/10.17742/IMAGE.p70s.9.1.3.
21. Williamson, "An Escape into Reality," 22.
22. Gere, *Digital Culture*, 74.
23. Carroll W. Pursell, *Technology in Postwar America: A History* (Columbia University Press, 2007).
24. Pursell, *Technology in Postwar America*, xv.

25. Cormac Deane, "The Control Room: A Media Archaeology," *Culture Machine* 16 (2015), https://culturemachine.net/drone-culture/the-control-room.

26. Reeves, "Yul Brynner's Hat," 278–279.

27. Senator Mark Warner of Virginia would famously comment on this in relation to the regulation of social media, stating, "The era of the Wild West in social media is coming to an end." Mark R. Warner, "Warner Social Media Hearing Opening Statement," Mark R. Warner, September 5, 2018, https://www.warner.senate.gov/public/index.cfm/2018/9/warner-social-media-hearing-opening-statement.

28. *"On Location with 'Westworld'" Featurette* (MGM Studios, 1973).

29. Anonymous, "Behind the Scenes of 'Westworld,'" *American Cinematographer* 54, no. 11 (November 1973): 1394–1397, 1420–1421, 1436–1437.

30. Michael Crichton, "The Official Site of Michael Crichton," https://www.michaelcrichton.com.

31. David A. Price, "How Michael Crichton's 'Westworld' Pioneered Modern Special Effects," *New Yorker*, May 14, 2013, https://www.newyorker.com/tech/annals-of-technology/how-michael-crichtons-westworld-pioneered-modern-special-effects.

32. Michael Crichton, "Letters," *Scientific American* 230, no. 1 (1974): 8; J. Whitney, "Creating the Special Effects for Westworld.," *American Cinematographer*, November 1973, 1480.

33. Michael Crichton, *Electronic Life: How to Think About Computers* (Knopf, 1983), 55.

34. Utterson, "To See Ourselves as Androids See Us," 140.

35. Williamson, "An Escape into Reality," 32.

36. Guy Lodge, "Feminist Twist on 'Frankenstein,'" *Variety*, January 20, 2015; veronica fitzpatrick, "'Can I Fuck This?': Alex Garland's Ex Machina," *Cléo* (blog), April 21, 2017, http://cleojournal.com/2017/04/21/can-i-fuck-this-alex-garlands-ex-machina/; Emily Yoshida, "Bodies Electric: Ex Machina Twists the History of Sexy Robots," *The Verge*, March 15, 2015, https://www.theverge.com/2015/3/15/8219231/ex-machina-review-sxsw-2015; Farihah Zaman, "Ex Machina," Reverse Shot, April 23, 2015, http://www.reverseshot.org/reviews/entry/2046/ex_machina.

37. David Sims, "'Ex Machina': Bad Romance, with Robots," *The Atlantic*, April 10, 2015, https://www.theatlantic.com/entertainment/archive/2015/04/ex-machina-review/390147.

38. Jake Coyle, "When Hollywood Needs a Movie Villain, the Tech Bro Answers," AP News, March 7, 2023, https://apnews.com/article/oscars-movie-villain-tech-bro-glass-onion-2eae1d6c3805d53339cdd7c1507f4687.

39. Lee Mackinnon discusses *Ex Machina*'s aesthetics in detail, although we differ on what the presence of these visual signals means. I see those aesthetic decisions as intentionally revealing and critiquing a problematic mindset, while Mackinnon argues they reify that mindset. See Lee Mackinnon, "Artificial Stupidity and the End of Men," *Third Text* 31, no. 5–6 (November 2017): 603–617.

40. Crichton, *Electronic Life*, 89.

41. Crichton, *Electronic Life*.
42. Crichton, *Electronic Life*, 5.
43. Crichton, *Electronic Life*, 5.

CHAPTER 5

1. Phil Graham, *Hypercapitalism: New Media, Language, and Social Perceptions of Value* (Peter Lang, 2005), ix. See also Philip Graham, "Hypercapitalism: A Political Economy of Informational Idealism," *New Media & Society* 2, no. 2 (June 2000): 131–156, https://doi.org/10.1177/14614440022225742; David Golumbia, "Hypercapital," *Postmodern Culture* 7, no. 1 (1996); Philip Graham, "Hypercapitalism: Language, New Media and Social Perceptions of Value," *Discourse & Society* 13, no. 2 (2002): 227–249, https://doi.org/10.1177/0957926502013002408.
2. Graham, *Hypercapitalism*, 2005, x.
3. Luis Suarez-Villa, *Technocapitalism: A Critical Perspective on Technological Innovation and Corporatism*, (repr., Temple University Press, 2009), 1–2.
4. Luis Suarez-Villa, *Globalization and Technocapitalism: The Political Economy of Corporate Power and Technological Domination* (Ashgate, 2012), 1.
5. This film was remade in 2002 by director John McTiernan. This version was universally panned for many reasons, the most significant being its removal of social critique. For an excellent comparison of the original versus the remake, see Adilifu Nama, "Humans Unite!: Race, Class, and Postindustrial Aliens," in *Black Space: Imagining Race in Science Fiction Film* (University of Texas Press, 2008), 96–122.
6. William Harrison, "Roller Ball Murder," *Esquire*, September 1973.
7. Bryan Senn, "Sport and Violence: Death Race 2000 and Rollerball," in *Science Fiction America: Essays on SF Cinema* (McFarland, 2011).
8. Michael Berman, "Corporate Challenges to the Recovery of the Individual and History in Rollerball (1975)," in *Heroes, Monsters and Values: Science Fiction Films of the 1970s*, ed. Rohit Dalvi and Michael Berman (Cambridge Scholars, 2011).
9. Berman, "Corporate Challenges," 25.
10. Berman, "Corporate Challenges," 26.
11. Graham, *Hypercapitalism*, 2005, x.
12. Charles Champlin, "It's Hell on Wheels in 'Rollerball,'" *Los Angeles Times*, June 22, 1975, sec. Calendar, 46.
13. Nama, "Black Space," 97.
14. Nama, "Black Space," 98.
15. Nama, "Black Space," 99–100.
16. Jonathan Rosenbaum, "Rollerball," *Monthly Film Bulletin; London*, January 1, 1975; Gene Siskel, "Movies: '*Rollerball*'s' Points Dull the Mind," *Chicago Tribune*,

June 27, 1975, sec. 3; Vincent Canby, "Film View: Sci-Fi: From Sports to Sharks," *New York Times*, 1975, sec. Arts & Leisure; Joy Gould Boyum, "The Blood Sports of Days to Come," *Wall Street Journal*, July 29, 1975, sec. 1; Gary Arnold, "It's a Game, but Is It a Movie?," *Washington Post*, July 2, 1975, sec. Style.

17. Norman Jewison, "Letters," *New York Times*, 1975, sec. Arts & Leisure.
18. Jewison, "Letters," 93.
19. James Monaco, review of *Review of Rollerball*, by Norman Jewison and William Harrison, *Cinéaste* 7, no. 1 (1975): 42.
20. Elizabeth Anne Hull, "Merging Madness: 'Rollerball' as a Cautionary Tale," in *In Clockwork Worlds: Mechanized Environments in SF* (Greenwood Press, 1983), 179.
21. Hull, "Merging Madness," 166.
22. Vincent Canby, "'Looker,' a Sinister-Computer Thriller," *New York Times*, late ed., October 30, 1981, sec. C.
23. Michael Crichton, "Coma," *Michael Crichton* (blog), n.g., accessed March 14, 2025, https://www.michaelcrichton.com/works/coma.
24. Michael Crichton, "Looker," author site, *Michael Crichton* (blog), n.g., accessed March 14, 2025, https://www.michaelcrichton.com/works/looker.
25. Michael Crichton, "Looker," author site, *Michael Crichton* (blog), n.g., accessed March 14, 2025, https://www.michaelcrichton.com/works/looker.
26. Philip H. Dougherty, "John H. Crichton Is Dead at 58; Led Advertising Agencies Group," *New York Times*, December 28, 1977, sec. Archives, https://www.nytimes.com/1977/12/28/archives/john-h-crichton-is-dead-at-58-led-advertising-agencies-group.html.
27. Alana Staiti gives an excellent history of how these effects were achieved. See Alana Staiti, "Before Body Scanning There Was Looker: Building the Proto-Digital Hollywood Actor, circa 1981," *Public* 30, no. 60 (March 2020): 222–235, https://doi.org/10.1386/public_00017_7.
28. Jason Sperb, "I'll (Always) Be Back: Virtual Performance and Post-Human Labor in the Age of Digital Cinema," *Culture, Theory and Critique* 53, no. 3 (November 2012): 383–397, https://doi.org/10.1080/14735784.2012.720441; Staiti, "Before Body Scanning."
29. Stuart Heritage, "Joan Is Awful: Black Mirror Episode Is Every Striking Actor's Worst Nightmare," *The Guardian*, July 13, 2023, sec. Television & Radio, https://www.theguardian.com/tv-and-radio/2023/jul/13/joan-is-awful-black-mirror-striking-actors-nightmare.
30. L.O.O.K.E.R. stands for Light Ocular-Oriented Kinetic Emotive Response
31. Gene Siskel, "Movies: 'Looker' Turns Ugly after Half-Hour," *Chicago Tribune*, October 30, 1981, sec. 3.
32. Canby, "Looker"; Pauline Kael, "The Current Cinema," *New Yorker*, November 9, 1981.
33. Staiti, "Before Body Scanning," 230.

CHAPTER 6

1. There are many important works about the presence of nuclear weapons in the American imagination. See, for example, H. Bruce Franklin, *War Stars: The Superweapon and the American Imagination* (University of Massachusetts Press, 2008); Mark Sachleben, "The War to End Humanity? Nuclear War and Film," in *World Politics on Screen*, Understanding International Relations through Popular Culture (University Press of Kentucky, 2014), 79–96; Sean M. Maloney, "Strategic Underground Command: The ICBM Force in Film and History," in *Deconstructing Dr. Strangelove: The Secret History of Nuclear War Films* (University of Nebraska Press, 2020).
2. J. Martin Corbett, "Celluloid Projections: Images of Technology and Organizational Futures in Contemporary Science Fiction Film," *Organization* 2, no. 3–4 (August 1995): 473, https://doi.org/10.1177/135050849523011.
3. Annie Jacobsen, *Operation Paperclip: The Secret Intelligence Program That Brought Nazi Scientists to America*, large print ed. (Little, Brown, 2014). Operation Paperclip was revealed in 1946.
4. Kevin Kelly, "'Colossus, the Forbin Project' Superior Space-Age Thriller," *Boston Globe*, October 14, 1970, 17.
5. Rick, "Film Reviews: 'The Forbin Project,'" *Variety*, April 1, 1970.
6. From the audio commentary by Jeff Bond.
7. Steven L. Goldman, "Images of Technology in Popular Films: Discussion and Filmography," *Science, Technology, & Human Values* 14, no. 3 (1989): 291.
8. Corbett, "Celluloid Projections," 472.
9. "Sleeper Sci-Fi Fare," *Newsday* (Nassau ed.), May 12, 1970, sec. In Review/II.
10. Louise Sweeney, "'Forbin Project' Film Stars Bossy Computer: Whirrs and Thunks Mechanized Society 'Getting Straight' Curiouser (Blue)," *Christian Science Monitor*, May 29, 1970, sec. Arts/Entertainment, 8.
11. Kevin Thomas, "Sci-Fact Theme in 'Colossus': 'PROJECT,'" *Los Angeles Times*, August 26, 1970, F1.
12. Langdon Winner, "Do Artifacts Have Politics?," in *The Whale and the Reactor: A Search for Limits in an Age of High Technology* (University of Chicago Press, 2001), 19–39.
13. Robert Martin, "Movies: Now Coitus Gets Computerized in Demon Seed," *Globe and Mail*, April 4, 1977, 17.
14. Dean Koontz, *Demon Seed* (New York: Bantam Books, 1977). Originally published in 1973.
15. Lawrence DeVine, "'Demon Seed' Takes Sci-Fi a Bit Too Far," *Philadelphia Inquirer*, April 2, 1977, 3B.
16. Gene Siskel, "'Demon Seed' Just Doesn't Compute," *Chicago Tribune*, April 5, 1977, sec. 2.

17. Tom McElfresh, "Christie Is Only Virtue of 'Demon Seed,'" *Cincinnati Enquirer*, May 4, 1977, A16.

18. Gary Arnold, "'Demon Seed': A Computerized Horror," *Washington Post*, April 8, 1977, sec. Style.

19. Per Schelde, "Disembodied Brains," in *Androids, Humanoids, and Other Folklore Monsters*, Science and Soul in Science Fiction Films (New York University Press, 1993), 140–143.

20. Many of the first to calculate data critical to the success of the Second World War and the space program were women. In fact, working with computers doing such mathematical calculations was initially considered "women's work." See David Alan Grier, *When Computers Were Human* (Princeton University Press, 2005); Margot Lee Shetterly, *Hidden Figures: The American Dream and the Untold Story of the Black Women Mathematicians Who Helped Win the Space Race* (William Morrow, 2016).

21. Cormac Deane, "The Control Room: A Media Archaeology," *Culture Machine* 16 (2015), https://culturemachine.net/drone-culture/the-control-room.

22. Deane, "The Control Room."

23. Gene Siskel, "'WarGames' Tale of Computer Evil Mushrooms into Top Entertainment," *Chicago Tribune*, June 3, 1983, 67.

24. Vincent Canby, "'Wargames,' A Computer Fantasy: [Review]," *New York Times*, June 3, 1983, C17.

25. "Computer Safety—'Wargames Hacking Fears,'" *CBS News Nightwatch* (CBS, 1983), https://youtu.be/ui8BejEVpz4?si=ZstS_VVWfcM6dT7w.

26. Kevin Bankston, "How Sci-Fi Like WarGames Led to Real Policy During the Reagan Administration—from Hacking Legislation to Missile Defense," *Slate*, October 8, 2018, https://slate.com/technology/2018/10/reagan-wargames-star-wars-science-fiction-policy.html.

27. Stephanie Ricker Schulte, "'The WarGames Scenario': Regulating Teenagers and Teenaged Technology (1980–1984)," *Television & New Media* 9, no. 6 (November 2008): 509, https://doi.org/10.1177/1527476408323345.

28. Paulina Borsook, "Cyberselfish: Ravers, Guilders, Cyberpunks, and Other Silicon Valley LifeForms," *Yale Journal of Law and Technology* 4 (January 2001), https://openyls.law.yale.edu/handle/20.500.13051/7831.

29. Mar Hicks, *Programmed Inequality: How Britain Discarded Women Technologists and Lost Its Edge in Computing* (MIT Press, 2018); Amanda C. Cote, *Gaming Sexism: Gender and Identity in the Era of Casual Video Games* (New York University Press, 2020); Amanda Phillips, *Gamer Trouble: Feminist Confrontations in Digital Culture* (New York University Press, 2020).

30. Carly Kocurek, *Coin-Operated Americans: Rebooting Boyhood at the Video Game Arcade* (University of Minnesota Press, 2015), xvii.

31. Kocurek, *Coin-Operated Americans*, xi.

32. Schulte, "WarGames Scenario," 488.
33. Schulte, "WarGames Scenario," 489.
34. Schulte, "WarGames Scenario," 489.
35. Schulte, "WarGames Scenario," 498.
36. Schulte, "WarGames Scenario," 502.
37. Schulte, "WarGames Scenario," 511.
38. Carly Kocurek, "Play Saves the Day: Tron, WarGames, and the Gamer as Protagonist," in *Coin-Operated Americans: Rebooting Boyhood at the Video Game Arcade* (University of Minnesota Press, 2015), 116.
39. Kocurek, "Play Saves the Day," 119.
40. Kocurek, "Play Saves the Day," 141.
41. Kocurek, "Play Saves the Day," 148.
42. Robert Kazel, "30 Years after 'WarGames,' Director John Badham Recalls His Nuclear-Brink Blockbuster," *Nuclear Age Peace Foundation* (blog), February 12, 2013, https://www.wagingpeace.org/30-years-after-wargames-director-john-badham-recalls-his-nuclear-brink-blockbuster.
43. Corbett, "Celluloid Projections," 476.
44. S. K, "Buying & Booking Guide: Demon Seed," *Independent Film Journal*, April 15, 1977.
45. Sobchack, *Screening Space*, 224–225.

CHAPTER 7

1. The film and the novel both appeared in the same year.
2. Bernard Weinraub, "At Lunch with: Michael Crichton; Scarier Than Dinosaurs: Men vs. Women," *New York Times*, January 5, 1994, C1.
3. Rene Rodriguez, "Unplug the Special Effects, and There's Really Nothing to See," *Miami Herald*, December 9, 1994.
4. Michael Crichton, interview by Charlie Rose, *Charlie Rose*, PBS, January 14, 1994, https://charlierose.com/videos/18483.
5. Michael Crichton, interview by Charlie Rose.
6. Kathy Kleiman, *Proving Ground: The Untold Story of the Six Women Who Programmed the World's First Modern Computer* (Grand Central, 2022).
7. Margot Lee Shetterly, *Hidden Figures: The American Dream and the Untold Story of the Black Women Mathematicians Who Helped Win the Space Race* (William Morrow, 2016).
8. Staff, "Women in Computer Science & Programming," ComputerScience.org, March 1, 2022, https://www.computerscience.org/resources/women-in-computer-science.

9. Steve Henn, "When Women Stopped Coding," *Planet Money*, NPR, October 21, 2014, https://www.npr.org/sections/money/2014/10/21/357629765/when-women-stopped-coding.
10. Sapna Cheryan, Allison Master, and Andrew Meltzoff, "There Are Too Few Women in Computer Science and Engineering," *Scientific American*, February 1, 2023, https://www.scientificamerican.com/article/there-are-too-few-women-in-computer-science-and-engineering.
11. Niki Panteli, Janet Stack, and Harvie Ramsay, "Gendered Patterns in Computing Work in the Late 1990s," *New Technology, Work and Employment* 16, no. 1 (2001): 3–17; See also: Mar Hicks, *Programmed Inequality: How Britain Discarded Women Technologists and Lost Its Edge in Computing* (MIT Press, 2018). For a useful overview of theorizing the link between gender and technology, see Judy Wajcman, "From Women and Technology to Gendered Technoscience," *Information, Communication & Society* 10, no. 3 (June 2007): 287–298, https://doi.org/10.1080/13691180701409770.
12. Sherry Turkle, *The Second Self: Computers and the Human Spirit* (MIT Press, 2005), 186–187. Originally published in 1984.
13. Turkle, *The Second Self*, 194.
14. Judy Wajcman, *Feminism Confronts Technology* (Pennsylvania State University Press, 1991), x.
15. Panteli, Stack, and Ramsay, "Gendered Patterns in Computing Work," 11.
16. Ellen Pao, *Reset: My Fight for Inclusion and Lasting Change* (Random House, 2017); Shira Chess and Adrienne Shaw, "A Conspiracy of Fishes, or, How We Learned to Stop Worrying About #GamerGate and Embrace Hegemonic Masculinity," *Journal of Broadcasting & Electronic Media* 59, no. 1 (January 2015): 208–220, https://doi.org/10.1080/08838151.2014.999917; Emily Chang, *Brotopia: Breaking up the Boys' Club of Silicon Valley* (Portfolio/Penguin, 2018).
17. Daisuke Wakabayashi, "Google Fires Engineer Who Wrote Memo Questioning Women in Tech," *New York Times*, August 7, 2017, sec. Business, https://www.nytimes.com/2017/08/07/business/google-women-engineer-fired-memo.html.
18. Liza Mundy, "Why Is Silicon Valley So Awful to Women?," *The Atlantic*, March 14, 2017, https://www.theatlantic.com/magazine/archive/2017/04/why-is-silicon-valley-so-awful-to-women/517788.
19. "The Late 1990s Dot-Com Bubble Implodes in 2000," Goldman Sachs, 2019, https://www.goldmansachs.com/our-firm/history/moments/2000-dot-com-bubble.html.
20. Anna Radulovski, "Women in Tech Stats 2024," https://www.womentech.net/en-us/women-in-tech-stats, accessed October 19, 2024.
21. Mundy, "Why Is Silicon Valley So Awful," 65.
22. Mar Hicks, "Sexism Is a Feature, Not a Bug," in *Your Computer Is on Fire*, ed. Thomas S. Mullaney, Benjamin Peters, Mar Hicks, and Kavita Philip (MIT Press, 2021), 137.

23. Michael Crichton, interview by Charlie Rose.

24. Sara-Jane Finlay and Natalie Fenton, "'If You've Got a Vagina and an Attitude, That's a Deadly Combination': Sex and Heterosexuality in Basic Instinct, Body of Evidence and Disclosure," *Sexualities* 8, no. 1 (2005): 53, https://doi.org/10.1177/1363460705049574; see also Jack Boozer, "The Lethal Femme Fatale in the Noir Tradition," *Journal of Film and Video* 51, no. 3–4 (Fall 1999): 20–35.

25. Valerie S. Terry and Edward Schiappa, "Disclosing Antifeminism in Michael Crichton's Postfeminist Disclosure," *Journal of Communication Inquiry* 23, no. 1 (January 1999): 68–89, https://doi.org/10.1177/0196859999023001004; see also Carol Watts, "Thinking Disclosure: Or, the Structure of Post-feminist Cynicism," *Women: A Cultural Review* 6, no. 3 (December 1995): 275–286, https://doi.org/10.1080/09574049508578245; Camille Nurka, "Exposing Power in Michael Crichton's Disclosure," *Continuum* 16, no. 2 (June 2002): 157–167, https://doi.org/10.1080/10304310220121028.

26. Desson Howe, "Unrevealing 'Disclosure,'" *Washington Post*, December 9, 1994, 55.

27. See film production notes on DVD.

28. Watts, "Thinking Disclosure," 277.

29. Caryn James, "'Disclosure' Is Silly, but It Reveals How Much Men Can Fear Powerful Women," *New York Times*, 1994, sec. Arts & Leisure, H1.

30. Jay Carr, "Hollywood Backlash," *Boston Globe*, December 11, 1994, B21.

31. James Verniere, "Movies: Fatal Attraction: The Best-Selling Novel 'Disclosure' Becomes a Coldly Calculated Paranoid Fantasy," *Boston Herald*, December 9, 1994, S03.

32. Lizzie Francke, "Disclosure," *Sight and Sound*, March 1995, 35.

33. Martin Kevorkian, *Color Monitors: The Black Face of Technology in America* (Cornell University Press, 2006), 65–66.

34. Jane Horowitz, "'Disclosure': All Is Not Revealed," *Washington Post*, December 15, 1994.

35. James, "'Disclosure' Is Silly," 27.

36. Rajani Sudan, "Technophalia," *Camera Obscura* 14, no. 1–2 (40–41) (May 997): 103–128, https://doi.org/10.1215/02705346-14-1-2_40-41-103.

37. Mark A. Stein, "Unwanted Suitor's Fixation on Woman Led to Carnage," *Los Angeles Times*, February 18, 1988, https://www.latimes.com/archives/la-xpm-1988-02-18-mn-43514-story.html; *Inside Edition of CA Mass Murderer Richard Farley Stalking Laura Black and Killing 7 People*, posted March 26, 2022, YouTube, 4:09, https://www.youtube.com/watch?v=teDYMj84Igg.

38. Niraj Chokshi, "What Is an Incel? A Term Used by the Toronto Van Attack Suspect, Explained," *New York Times*, April 25, 2018, sec. World, https://www.nytimes.com/2018/04/24/world/canada/incel-reddit-meaning-rebellion.html. The term was first coined in 1997.

CHAPTER 8

1. *M3GAN* premiered in Los Angeles in December 2022, but was released in the United States in January 2023.
2. Will Douglas Heaven, "Google DeepMind Wants to Define What Counts as Artificial General Intelligence," *MIT Technology Review*, November 16, 2023, https://www.technologyreview.com/2023/11/16/1083498/google-deepmind-what-is-artificial-general-intelligence-agi.
3. Matt O'Brien and Barbara Ortutay, "White House Pushes Tech Industry to Shut Down Market for Sexually Abusive AI Deepfakes," *AP News*, May 23, 2024, https://apnews.com/article/ai-deepfake-biden-nonconsensual-sexual-images-c76c46b48e872cf79ded5430e098e65b.
4. European Commission, "AI Act," Shaping Europe's Digital Future, April 23, 2024, https://digital-strategy.ec.europa.eu/en/policies/regulatory-framework-ai.
5. The White House, "Administration Announces Key Actions to Advance Tech Accountability and Protect the Rights of the American Public," White House, October 4, 2022, https://www.whitehouse.gov/ostp/news-updates/2022/10/04/fact-sheet-biden-harris-administration-announces-key-actions-to-advance-tech-accountability-and-protect-the-rights-of-the-american-public.
6. Cade Metz and Gregory Schmidt, "Elon Musk and Others Call for Pause on A.I., Citing 'Profound Risks to Society,'" *New York Times*, March 29, 2023, sec. Technology, https://www.nytimes.com/2023/03/29/technology/ai-artificial-intelligence-musk-risks.html.
7. Talha Burki, "Crossing the Frontier: The First Global AI Safety Summit," *The Lancet Digital Health* 6, no. 2 (February 2024): e91–92, https://doi.org/10.1016/S2589-7500(24)00001-3.
8. Dawn Chmielewski and Lisa Richwine, "Hollywood Actors Secure Safeguards around AI Use on Screen," *Reuters*, November 9, 2023, https://www.reuters.com/business/media-telecom/hollywood-actors-secure-safeguards-around-ai-use-screen-2023-11-09.
9. For a good, brief overview of debates around AI in the film industry and film pedagogy, see Craig Erpelding, Jack Beck, J. D. Swerzenski, and Thomas Brecheisen, "Forum on Artificial Intelligence," *Journal of Film and Video* 76, no. 1 (2024): 44–55.
10. *True Love: Making The Creator*, Blu-Ray Featurette, Featurette (20th Century Studios, 2023); Brian Davids, "'The Creator' Director Gareth Edwards Believes Big-Budget Franchises Can Adopt His More Affordable Approach," *Hollywood Reporter* (blog), October 4, 2023, https://www.hollywoodreporter.com/movies/movie-features/the-creator-budget-gareth-edwards-1235609000.
11. David S. Roh, Betsy Huang, and Greta A. Niu, eds., *Techno-Orientalism: Imagining Asia in Speculative Fiction, History, and Media* (Rutgers University Press, 2015), 2.
12. Lisa Nakamura, *Cybertypes: Race, Ethnicity, and Identity on the Internet* (Routledge, 2002); see especially chapter 3, "Race in the Construct and the Construction of Race"; Roh, Huang, and Niu, *Techno-Orientalism*.

13. This resonates with Denis Villeneuve's 2017 film, *Blade Runner 2049*, a key theme of which is the discovery that a "replicant" was imbued with the power of reproduction.

14. J. William Gibson, "Redeeming Vietnam: Techno-Thriller Novels of the 1980s," *Cultural Critique*, no. 19 (1991): 179–202, https://doi.org/10.2307/1354313.

15. Peter Bradshaw, "The Creator Review—Vast and Exhilarating Sci-Fi Actioner Rages against the AI Machine," *The Guardian*, September 26, 2023, sec. Film, https://www.theguardian.com/film/2023/sep/26/the-creator-review-sci-fi-actioner-ai-gareth-edwards; see also Michael Phillips, "'The Creator' Review: Rise of the Machines! But Who's the Real Enemy Here?," *Chicago Tribune* (online), September 27, 2023, https://www.chicagotribune.com/2023/09/27/the-creator-review-rise-of-the-machines-but-whos-the-real-enemy-here.

16. David Sims, "'The Creator' Is Worth Catching on a Big Screen," *The Atlantic* (online), September 27, 2023, https://www.theatlantic.com/culture/archive/2023/09/the-creator-movie-review/675462.

17. Kyle Smith, "'The Creator' Review: On the Run in a Sci-Fi AI Empire," *Wall Street Journal* (online), September 28, 2023.

18. Josh Rotttenberg, "Sympathy for 'The Creator': Gareth Edwards Reflects on AI's Point of View and His Film's Sudden Timeliness," *Los Angeles Times*, October 2, 2023.

19. David Rooney, "'The Creator': John David Washington Stars as a Former Special Forces Op Caught up in an AI War in Gareth Edwards' Ambitious but Baggy and Sentimental Sci-Fi Epic," *Hollywood Reporter*, September 27, 2023.

20. Sobchack, *Screening Space*; see especially chapter 4, "Postfuturism," 223–305.

21. Sobchack, *Screening Space*, 226.

22. Sobchack, *Screening Space*, 226.

23. Sobchack, *Screening Space*, 229.

24. Tom Williams, "Oren Soffer and Greig Fraser ASC ACS / 'The Creator,'" British Cinematographer, December 22, 2023, https://britishcinematographer.co.uk/oren-soffer-and-greig-fraser-asc-acs-the-creator/; Jay Holben, "The Creator: Hope for the Future.," *American Cinematographer* (Federation Internationale des Archives [FIAF], November 2023).

25. Williams, "Oren Soffer and Greig Fraser."

26. *True Love: Making "The Creator."*

27. Anne Balsamo, "Gendering the Technological Imagination," in *Science Fiction and Cultural Theory: A Reader*, ed. Sherryl Vint, Routledge Literature Readers (Routledge, 2016), 78.

28. Hans Moravec, *Mind Children: The Future of Robot and Human Intelligence* (Harvard University Press, 1990). Originally published in 1988.

29. Angelica Jade Bastién, "Oscar Isaac and the Case Against Colorblind Casting," *The Atlantic* (online), December 26, 2015, https://www.theatlantic.com/entertainment/archive/2015/12/oscar-isaac-and-the-case-against-colorblind-casting

/421668/; Rebecca Keegan, "'Star Wars: The Force Awakens' Reflects Our Diverse, Modern World," *Los Angeles Times*, December 21, 2015, https://www.latimes.com/entertainment/movies/la-et-mn-star-wars-diversity-20151221-story.html; Armond White, "Christopher Nolan Pursues Hollywood's New Tenets," *National Review* (online), December 23, 2020, https://www.nationalreview.com/2020/12/christopher-nolan-pursues-hollywoods-new-tenets.

30. Glenn Whipp, "Movie Review: 'The Creator' Is Not Especially Creative; the Sci-Fi Visuals Are Gorgeous, but the Story Is One You've Probably Seen Before," *Los Angeles Times*, September 27, 2023, sec. Calendar.
31. David Ehrlich, "'The Creator' Review: 'A.I.' Meets 'Children of Men' in a Sci-Fi Epic That Should Change Hollywood Forever," *IndieWire* (blog), September 26, 2023, https://www.indiewire.com/criticism/movies/the-creator-movie-review-1234908583.
32. Gerard Johnstone, as cited in *M3GAN* BluRay featurette "A New Vision of Horror," Universal Pictures, 2022.
33. For more on this, see Stephanie Ricker Schulte, "'The WarGames Scenario': Regulating Teenagers and Teenaged Technology (1980–1984)" *Television & New Media* 9, no. 6 (November 2008): 509, https://doi.org/10.1177/1527476408323345; Carly Kocurek, "Play Saves the Day: Tron, WarGames, and the Gamer as Protagonist," in *Coin-Operated Americans: Rebooting Boyhood at the Video Game Arcade* (University of Minnesota Press, 2015)." See discussion of *WarGames* in chapter 6.
34. Peter Bradshaw, "M3gan Review—Girlbot Horror Offers Entertaining Spin on Teenage Growing Pains," *The Guardian*, January 4, 2023, sec. Film, https://www.theguardian.com/film/2023/jan/04/m3gan-review-girlbot-horror-offers-entertaining-spin-on-teenage-growing-pains.
35. Anne Balsamo, *Designing Culture: The Technological Imagination at Work* (Duke University Press, 2011), 7, https://doi.org/10.1515/9780822392149.

CHAPTER 9

1. Martin Kevorkian, *Color Monitors: The Black Face of Technology in America* (Cornell University Press, 2006).
2. Kevorkian, *Color Monitors*, 13, 1–2.
3. Tony Baer, "Getting the Picture: The Computer Graphics Techniques That Produced Dazzling Special Effects in 'Terminator 2' Are Also Valuable Research Tools. They Enable Scientists and Engineers to Put Complex Data into a Form They Can Visualize," *Los Angeles Times*, September 16, 1991, sec. Metro.
4. Joe Brown, "Wrecking Ball: 'Terminator 2,'" *Washington Post*, July 5, 1991, sec. On Screen, 31.
5. Robert F. Arnold, "Termination or Transformation? The 'Terminator' Films and Recent Changes in the U.S. Auto Industry," *Film Quarterly* 52, no. 1 (Autumn 1998): 20–30.

6. Ellexis Boyle, "The Intertextual Terminator: The Role of Film in Branding 'Arnold Schwarzenegger,'" *Journal of Communication Inquiry* 34, no. 1 (January 2010): 42–60, https://doi.org/10.1177/0196859909340054.
7. Mark Duckenfield, "Terminator 2: A Call to Economic Arms?," *Studies in Popular Culture* 17, no. 1 (October 1994): 1–16.
8. Ziauddin Sardar, "Terminator 2 Modernity, Postmodernism and the 'Other,'" *Futures* 24, no. 5 (June 1992): 493–506, https://doi.org/10.1016/0016-3287(92)90019-C.
9. J. P. Telotte, "The Terminator, Terminator 2, & the Exposed Body," *Journal of Popular Film & Television; Washington* 20, no. 2 (Summer 1992): 26, http://dx.doi.org/10.1080/01956051.1992.9943966.
10. Sharon Willis, "Combative Femininity: *Thelma and Louise* and *Terminator 2*," in *High Contrast: Race and Gender in Contemporary Hollywood Film* (Duke University Press, 1997), 98–128.
11. David Greven, "Cyborg Masochism, Homo-Fascism: Rereading Terminator 2," *Postmodern Culture* 19, no. 1 (September 2008).
12. The association is literal. Sarah Connor, at one point in the film says, "Men like you built the hydrogen bomb. Men like you thought it up." J. Robert Oppenheimer innovated the hydrogen bomb, and has become a tragic symbol for scientific and innovative responsibility to humanity.
13. Kevorkian, *Color Monitors*, x. Please note the author uses a lowercase *b* in *black* and *blackness* which is in keeping with the convention of his time. As such, I have kept the original quotes as-is.
14. Kevorkian, *Color Monitors*, 9.
15. Kevorkian, *Color Monitors*, 9, 13.
16. Kevorkian, *Color Monitors*, 15.
17. Kevorkian, *Color Monitors*, 192, note 42.
18. Lisa Nakamura, "The Unwanted Labour of Social Media: Women of Colour Call Out Culture as Venture Community Management," *New Formations: A Journal of Culture/Theory/Politics* 86, no. 1 (December 2015): 106–112; Lisa Nakamura, "Indigenous Circuits: Navajo Women and the Racialization of Early Electronic Manufacture," *American Quarterly* 66, no. 4 (2014): 919–941, https://doi.org/10.1353/aq.2014.0070; Lisa Nakamura, "Don't Hate the Player, Hate the Game: The Racialization of Labor in World of Warcraft," *Critical Studies in Media Communication* 26, no. 2 (June 2009): 128–144. Here, I am not suggesting that Nakamura's work is in alignment with Kevorkian's, necessarily.
19. Kevorkian, *Color Monitors*, 27.
20. Willis, "Combative Femininity," 125–126.
21. Margot Lee Shetterly, *Hidden Figures: The American Dream and the Untold Story of the Black Women Mathematicians Who Helped Win the Space Race* (William Morrow, 2016); Clarence G. Williams, *Technology and the Dream: Reflections on the Black Experience at MIT, 1941–1999* (MIT Press, 2001).

22. "President Bush Honors Excellence in Science, Mathematics and Engineering Mentoring," accessed June 6, 2024, https://www.nsf.gov/news/news_summ.jsp?cntn_id=100381.

23. Stuart Hall, "Encoding, Decoding," in *The Cultural Studies Reader*, ed. Simon During (Routledge, 1993), 90–103.

24. Abdul Alkalimat, "Martin Kevorkian, *Color Monitors: The Black Face of Technology in America*," *Journal of African American History* 92, no. 1 (Winter 2007): 147, https://doi.org/10.1086/JAAHv92n1p146.

25. Note that Rhames has only a cameo at the end of the fourth film, *Ghost Protocol*. *Mission: Impossible* is based on a television show of the same name from 1966 (Bruce Geller). As of 2025 there have been eight films.

26. This contradicts Kevorkian's understanding of this character. See Kevorkian, *Color Monitors*, 32–34.

27. Kevorkian, *Color Monitors*, 33.

28. Ross Andersen, "Christopher Nolan on the Promise and Peril of Technology," Atlantic Online, November 20, 2023, https://www.theatlantic.com/technology/archive/2023/11/christopher-nolan-interview-technology-oppenheimer-interstellar/676044.

29. Armond White, "Christopher Nolan Pursues Hollywood's New Tenets," *National Review* (online), December 23, 2020, https://www.nationalreview.com/2020/12/christopher-nolan-pursues-hollywoods-new-tenets

30. White, "Christopher Nolan Pursues."

31. Scott Mendelson, "'Tenet' Review: A Disappointing Step Backward For Chris Nolan," *Forbes*, September 1, 2020, https://www.forbes.com/sites/scottmendelson/2020/09/01/tenet-movie-review-chris-nolan-john-david-washington-robert-pattinson-imax.

32. Mendelson, "'Tenet' Review."

33. *Bokeh* is a common term in photography for the pleasing blur that may occur when shooting objects with a shallow focus, often resulting in painterly swirls or visually appealing circular points of color in the background.

34. White, "Christopher Nolan Pursues."

35. hooks, "The Oppositional Gaze." See also my discussion of this in the introduction.

36. John Connor in *Terminator 2: Judgment Day* (James Cameron, 1991).

INDEX

Note: Page numbers in italics indicate illustrations.